MARVEL ZOMBIES 4

WRITER: FRED VAN LENTE • ARTIST: KEV WALKER
COLORIST: JEAN-FRANCOIS BEAULIEU
LETTERER: VC's RUS WOOTON

COVER ARTISTS: GREG LAND & ARTHUR SUYDAM
ASSISTANT EDITOR: MICHAEL HORWITZ • EDITOR: BILL ROSEMANN
SENIOR EDITOR: RALPH MACCHIO

TALES OF THE ZOMBIE #1
"ALTAR OF THE DAMNED"
WRITER: STEVE GERBER • CO-PLOTTER: ROY THOMAS
LAYOUTS: JOHN BUSCEMA • FINISHES: TOM PALMER

"ZOMBIE!"
WRITER: STAN LEE • ARTIST: BILL EVERETT

"NIGHT OF THE WALKING DEAD"
WRITER: STEVE GERBER
LAYOUTS: JOHN BUSCEMA
FINISHES: SYD SHORES

COLLECTION EDITOR: MARK D. BEAZLEY
ASSISTANT EDITORS: JOHN DENNING & ALEX STARBUCK
EDITOR, SPECIAL PROJECTS: JENNIFER GRÜNWALD
SENIOR EDITOR, SPECIAL PROJECTS: JEFF YOUNGQUIST
SENIOR VICE PRESIDENT OF SALES: DAVID GABRIEL
PRODUCTION: JERRY KALINOWSKI
BOOK DESIGN: RODOLFO MURAGUCHI

EDITOR IN CHIEF: JOE QUESADA
PUBLISHER: DAN BUCKLEY
EXECUTIVE PRODUCER: ALAN FINE

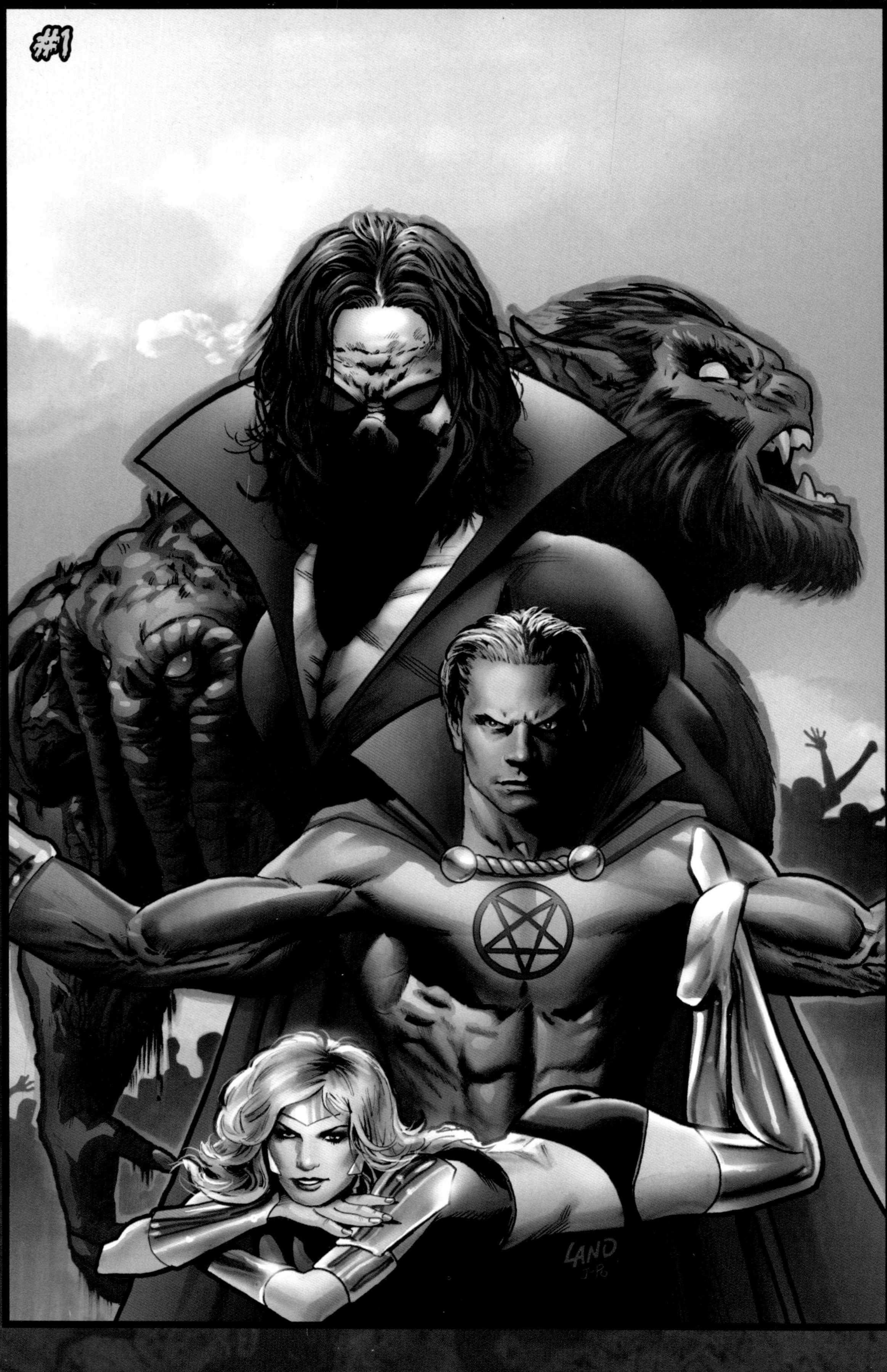
#1
LAND

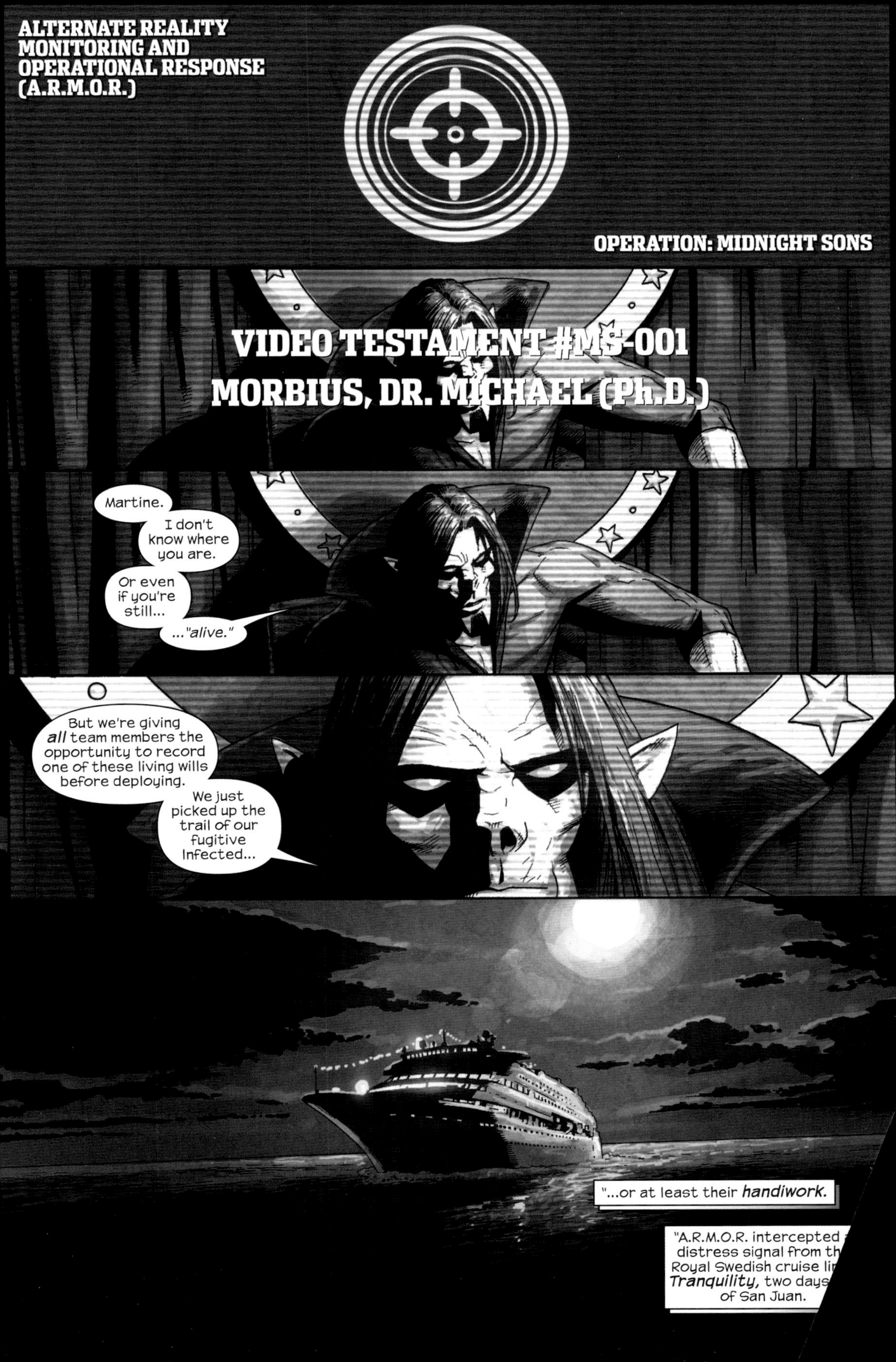
ALTERNATE REALITY MONITORING AND OPERATIONAL RESPONSE (A.R.M.O.R.)
OPERATION: MIDNIGHT SONS
VIDEO TESTAMENT #MS-001
MORBIUS, DR. MICHAEL (Ph.D.)
Martine.
I don't know where you are.
Or even if you're still...
..."alive."
But we're giving *all* team members the opportunity to record one of these living wills before deploying.
We just picked up the trail of our fugitive Infected...
"...or at least their *handiwork.*
"A.R.M.O.R. intercepted a distress signal from th Royal Swedish cruise li *Tranquility,* two days of San Juan.

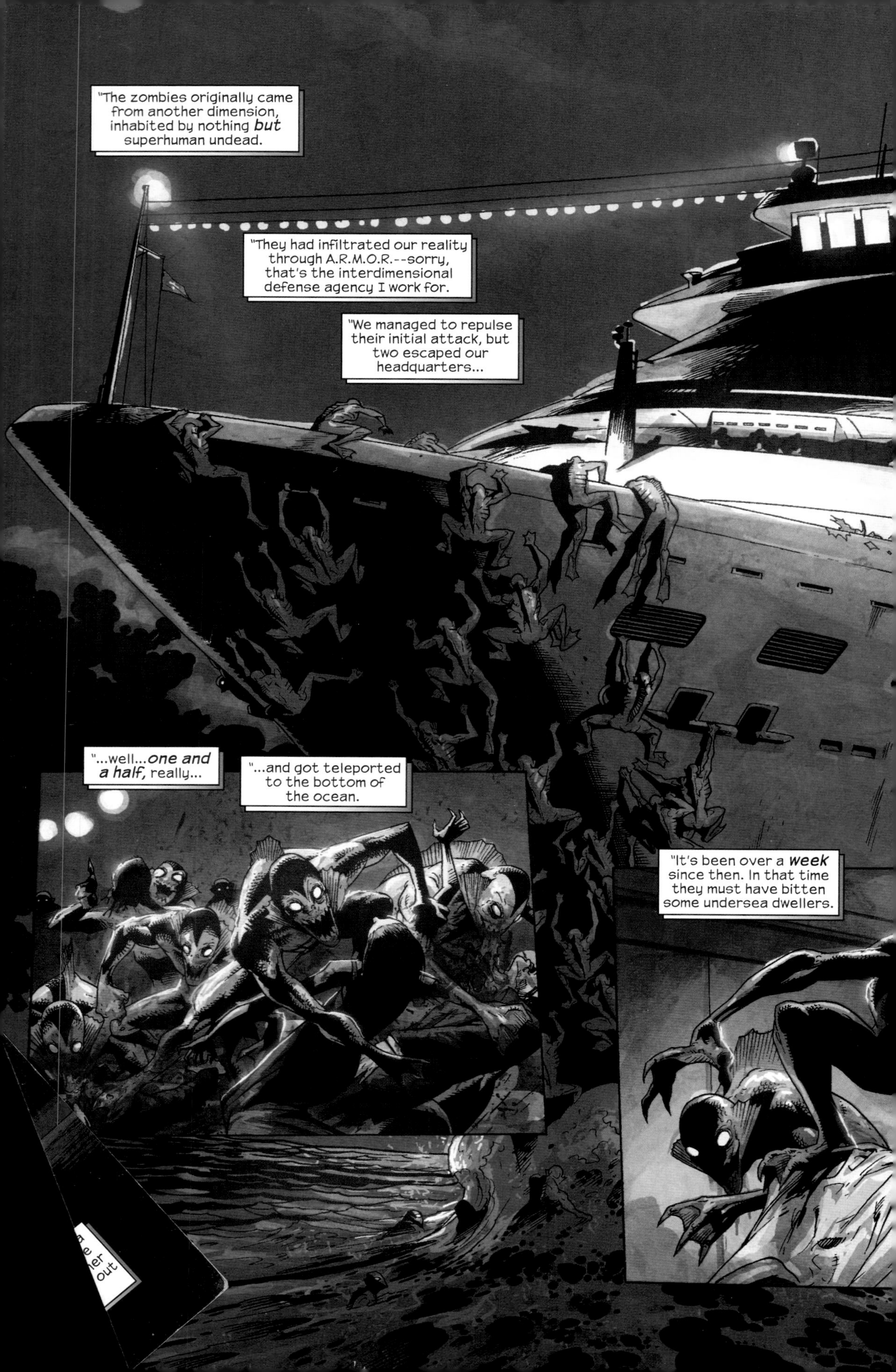
"The zombies originally came from another dimension, inhabited by nothing *but* superhuman undead.
"They had infiltrated our reality through A.R.M.O.R.--sorry, that's the interdimensional defense agency I work for.
"We managed to repulse their initial attack, but two escaped our headquarters...
"...well...*one and a half,* really...
"...and got teleported to the bottom of the ocean.
"It's been over a *week* since then. In that time they must have bitten some undersea dwellers.

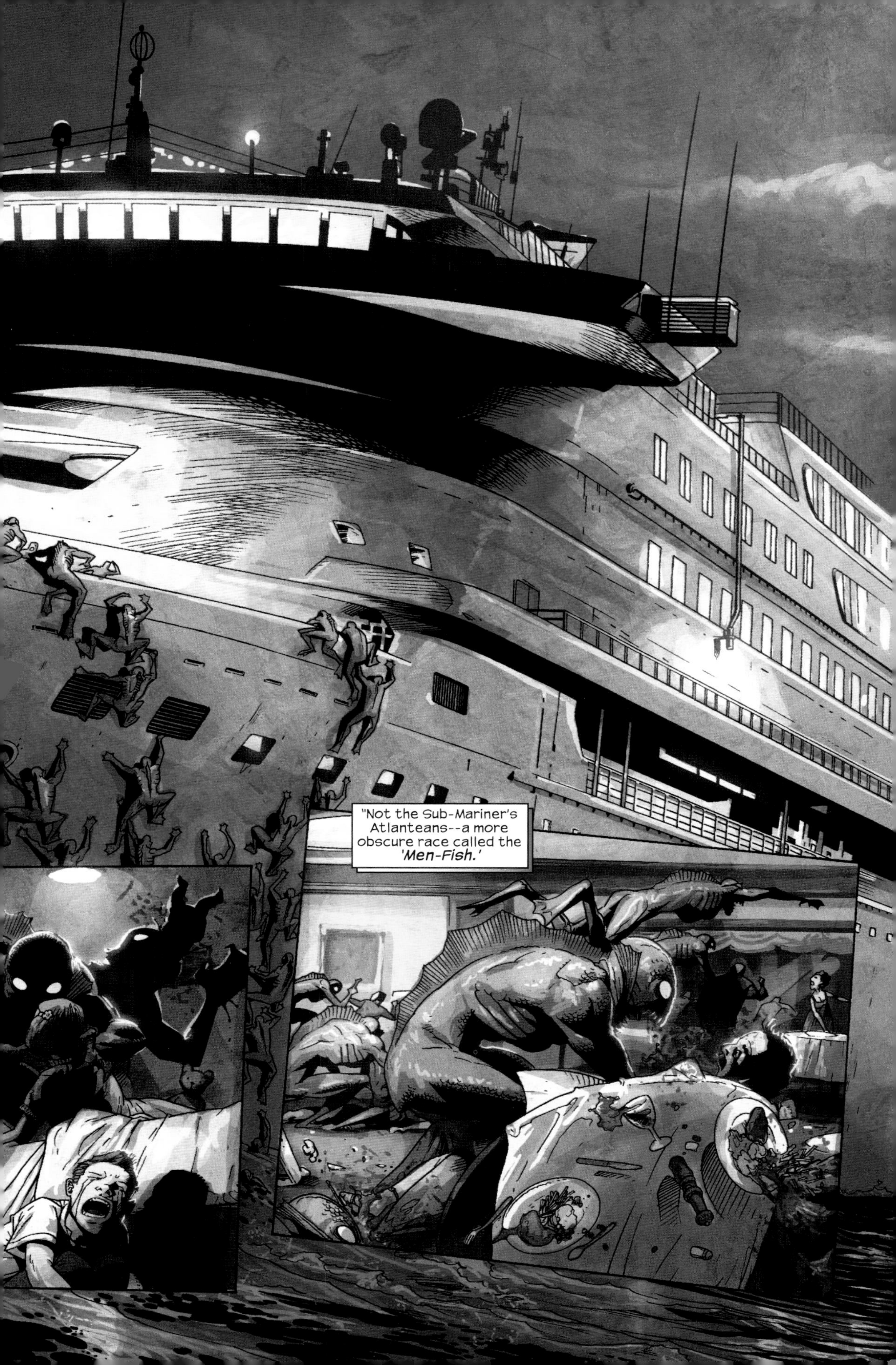
"Not the Sub-Mariner's Atlanteans--a more obscure race called the *'Men-Fish.'*

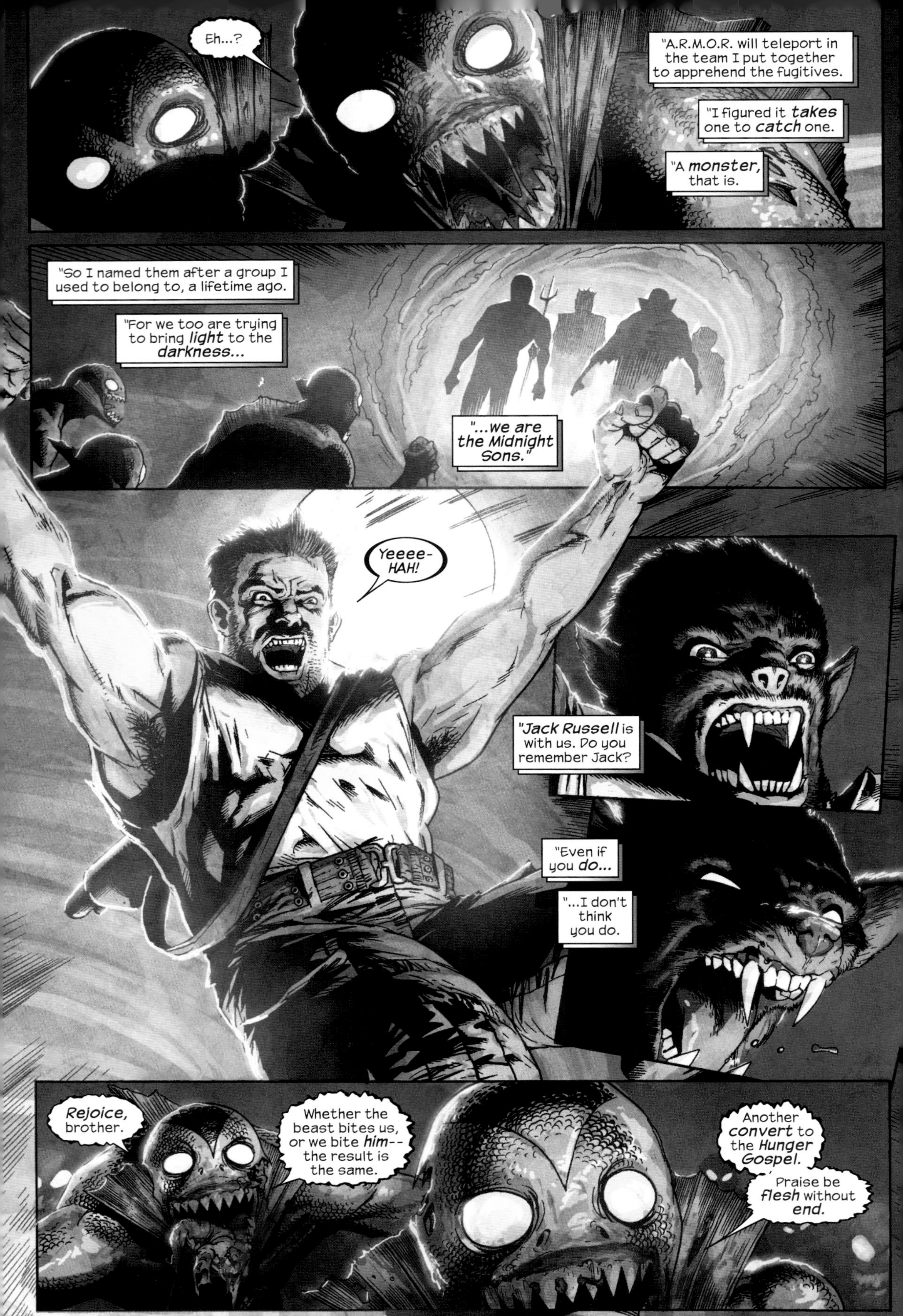
Eh...?
"A.R.M.O.R. will teleport in the team I put together to apprehend the fugitives.
"I figured it *takes* one to *catch* one.
"A *monster,* that is.
"So I named them after a group I used to belong to, a lifetime ago.
"For we too are trying to bring *light* to the *darkness...*
"...we are the Midnight Sons."
Yeeee-HAH!
"*Jack Russell* is with us. Do you remember Jack?
"Even if you *do...*
"...I don't think you do.
Rejoice, brother.
Whether the beast bites us, or we bite *him*-- the result is the same.
Another *convert* to the *Hunger Gospel.*
Praise be *flesh* without *end.*

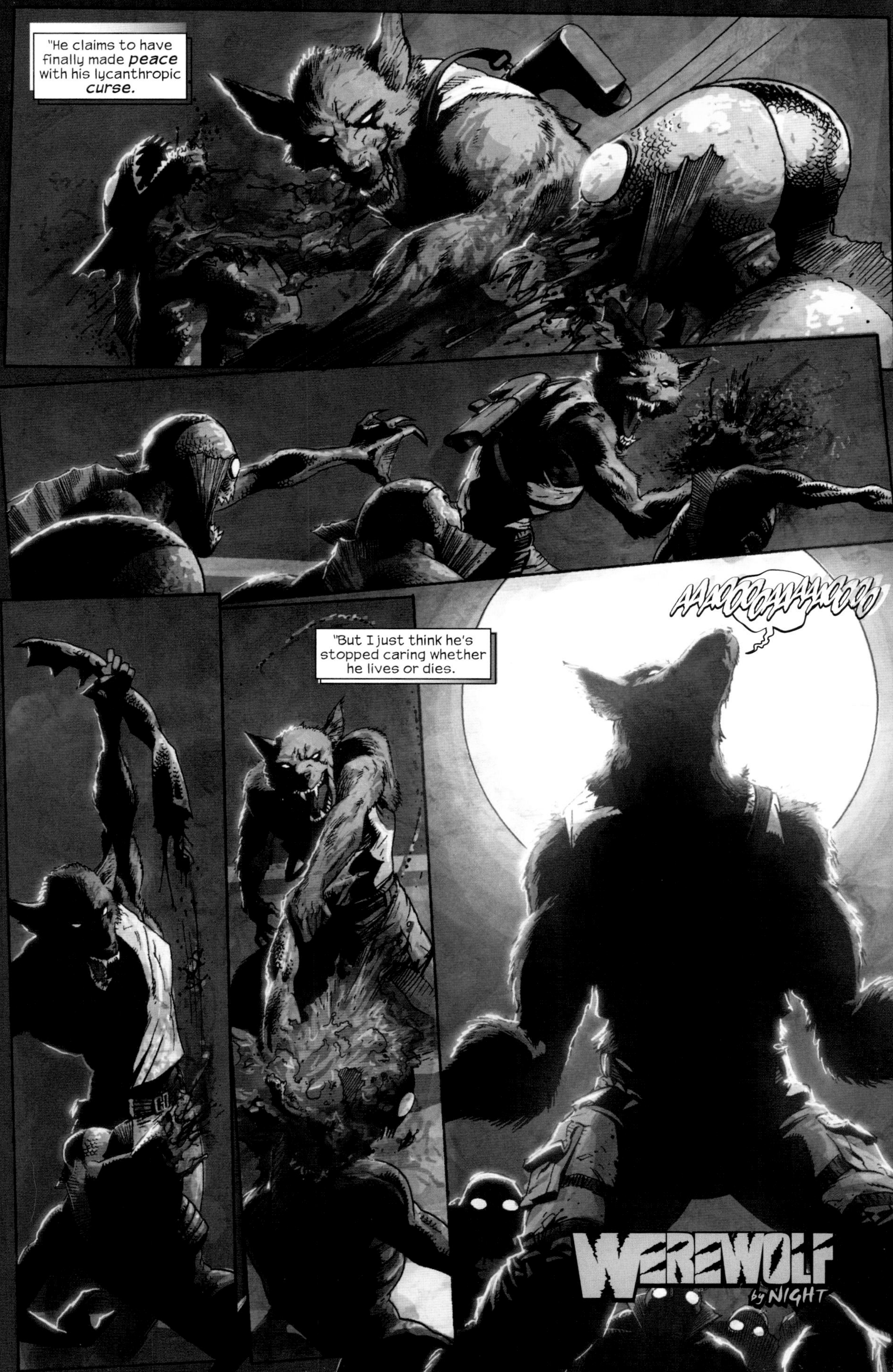
"He claims to have finally made *peace* with his lycanthropic *curse.*
"But I just think he's stopped caring whether he lives or dies.
AAAOOOOAAAAOOOO
WEREWOLF by NIGHT

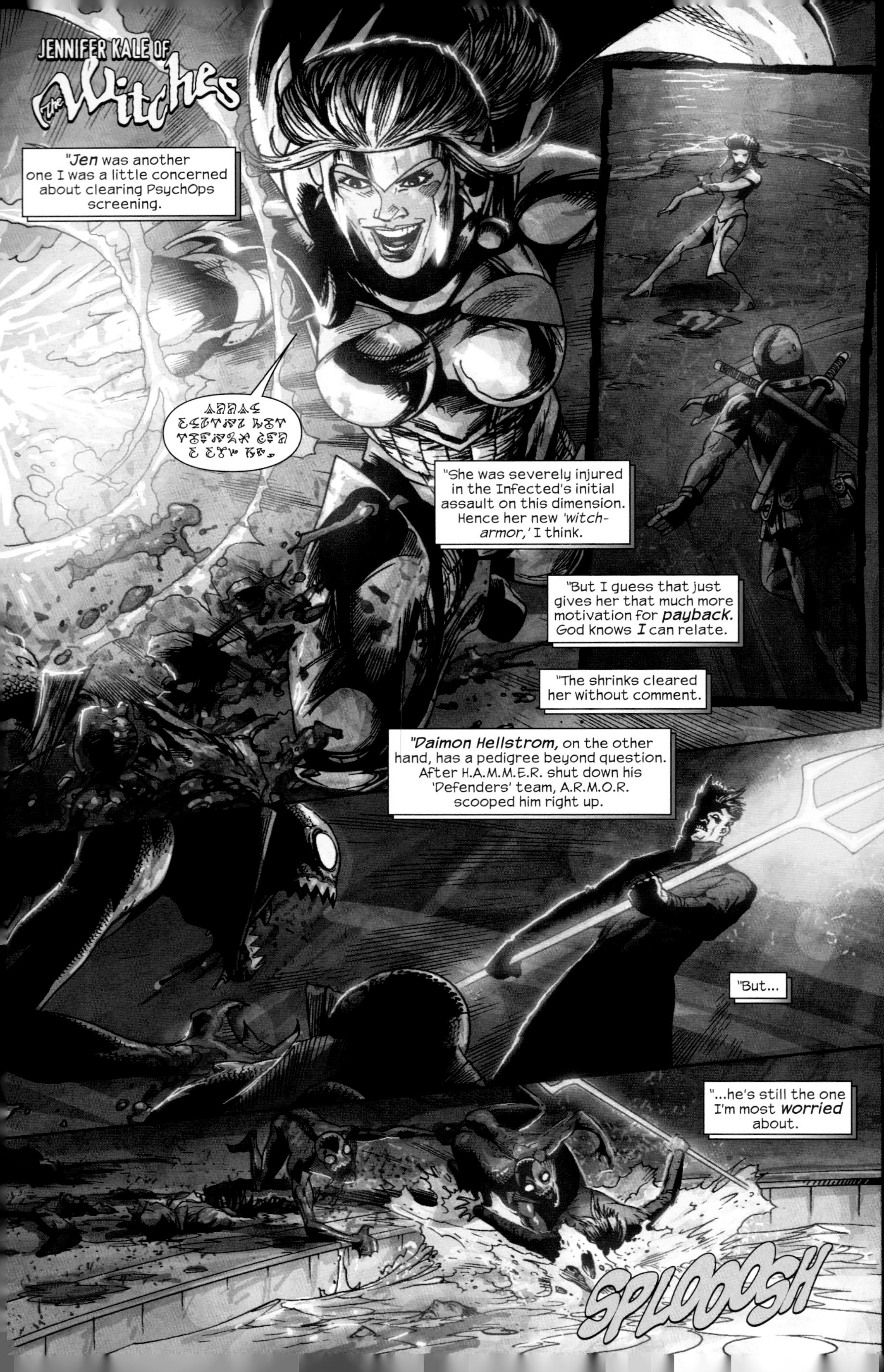
JENNIFER KALE OF the Witches
"Jen was another one I was a little concerned about clearing PsychOps screening.
"She was severely injured in the Infected's initial assault on this dimension. Hence her new 'witch-armor,' I think.
"But I guess that just gives her that much more motivation for payback. God knows I can relate.
"The shrinks cleared her without comment.
"Daimon Hellstrom, on the other hand, has a pedigree beyond question. After H.A.M.M.E.R. shut down his 'Defenders' team, A.R.M.O.R. scooped him right up.
"But...
"...he's still the one I'm most worried about.
SPLOOOSH

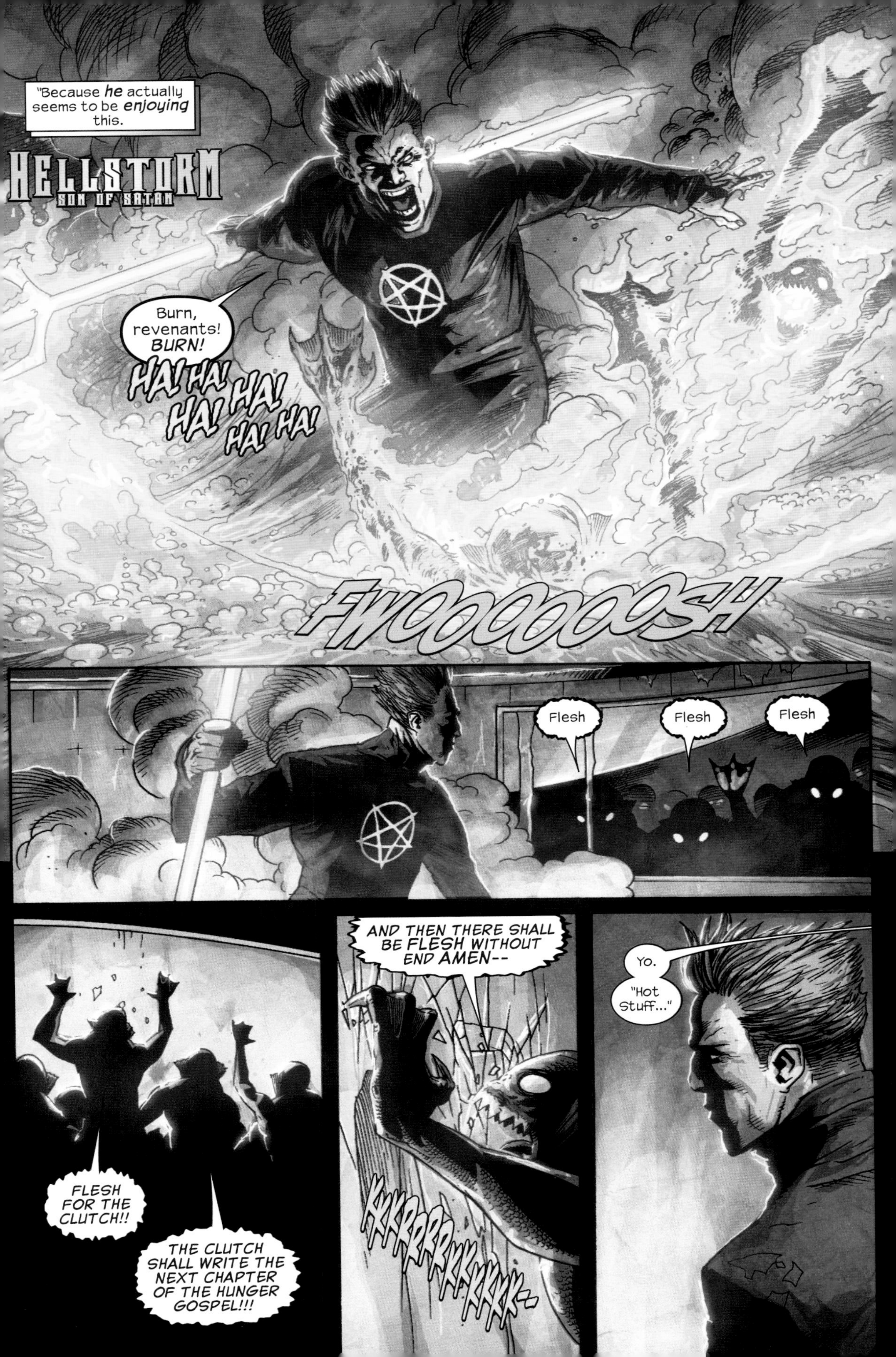
"Because he actually seems to be enjoying this.
HELLSTORM
SON OF SATAN
Burn, revenants! BURN!
HA! HA! HA! HA! HA! HA!
FWOOOOOOOSH
Flesh
Flesh
Flesh
FLESH FOR THE CLUTCH!!
THE CLUTCH SHALL WRITE THE NEXT CHAPTER OF THE HUNGER GOSPEL!!!
AND THEN THERE SHALL BE FLESH WITHOUT END AMEN--
KKKRRRRKKKKKK--
Yo.
"Hot Stuff..."

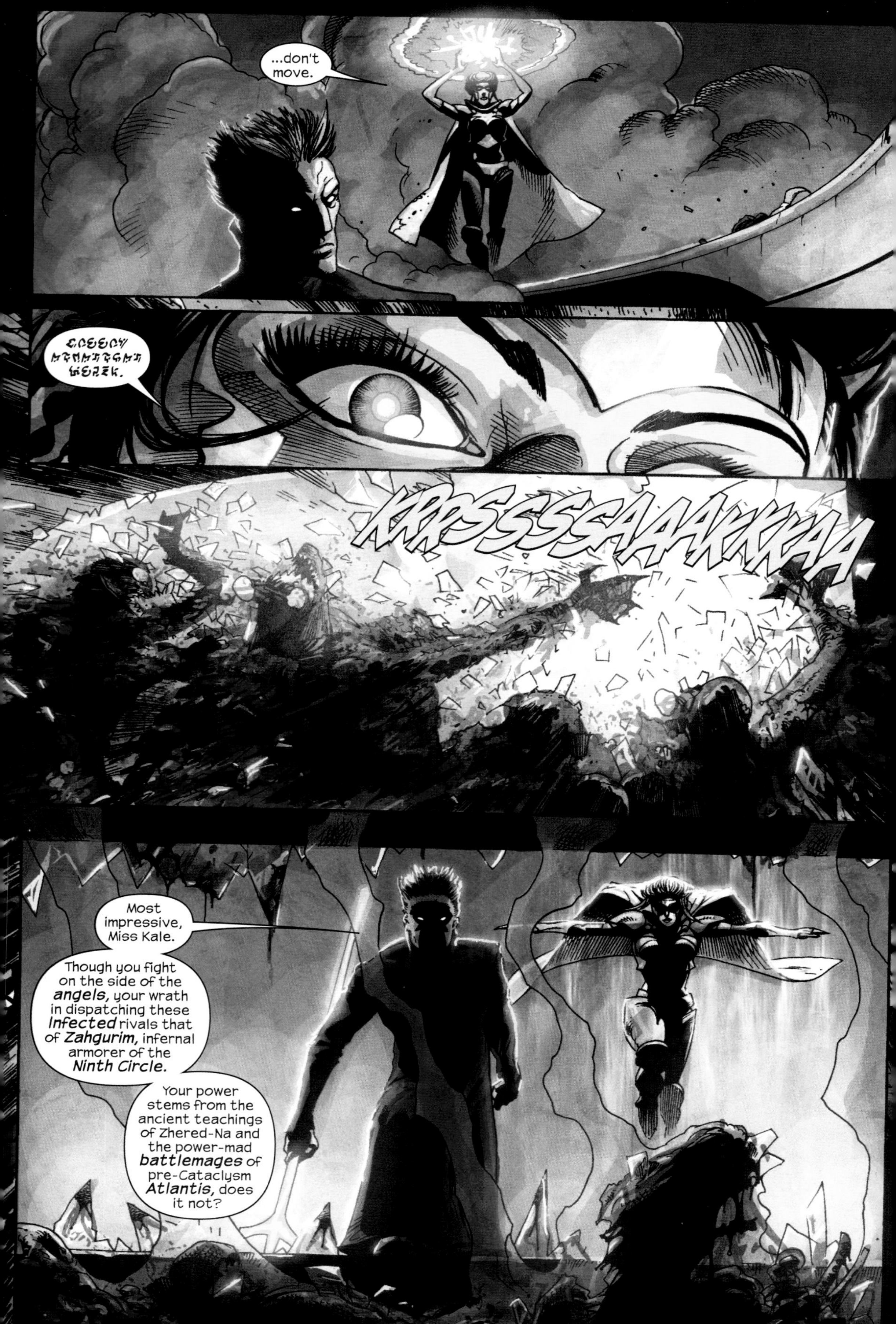
...don't move.
KRRSSSSAAAKKKAA
Most impressive, Miss Kale.
Though you fight on the side of the *angels*, your wrath in dispatching these *Infected* rivals that of *Zahgurim*, infernal armorer of the *Ninth Circle*.
Your power stems from the ancient teachings of Zhered-Na and the power-mad *battlemages* of pre-Cataclysm *Atlantis*, does it not?

When I see the fire of those ruthless conquerors ignite in your soul in the heat of battle...

...it is *quite* beautiful.

Um. I think you may have *misinterpreted* my use of the term *"Hot Stuff"*...

If you're hitting on me, you're wasting your time--

HA HA HA HA HA HA HA HA HA HA

Oh, my, no.

I am merely a connoisseur...

...of darker *halves*.

Do me a favor.

Don't ever laugh again.

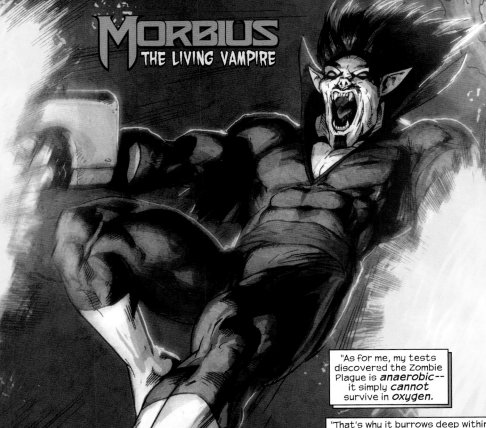

MORBIUS
THE LIVING VAMPIRE

"As for me, my tests discovered the Zombie Plague is *anaerobic*-- it simply *cannot* survive in *oxygen*.

"That's why it burrows deep within the *bone marrow*, distributes a *secondary nervous system* in the Infected, which *animates* the corpse.

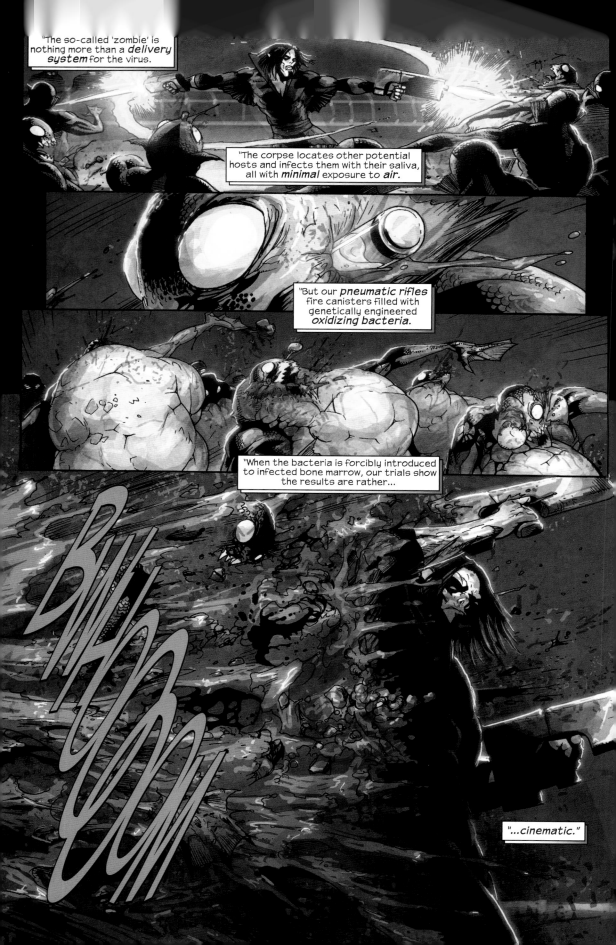

"The so-called 'zombie' is nothing more than a *delivery system* for the virus.

"The corpse locates other potential hosts and infects them with their saliva, all with *minimal* exposure to *air*.

"But our *pneumatic rifles* fire canisters filled with genetically engineered *oxidizing bacteria*.

"When the bacteria is forcibly introduced to infected bone marrow, our trials show the results are rather...

"...cinematic."

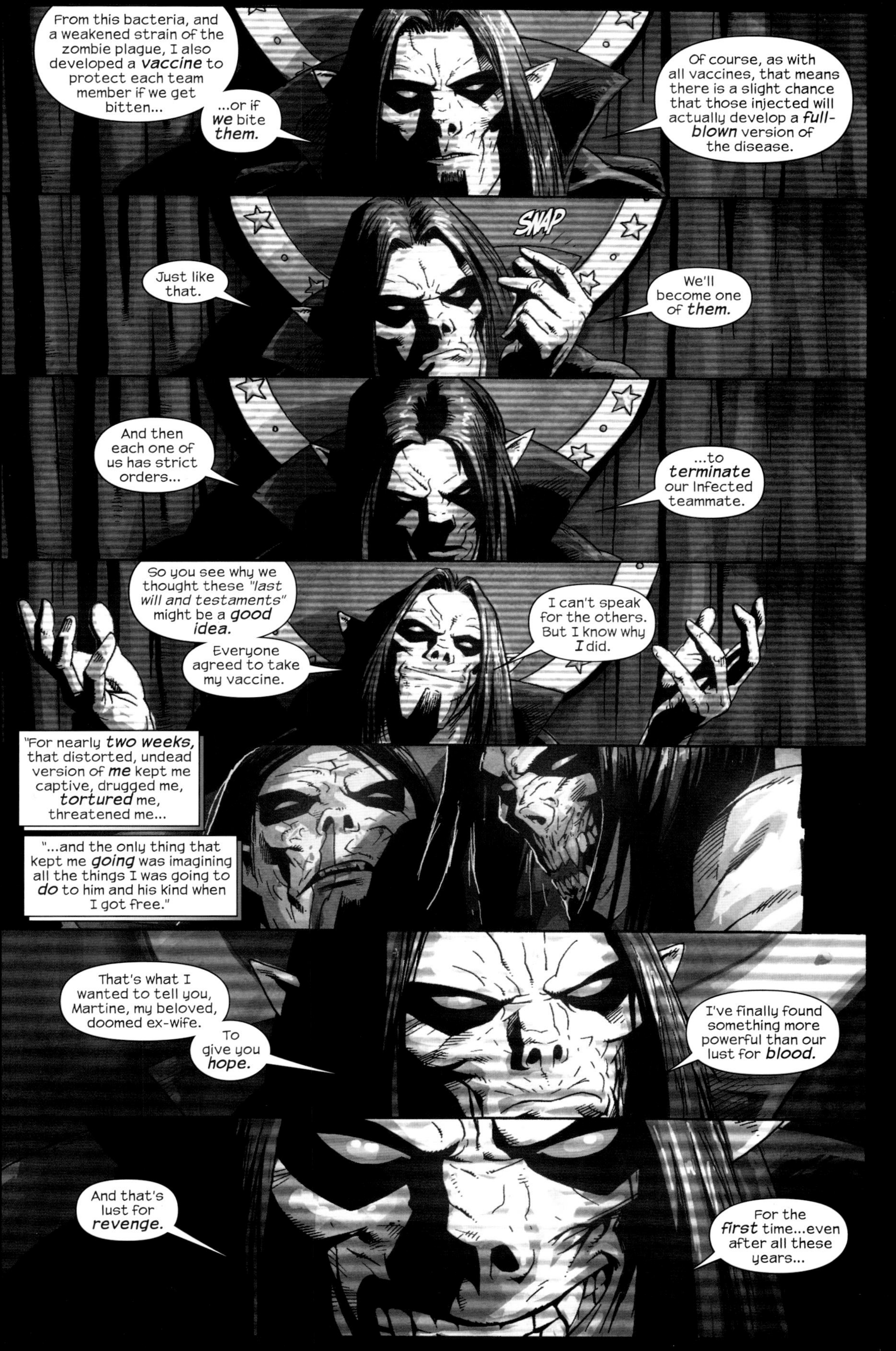
From this bacteria, and a weakened strain of the zombie plague, I also developed a *vaccine* to protect each team member if we get bitten...
...or if *we* bite *them.*
Of course, as with all vaccines, that means there is a slight chance that those injected will actually develop a *full-blown* version of the disease.
SNAP
Just like that.
We'll become one of *them.*
And then each one of us has strict orders...
...to *terminate* our Infected teammate.
So you see why we thought these *"last will and testaments"* might be a *good idea.*
Everyone agreed to take my vaccine.
I can't speak for the others. But I know why *I* did.
"For nearly *two weeks,* that distorted, undead version of *me* kept me captive, drugged me, *tortured* me, threatened me...
"...and the only thing that kept me *going* was imagining all the things I was going to *do* to him and his kind when I got free."
That's what I wanted to tell you, Martine, my beloved, doomed ex-wife.
To give you *hope.*
I've finally found something more powerful than our lust for *blood.*
And that's lust for *revenge.*
For the *first* time...even after all these years...

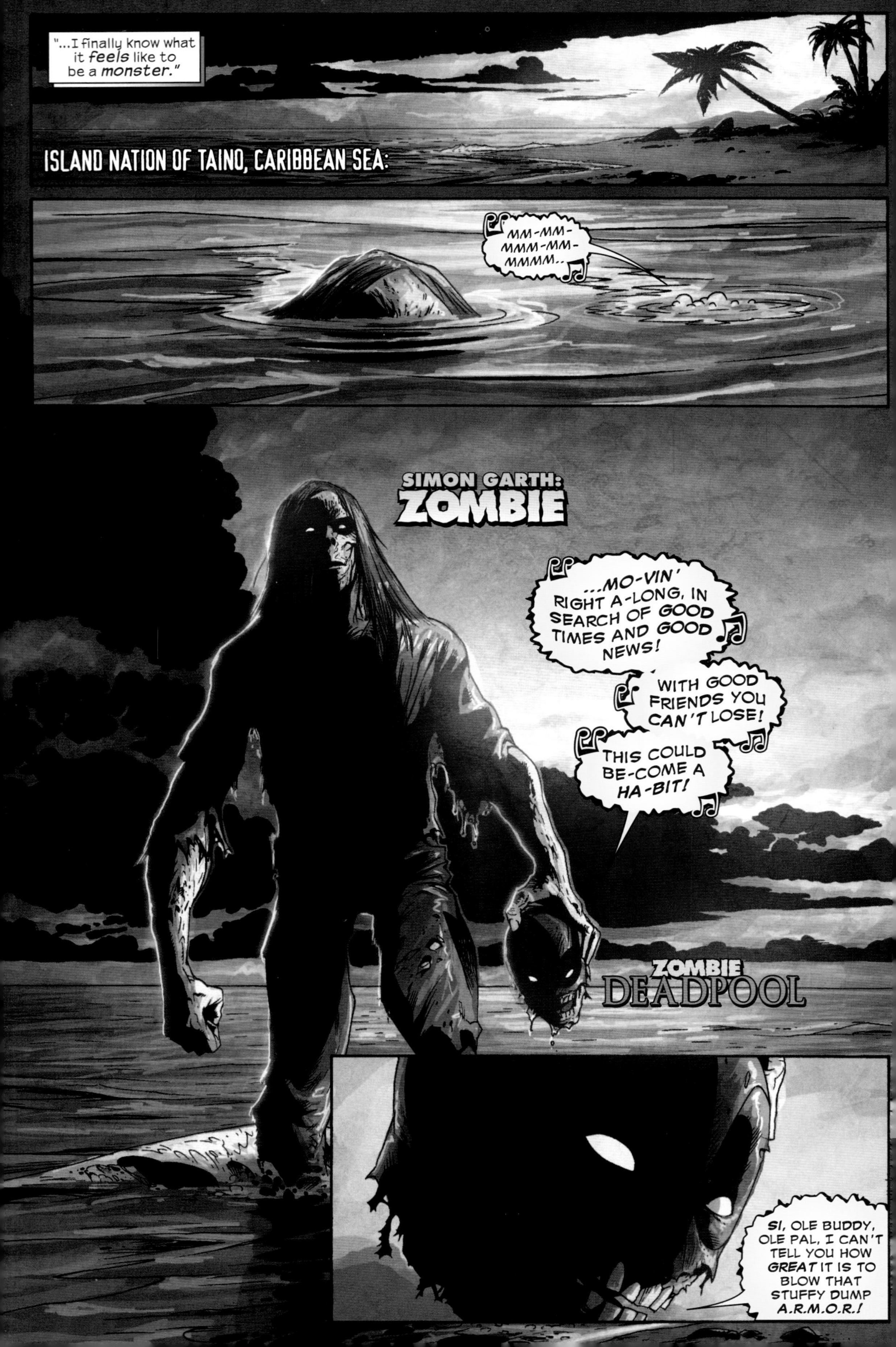
"...I finally know what it *feels* like to be a *monster.*"
ISLAND NATION OF TAINO, CARIBBEAN SEA:
MM-MM-MMM-MM-MMMM..
SIMON GARTH: ZOMBIE
...MO-VIN' RIGHT A-LONG, IN SEARCH OF GOOD TIMES AND GOOD NEWS!
WITH GOOD FRIENDS YOU CAN'T LOSE!
THIS COULD BE-COME A HA-BIT!
ZOMBIE DEADPOOL
SI, OLE BUDDY, OLE PAL, I CAN'T TELL YOU HOW GREAT IT IS TO BLOW THAT STUFFY DUMP A.R.M.O.R.!

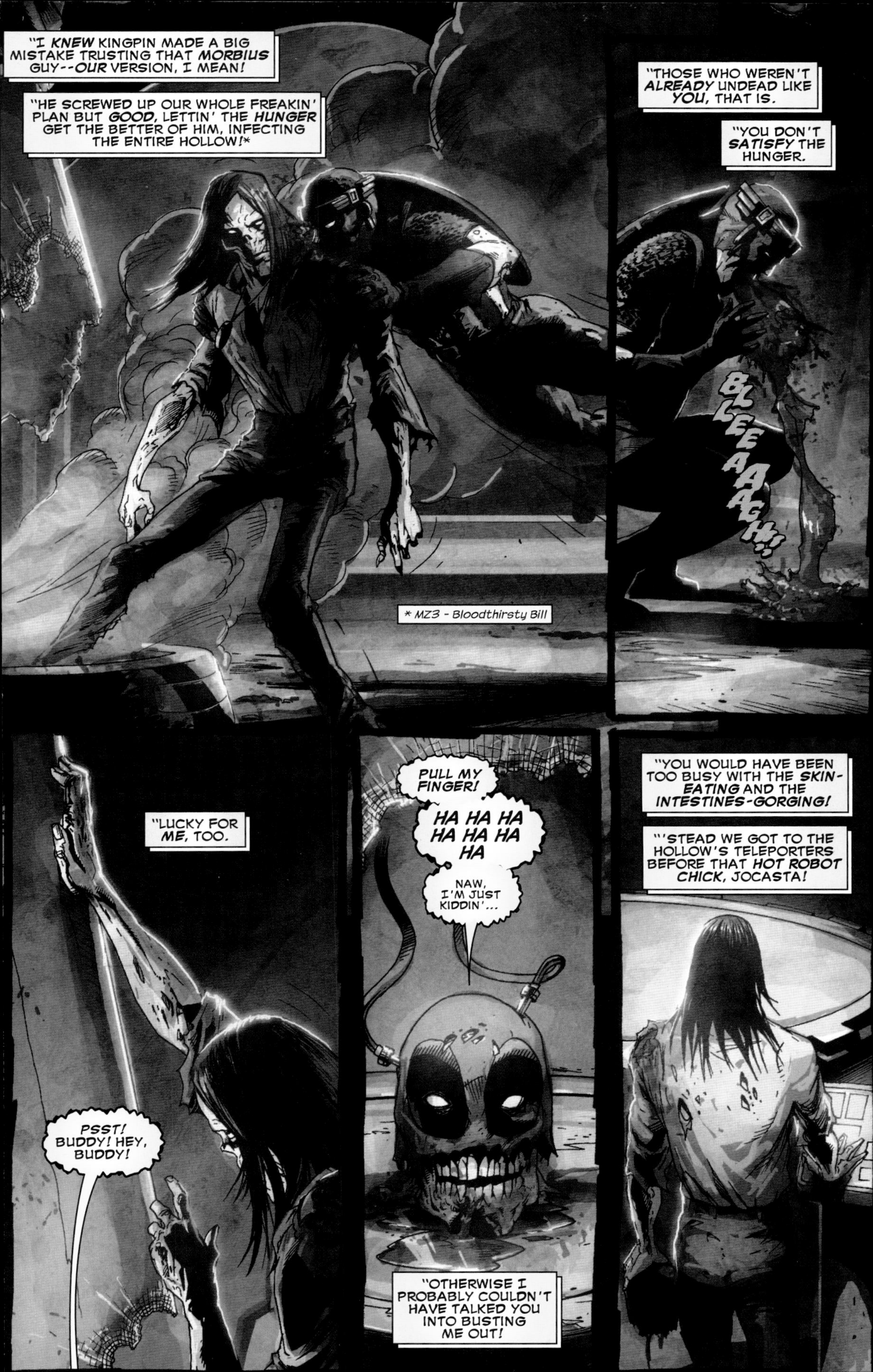
"I KNEW KINGPIN MADE A BIG MISTAKE TRUSTING THAT MORBIUS GUY--OUR VERSION, I MEAN!
"HE SCREWED UP OUR WHOLE FREAKIN' PLAN BUT GOOD, LETTIN' THE HUNGER GET THE BETTER OF HIM, INFECTING THE ENTIRE HOLLOW!*
* MZ3 - Bloodthirsty Bill
"THOSE WHO WEREN'T ALREADY UNDEAD LIKE YOU, THAT IS.
"YOU DON'T SATISFY THE HUNGER.
BLLEEAAAAGH!!
"LUCKY FOR ME, TOO.
PSST! BUDDY! HEY, BUDDY!
PULL MY FINGER!
HA HA HA HA HA HA HA
NAW, I'M JUST KIDDIN'...
"OTHERWISE I PROBABLY COULDN'T HAVE TALKED YOU INTO BUSTING ME OUT!
"YOU WOULD HAVE BEEN TOO BUSY WITH THE SKIN-EATING AND THE INTESTINES-GORGING!
"'STEAD WE GOT TO THE HOLLOW'S TELEPORTERS BEFORE THAT HOT ROBOT CHICK, JOCASTA!

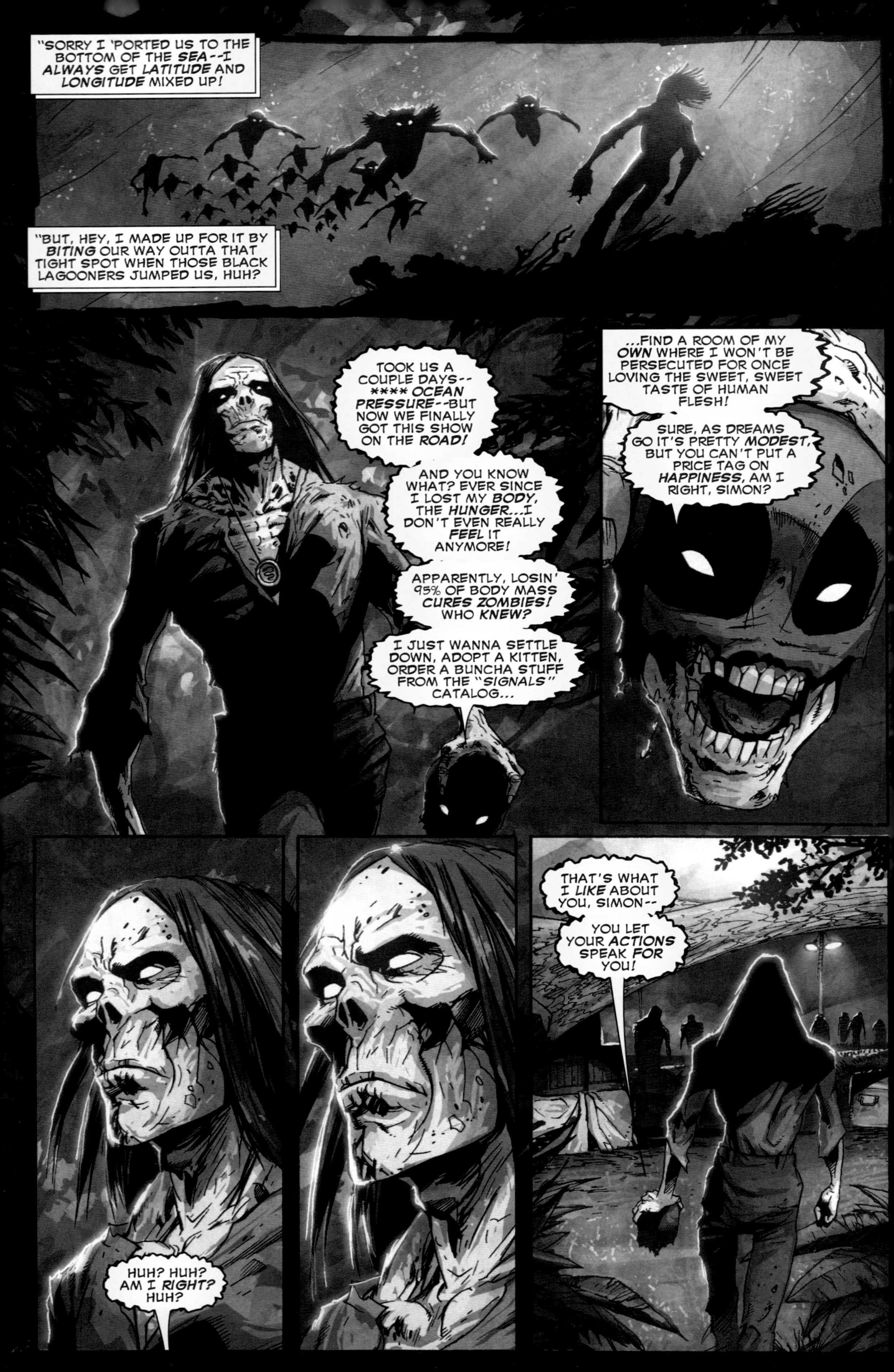
"SORRY I 'PORTED US TO THE BOTTOM OF THE SEA--I ALWAYS GET LATITUDE AND LONGITUDE MIXED UP!
"BUT, HEY, I MADE UP FOR IT BY BITING OUR WAY OUTTA THAT TIGHT SPOT WHEN THOSE BLACK LAGOONERS JUMPED US, HUH?
TOOK US A COUPLE DAYS-- **** OCEAN PRESSURE--BUT NOW WE FINALLY GOT THIS SHOW ON THE ROAD!
AND YOU KNOW WHAT? EVER SINCE I LOST MY BODY, THE HUNGER...I DON'T EVEN REALLY FEEL IT ANYMORE!
APPARENTLY, LOSIN' 95% OF BODY MASS CURES ZOMBIES! WHO KNEW?
I JUST WANNA SETTLE DOWN, ADOPT A KITTEN, ORDER A BUNCHA STUFF FROM THE "SIGNALS" CATALOG...
...FIND A ROOM OF MY OWN WHERE I WON'T BE PERSECUTED FOR ONCE LOVING THE SWEET, SWEET TASTE OF HUMAN FLESH!
SURE, AS DREAMS GO IT'S PRETTY MODEST, BUT YOU CAN'T PUT A PRICE TAG ON HAPPINESS, AM I RIGHT, SIMON?
HUH? HUH? AM I RIGHT? HUH?
THAT'S WHAT I LIKE ABOUT YOU, SIMON--
YOU LET YOUR ACTIONS SPEAK FOR YOU!

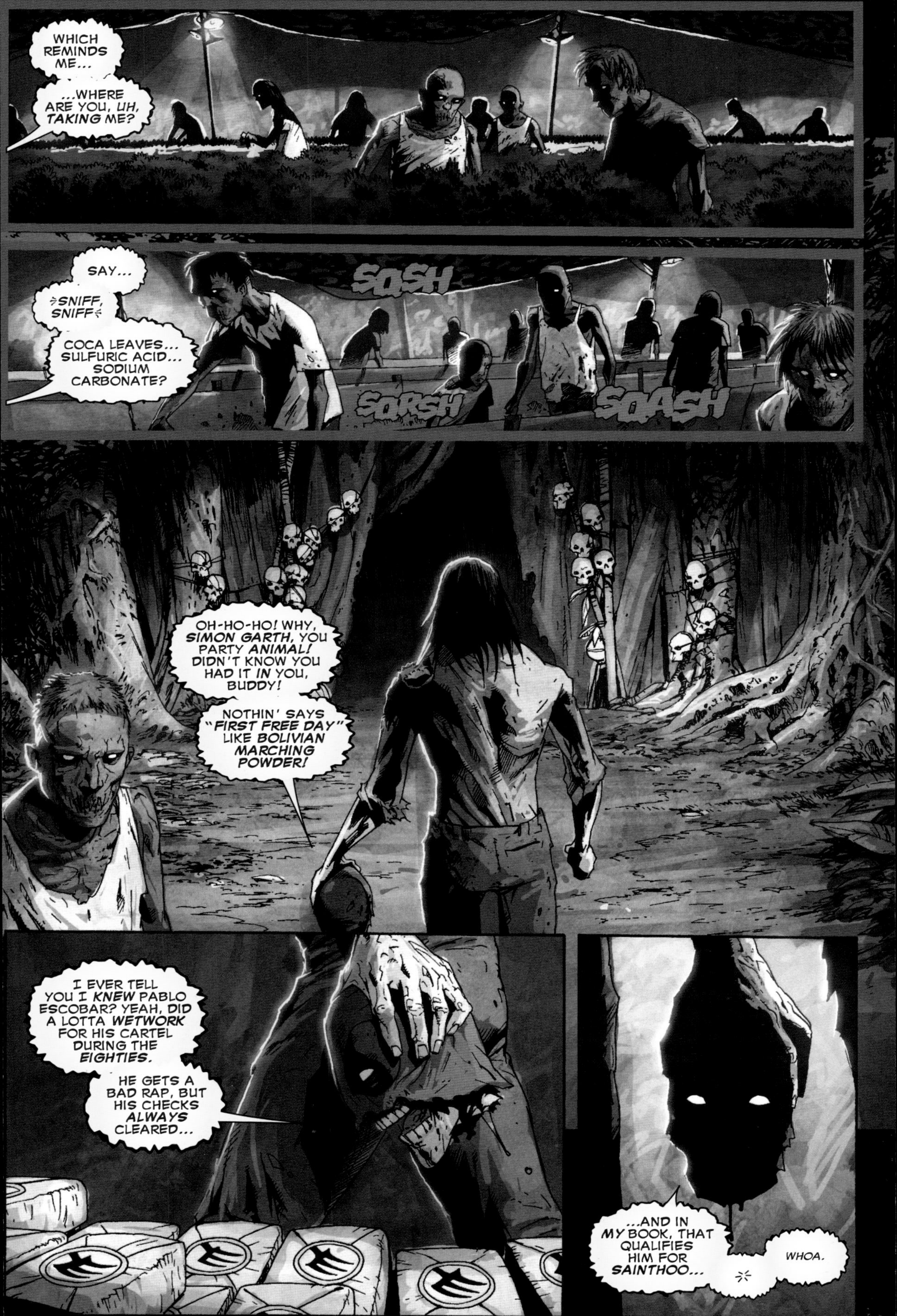
WHICH REMINDS ME...
...WHERE ARE YOU, UH, TAKING ME?
SAY...
SNIFF, SNIFF
COCA LEAVES... SULFURIC ACID... SODIUM CARBONATE?
SQSH
SQRSH
SQASH
OH-HO-HO! WHY, SIMON GARTH, YOU PARTY ANIMAL! DIDN'T KNOW YOU HAD IT IN YOU, BUDDY!
NOTHIN' SAYS "FIRST FREE DAY" LIKE BOLIVIAN MARCHING POWDER!
I EVER TELL YOU I KNEW PABLO ESCOBAR? YEAH, DID A LOTTA WETWORK FOR HIS CARTEL DURING THE EIGHTIES.
HE GETS A BAD RAP, BUT HIS CHECKS ALWAYS CLEARED...
...AND IN MY BOOK, THAT QUALIFIES HIM FOR SAINTHOO...
WHOA.

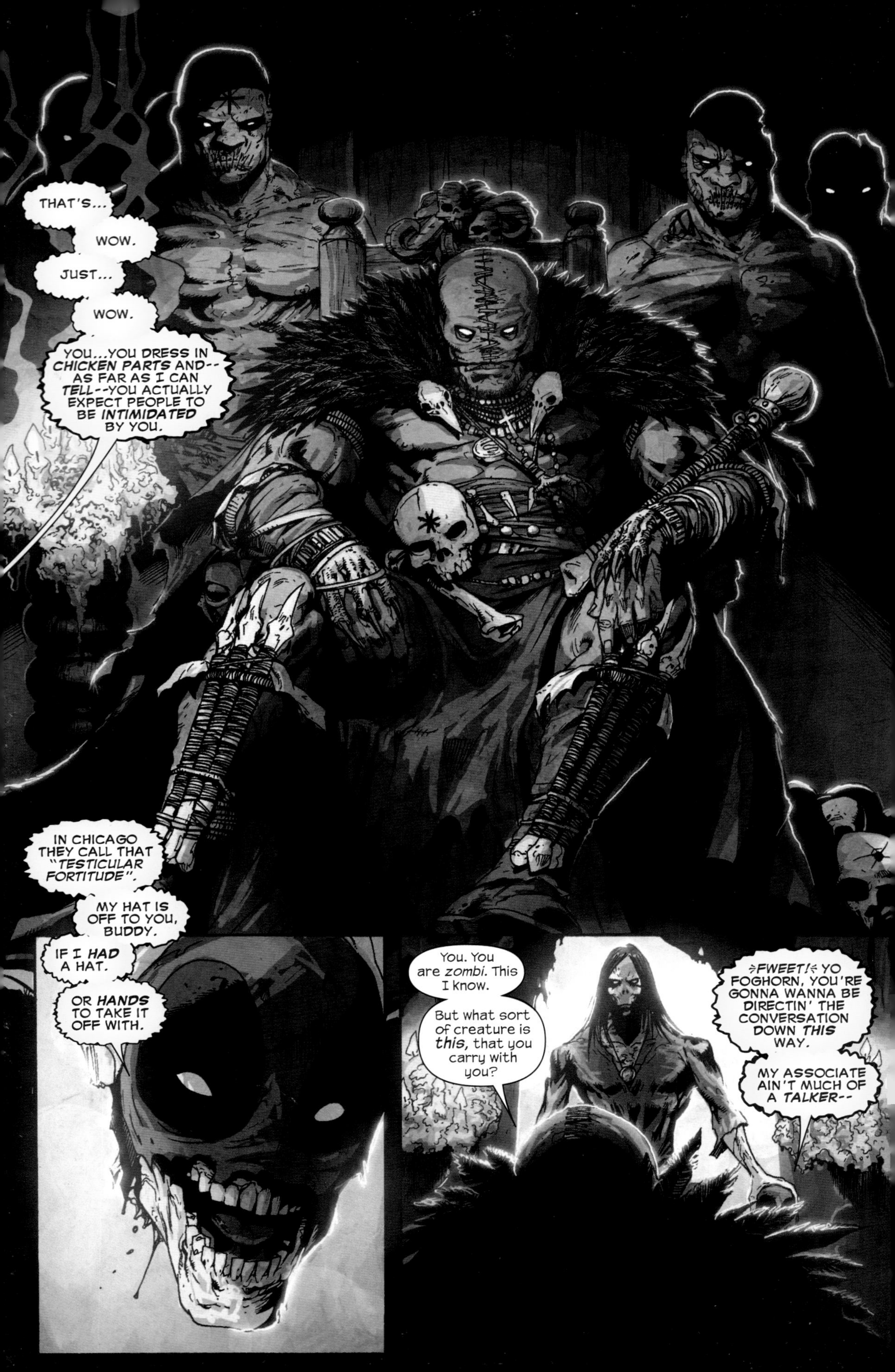
THAT'S...
WOW.
JUST...
WOW.
YOU...YOU **DRESS** IN ***CHICKEN PARTS*** AND--AS FAR AS I CAN ***TELL***--YOU ACTUALLY EXPECT PEOPLE TO BE ***INTIMIDATED*** BY YOU.
IN CHICAGO THEY CALL THAT "***TESTICULAR FORTITUDE***".
MY HAT IS OFF TO YOU, BUDDY.
IF I ***HAD*** A HAT.
OR ***HANDS*** TO TAKE IT OFF WITH.
You. You are *zombi*. This I know.
But what sort of creature is **this**, that you carry with you?
FWEET! YO FOGHORN, YOU'RE GONNA WANNA BE DIRECTIN' THE CONVERSATION DOWN ***THIS*** WAY.
MY ASSOCIATE AIN'T MUCH OF A ***TALKER***--

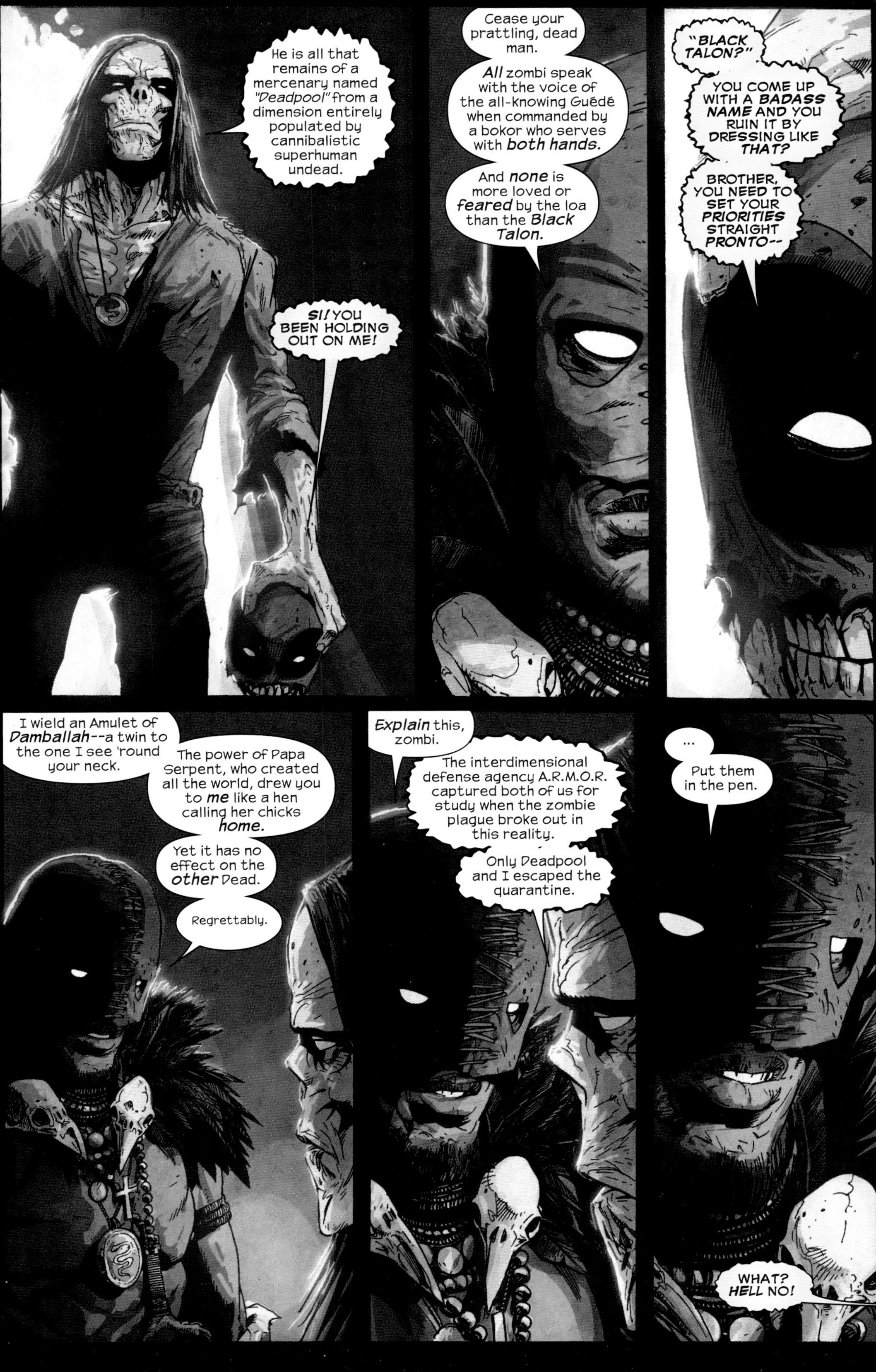

He is all that remains of a mercenary named "Deadpool" from a dimension entirely populated by cannibalistic superhuman undead.
SI! YOU BEEN HOLDING OUT ON ME!
Cease your prattling, dead man.
All zombi speak with the voice of the all-knowing Guédé when commanded by a bokor who serves with both hands.
And none is more loved or feared by the loa than the Black Talon.
"BLACK TALON?"
YOU COME UP WITH A BADASS NAME AND YOU RUIN IT BY DRESSING LIKE THAT?
BROTHER, YOU NEED TO SET YOUR PRIORITIES STRAIGHT PRONTO--
I wield an Amulet of Damballah--a twin to the one I see 'round your neck.
The power of Papa Serpent, who created all the world, drew you to me like a hen calling her chicks home.
Yet it has no effect on the other Dead.
Regrettably.
Explain this, zombi.
The interdimensional defense agency A.R.M.O.R. captured both of us for study when the zombie plague broke out in this reality.
Only Deadpool and I escaped the quarantine.
...
Put them in the pen.
WHAT? HELL NO!

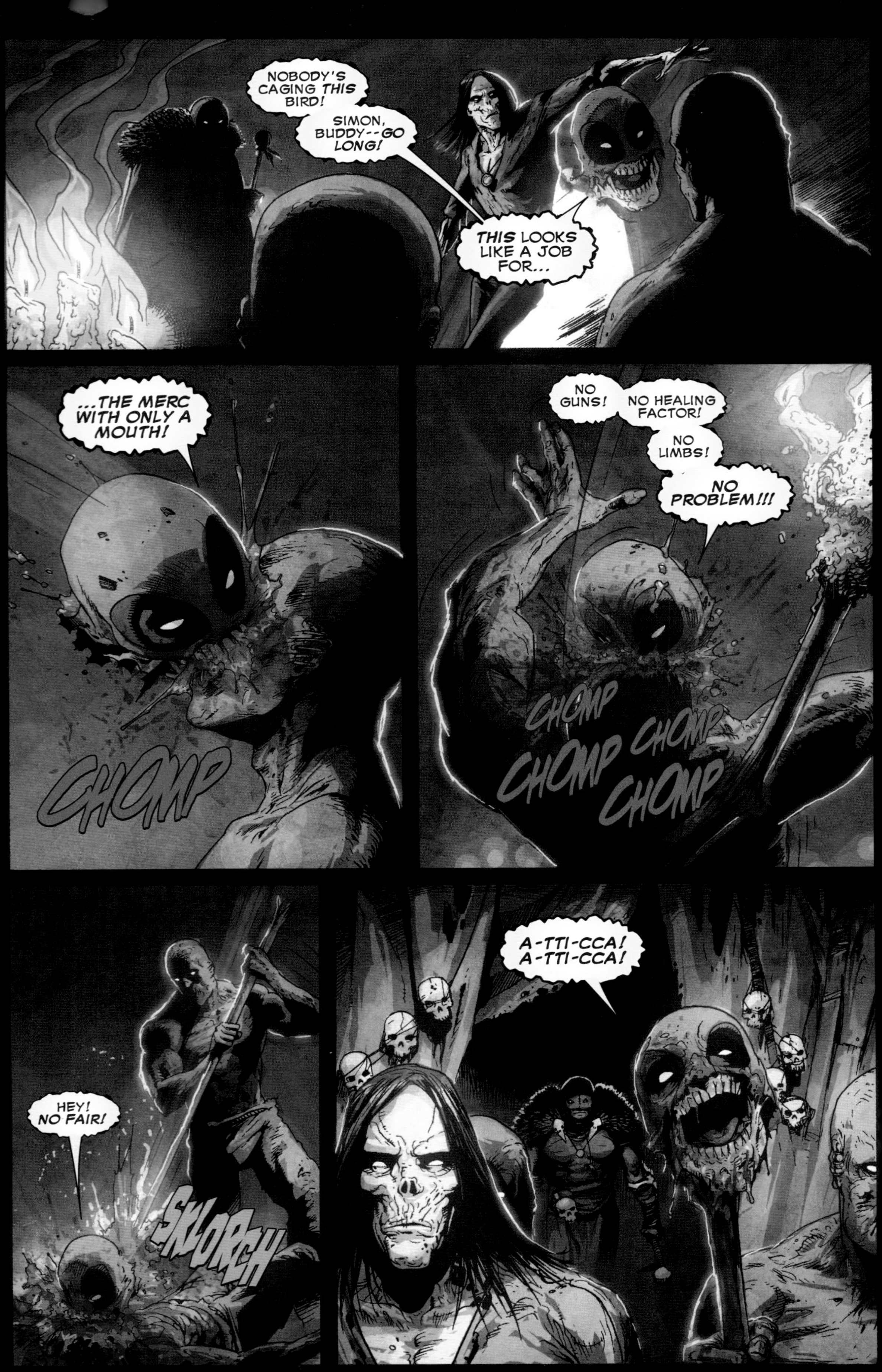
NOBODY'S CAGING THIS BIRD!
SIMON, BUDDY--GO LONG!
THIS LOOKS LIKE A JOB FOR...
...THE MERC WITH ONLY A MOUTH!
CHOMP
NO GUNS!
NO HEALING FACTOR!
NO LIMBS!
NO PROBLEM!!!
CHOMP
CHOMP CHOMP
CHOMP
HEY! NO FAIR!
SKLORCH
A-TTI-CCA! A-TTI-CCA!

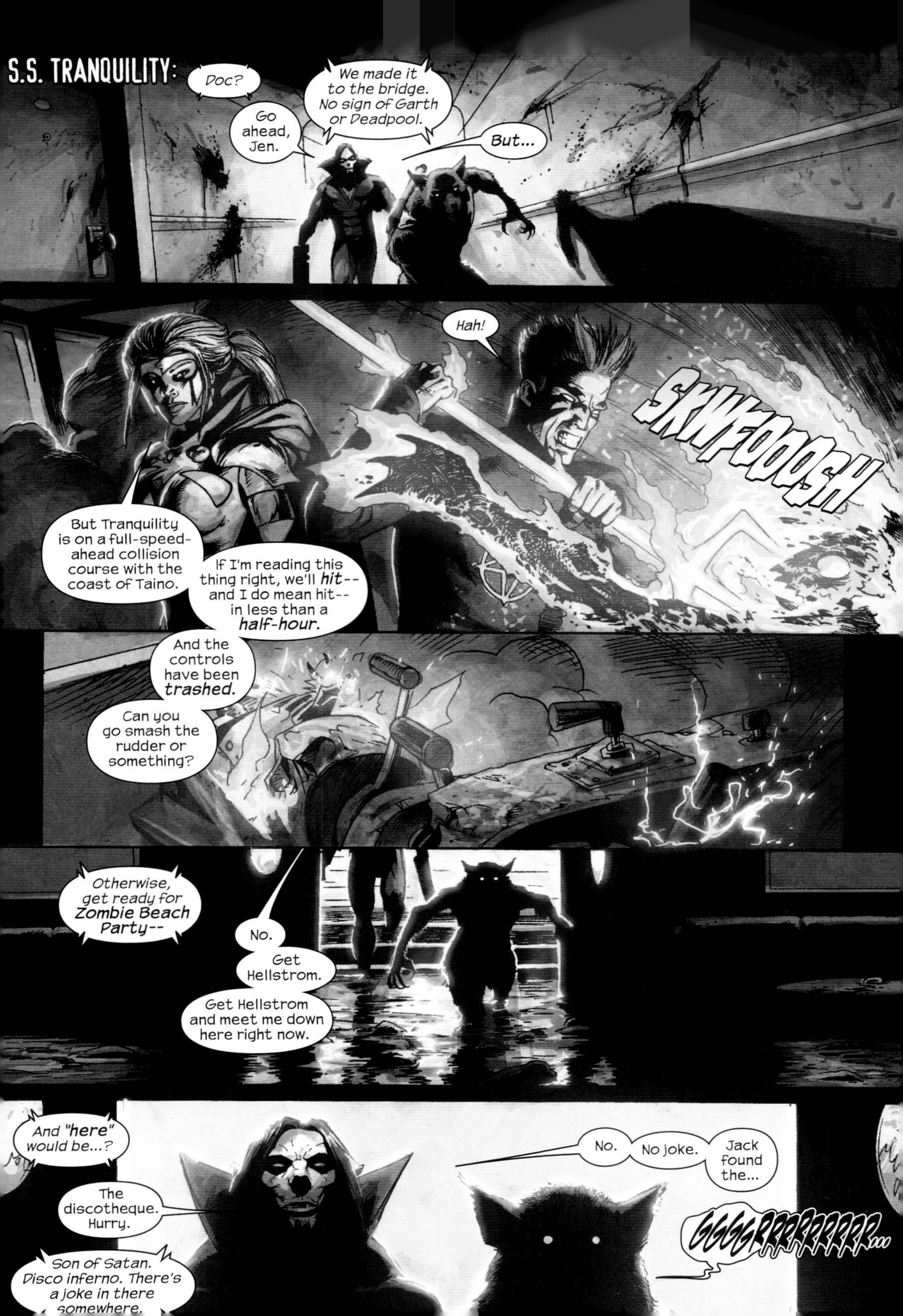
S.S. TRANQUILITY:
Doc?
We made it to the bridge. No sign of Garth or Deadpool.
Go ahead, Jen.
But...
Hah!
SKWFOOOSH
But Tranquility is on a full-speed-ahead collision course with the coast of Taino.
If I'm reading this thing right, we'll hit--and I do mean hit--in less than a half-hour.
And the controls have been trashed.
Can you go smash the rudder or something?
Otherwise, get ready for Zombie Beach Party--
No.
Get Hellstrom.
Get Hellstrom and meet me down here right now.
And "here" would be...?
The discotheque. Hurry.
Son of Satan. Disco inferno. There's a joke in there somewhere.
No.
No joke.
Jack found the...
GGGGRRRRRRRRRR...

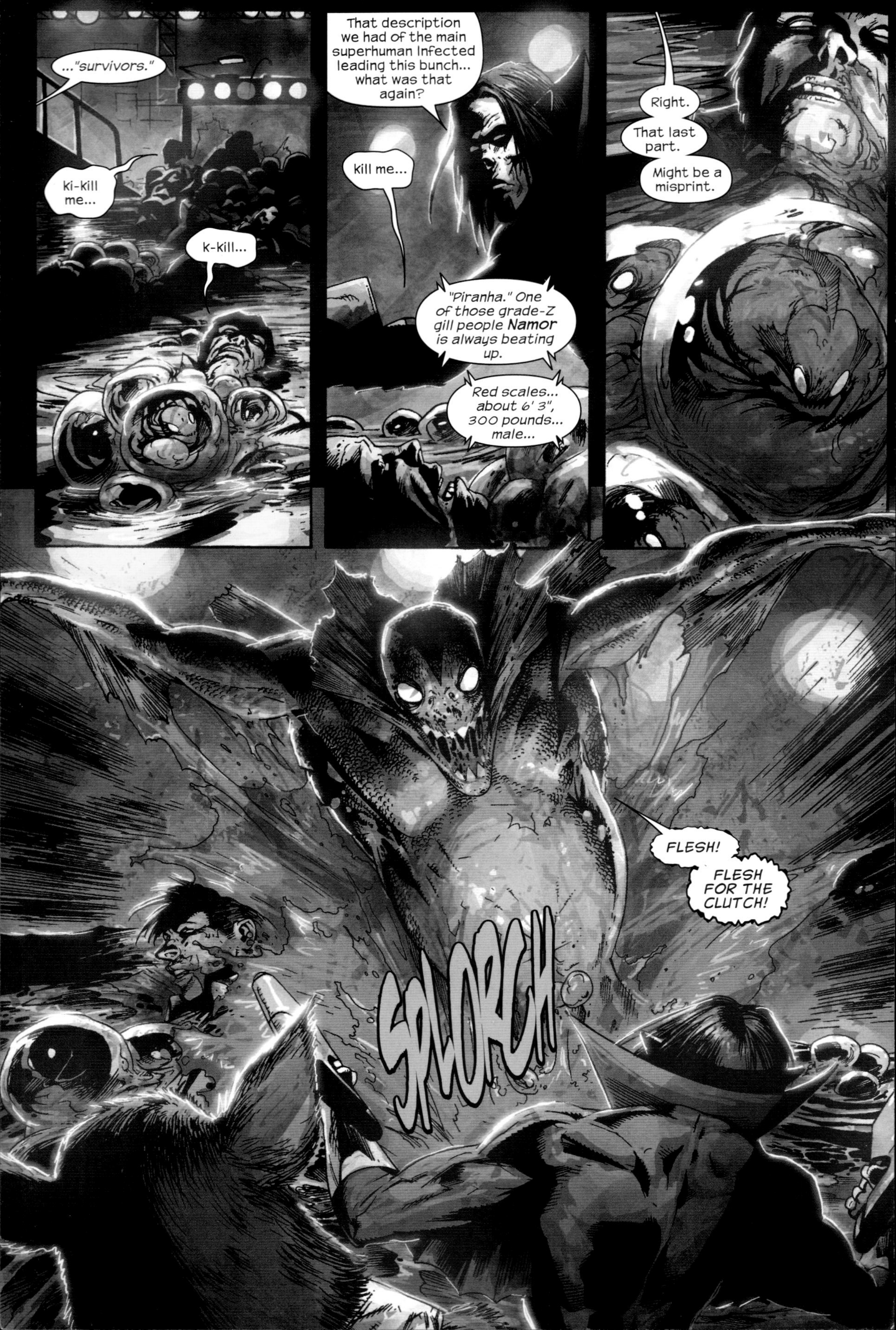

..."survivors."
ki-kill me...
K-kill...
That description we had of the main superhuman Infected leading this bunch... what was that again?
kill me...
"Piranha." One of those grade-Z gill people Namor is always beating up.
Red scales... about 6' 3", 300 pounds... male...
Right.
That last part.
Might be a misprint.
FLESH!
FLESH FOR THE CLUTCH!
SPLORCH

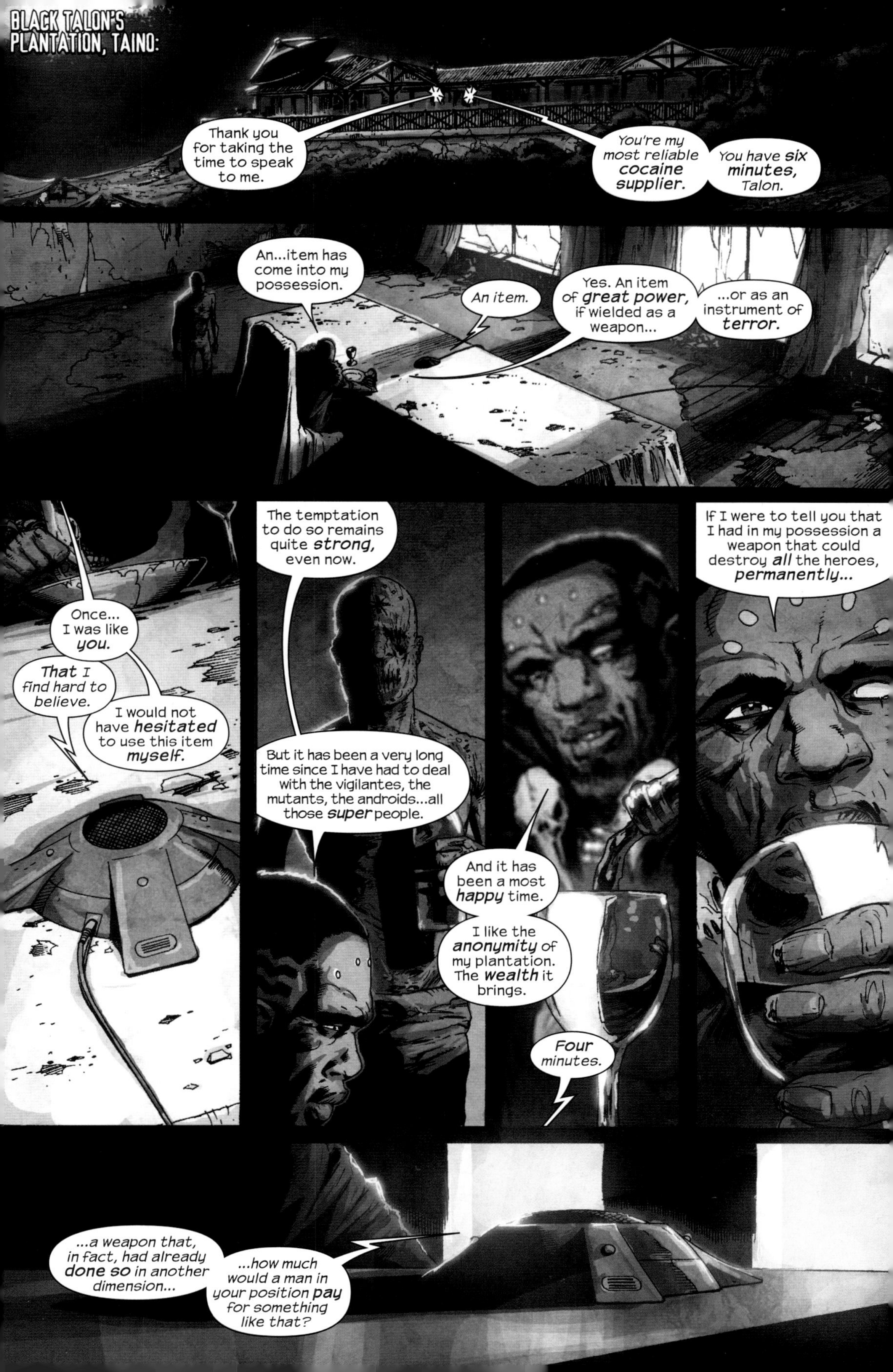
BLACK TALON'S PLANTATION, TAINO:
Thank you for taking the time to speak to me.
You're my most reliable cocaine supplier.
You have six minutes, Talon.
An...item has come into my possession.
An item.
Yes. An item of great power, if wielded as a weapon...
...or as an instrument of terror.
Once... I was like you.
That I find hard to believe.
I would not have hesitated to use this item myself.
The temptation to do so remains quite strong, even now.
But it has been a very long time since I have had to deal with the vigilantes, the mutants, the androids...all those super people.
And it has been a most happy time.
I like the anonymity of my plantation. The wealth it brings.
Four minutes.
If I were to tell you that I had in my possession a weapon that could destroy all the heroes, permanently...
...a weapon that, in fact, had already done so in another dimension...
...how much would a man in your position pay for something like that?

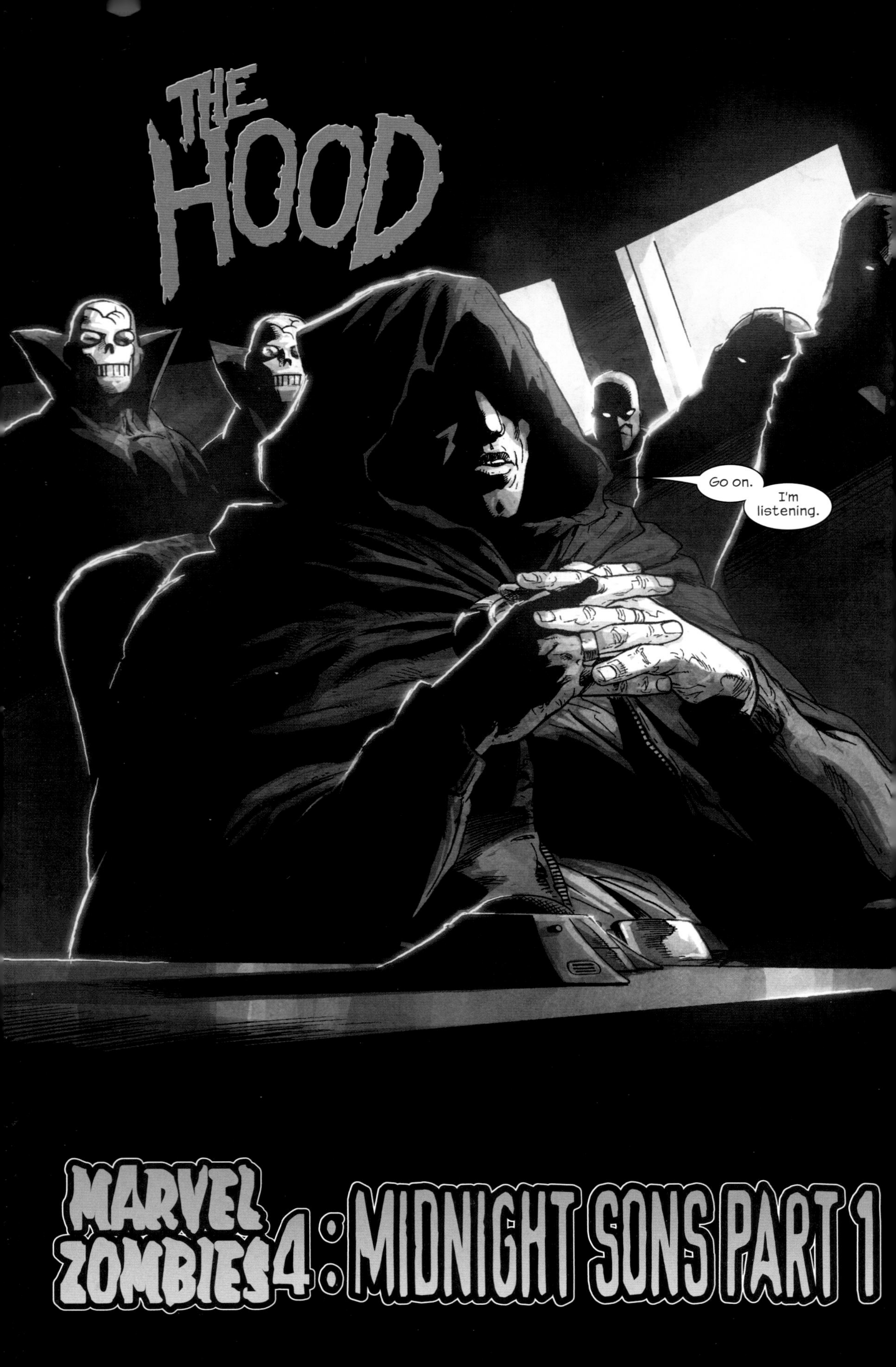
THE HOOD
Go on.
I'm listening.
MARVEL ZOMBIES 4: MIDNIGHT SONS PART 1

#1 VARIANT BY ARTHUR SUYDAM

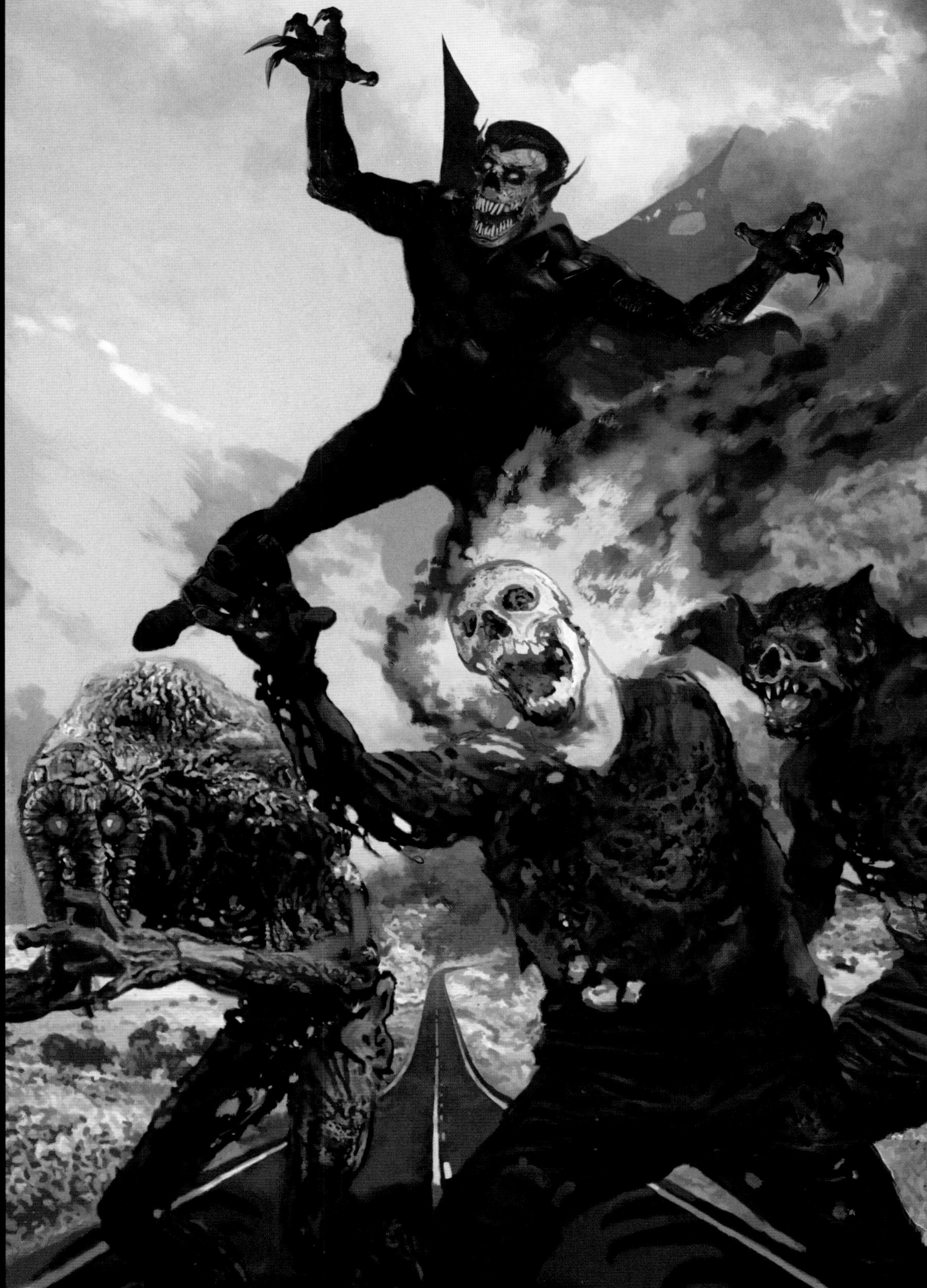

#2

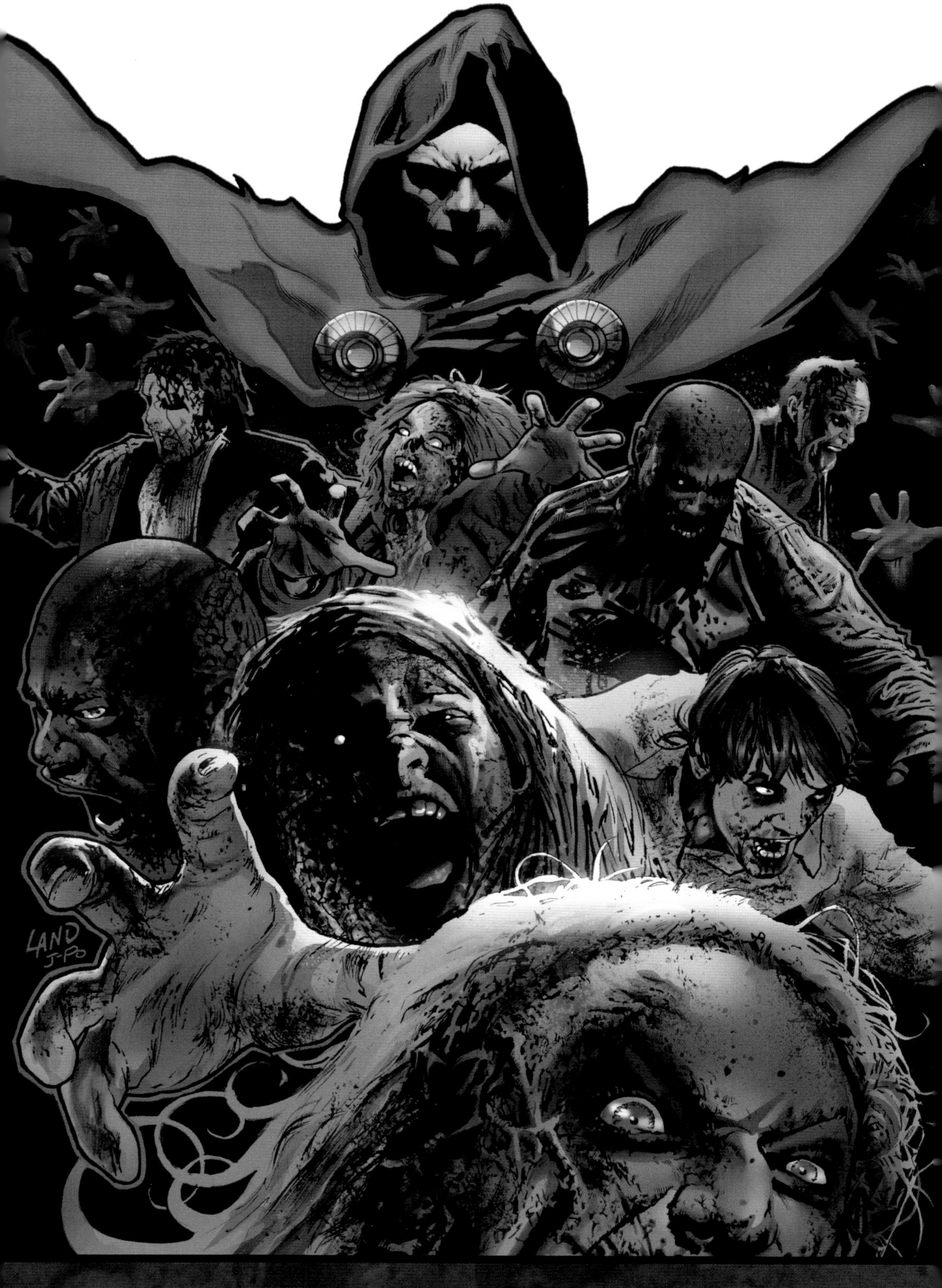
LAND
J-Po

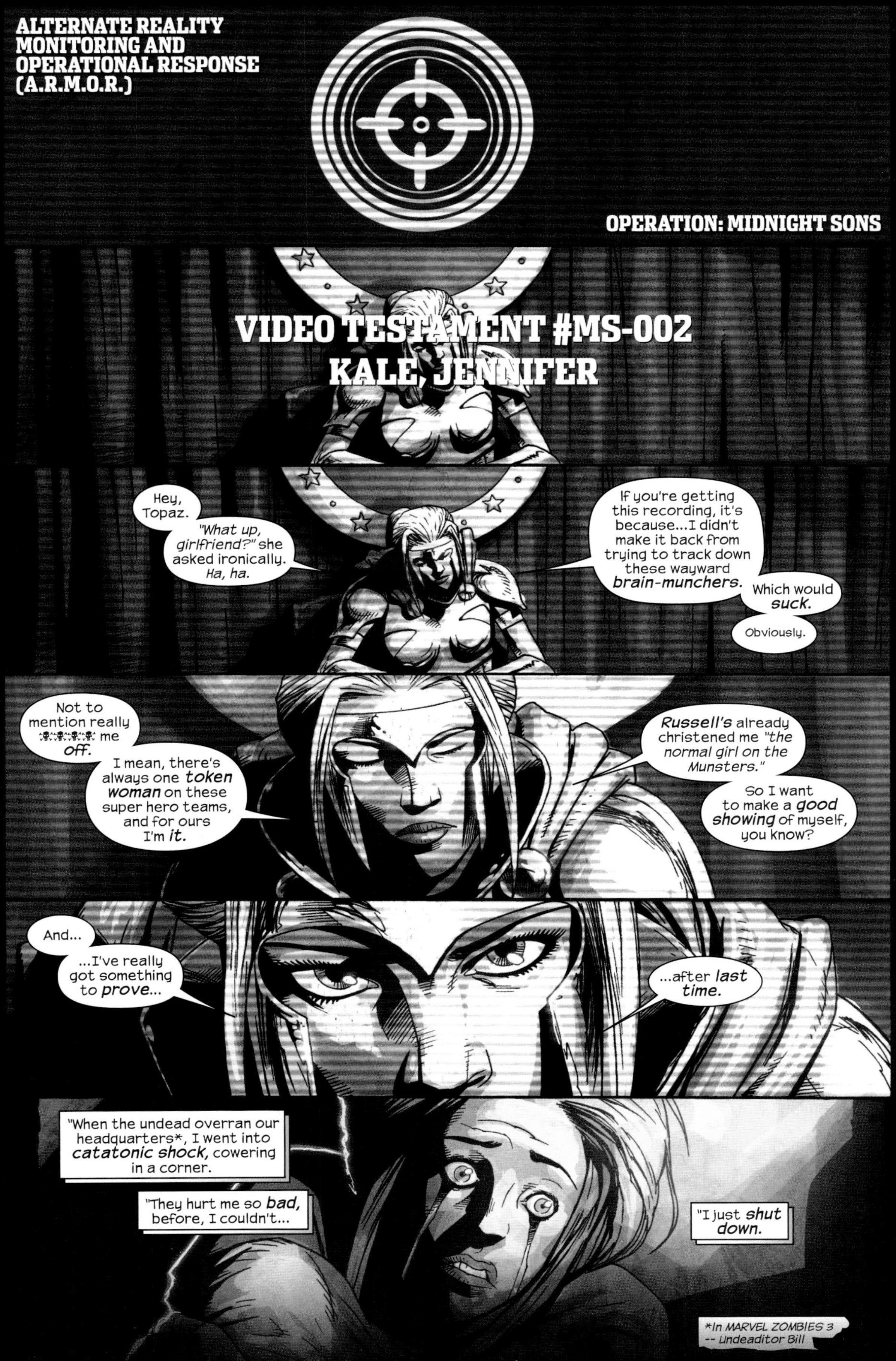
ALTERNATE REALITY MONITORING AND OPERATIONAL RESPONSE (A.R.M.O.R.)
OPERATION: MIDNIGHT SONS
VIDEO TESTAMENT #MS-002
KALE, JENNIFER
Hey, Topaz.
"What up, girlfriend?" she asked ironically. Ha, ha.
If you're getting this recording, it's because...I didn't make it back from trying to track down these wayward brain-munchers.
Which would suck.
Obviously.
Not to mention really ☠☠☠☠ me off.
I mean, there's always one token woman on these super hero teams, and for ours I'm it.
Russell's already christened me "the normal girl on the Munsters."
So I want to make a good showing of myself, you know?
And...
...I've really got something to prove...
...after last time.
"When the undead overran our headquarters*, I went into catatonic shock, cowering in a corner.
"They hurt me so bad, before, I couldn't...
"I just shut down.
*In MARVEL ZOMBIES 3 -- Undeaditor Bill

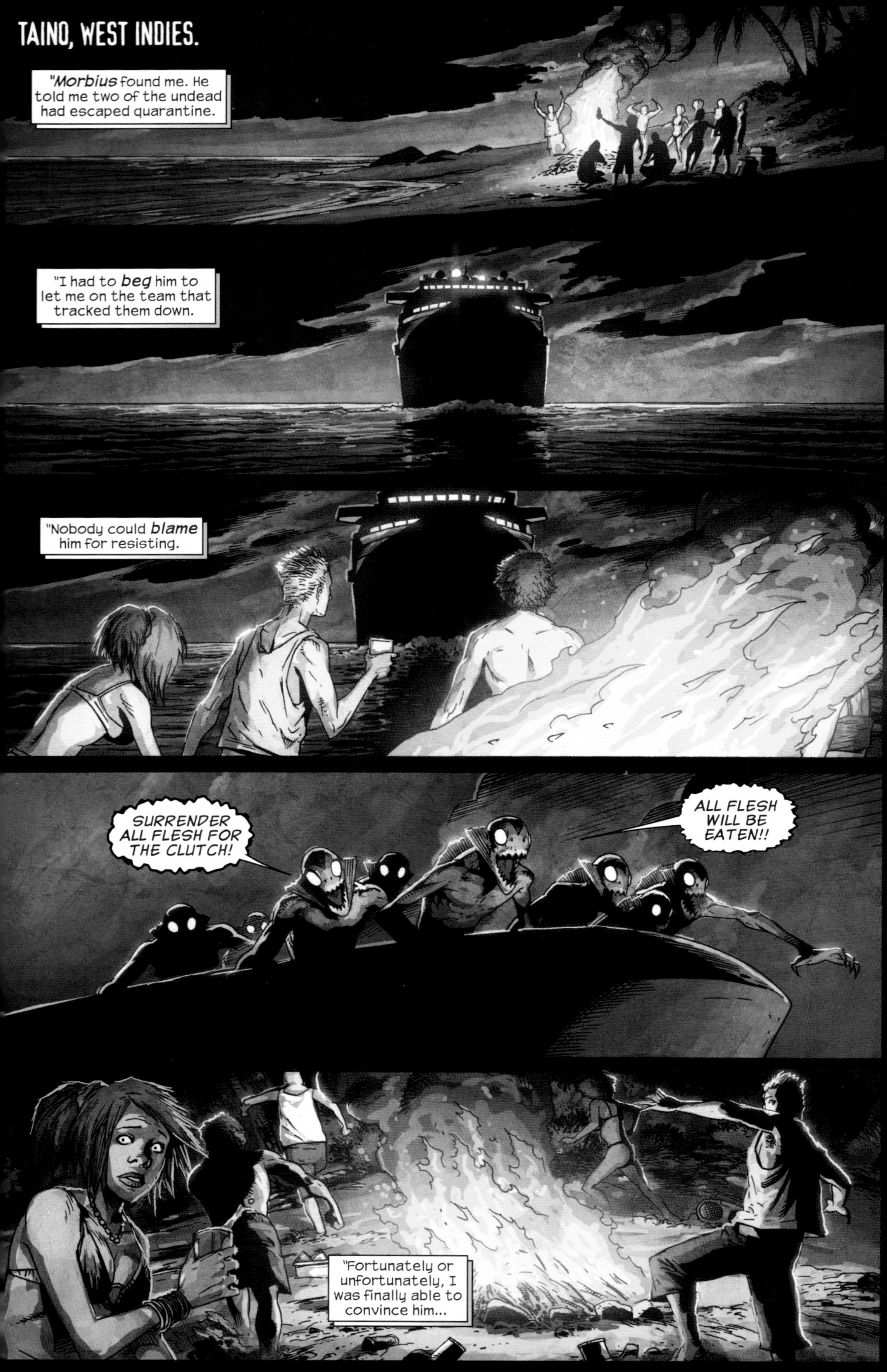
TAINO, WEST INDIES.
"Morbius found me. He told me two of the undead had escaped quarantine.
"I had to beg him to let me on the team that tracked them down.
"Nobody could blame him for resisting.
SURRENDER ALL FLESH FOR THE CLUTCH!
ALL FLESH WILL BE EATEN!!
"Fortunately or unfortunately, I was finally able to convince him...

"...I could still be of some *use.*
"*And* I was willing to inject the zombie virus *vaccine* he developed into my body."
You snagged *us* off the ship with your teleportation spell, Jen...
...but where's *Hellstrom?*

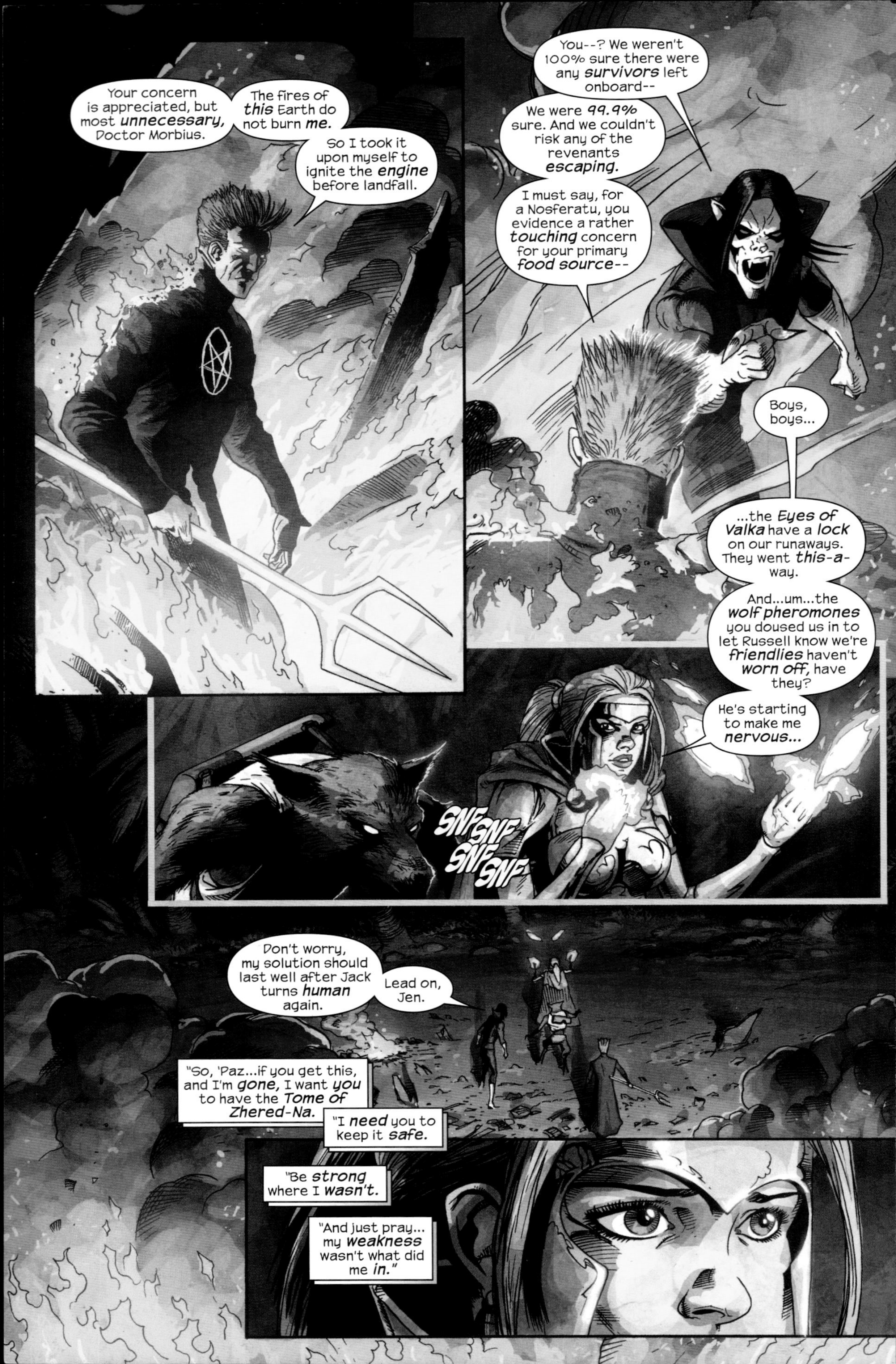

Your concern is appreciated, but most *unnecessary,* Doctor Morbius.
The fires of *this* Earth do not burn *me.*
So I took it upon myself to ignite the *engine* before landfall.
You--? We weren't 100% sure there were any *survivors* left onboard--
We were *99.9%* sure. And we couldn't risk any of the revenants *escaping.*
I must say, for a Nosferatu, you evidence a rather *touching* concern for your primary *food source*--
Boys, boys...
...the *Eyes of Valka* have a *lock* on our runaways. They went *this-a*-way.
And...um...the *wolf pheromones* you doused us in to let Russell know we're *friendlies* haven't *worn off,* have they?
He's starting to make me *nervous...*
SNF SNF SNF SNF
Don't worry, my solution should last well after Jack turns *human* again.
Lead on, Jen.
"So, 'Paz...if you get this, and I'm *gone,* I want *you* to have the *Tome of Zhered-Na.*
"I *need* you to keep it *safe.*
"Be *strong* where I *wasn't.*
"And just pray... my *weakness* wasn't what did me *in.*"

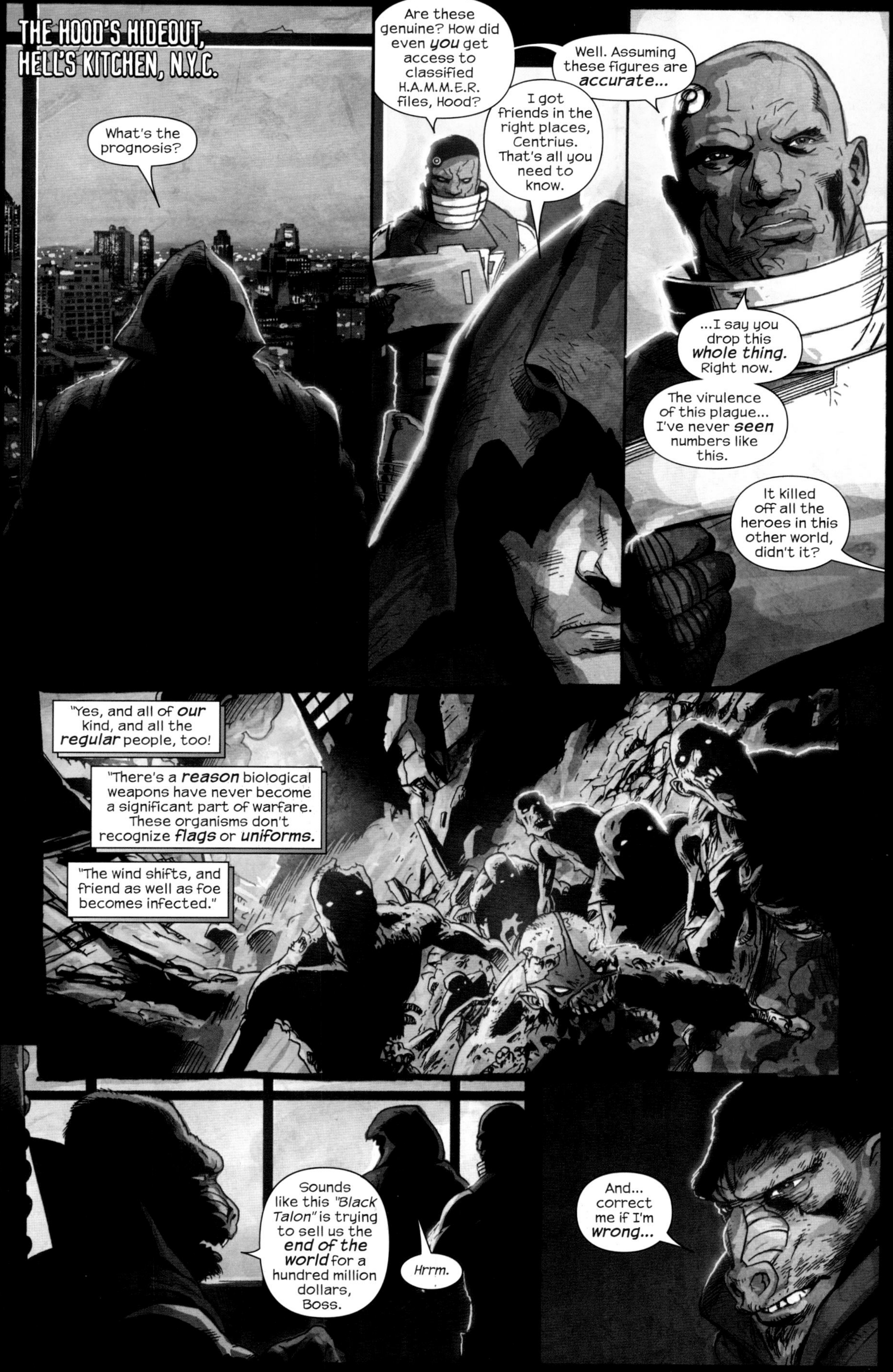
THE HOOD'S HIDEOUT, HELL'S KITCHEN, N.Y.C.
What's the prognosis?
Are these genuine? How did even you get access to classified H.A.M.M.E.R. files, Hood?
I got friends in the right places, Centrius. That's all you need to know.
Well. Assuming these figures are accurate...
...I say you drop this whole thing. Right now.
The virulence of this plague... I've never seen numbers like this.
It killed off all the heroes in this other world, didn't it?
"Yes, and all of our kind, and all the regular people, too!
"There's a reason biological weapons have never become a significant part of warfare. These organisms don't recognize flags or uniforms.
"The wind shifts, and friend as well as foe becomes infected."
Sounds like this "Black Talon" is trying to sell us the end of the world for a hundred million dollars, Boss.
Hrrm.
And... correct me if I'm wrong...

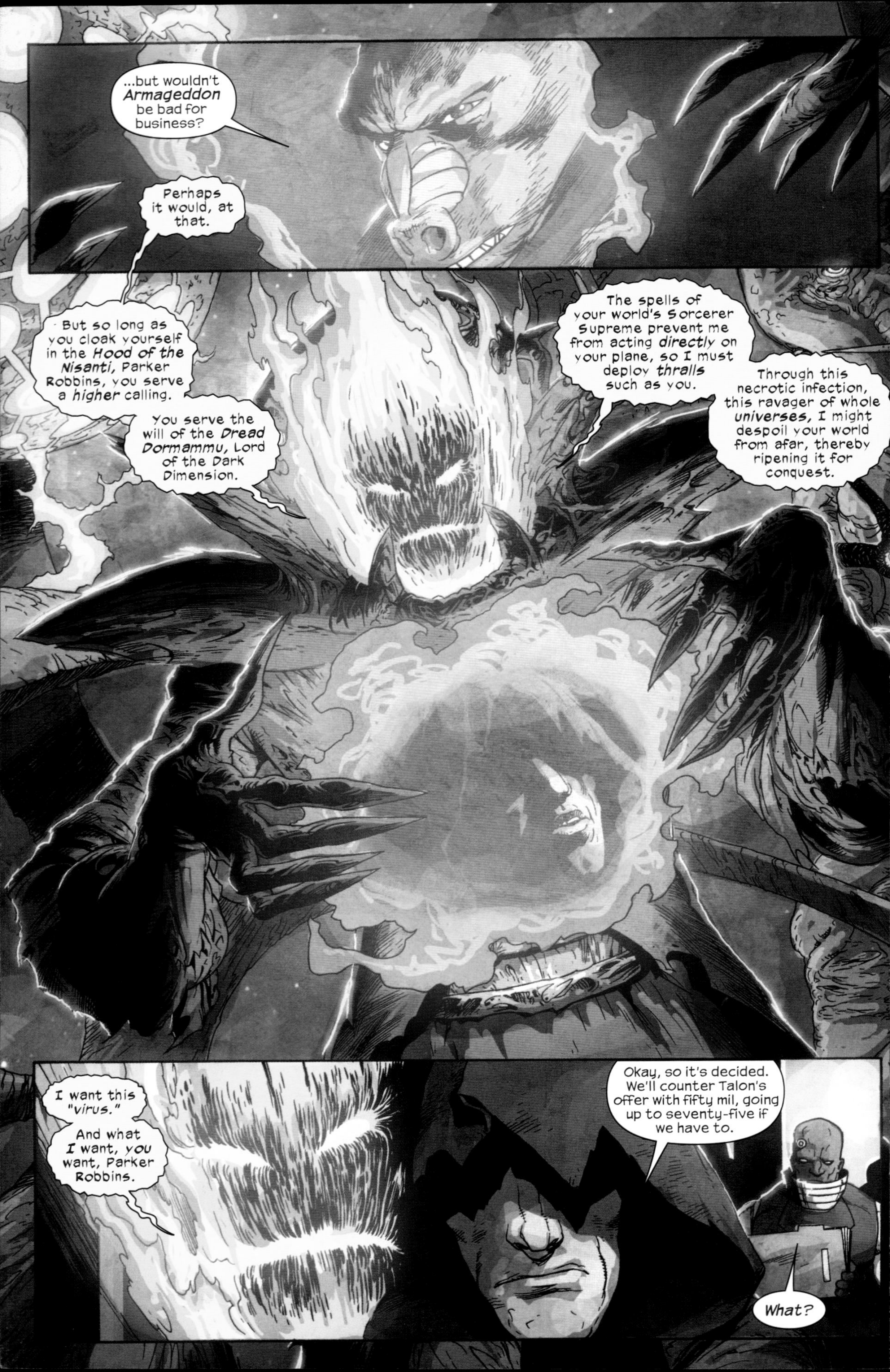
...but wouldn't *Armageddon* be bad for business?
Perhaps it would, at that.
But so long as you cloak yourself in the *Hood of the Nisanti*, Parker Robbins, you serve a *higher* calling.
You serve the will of the *Dread Dormammu*, Lord of the Dark Dimension.
The spells of your world's Sorcerer Supreme prevent me from acting *directly* on your plane, so I must deploy *thralls* such as you.
Through this necrotic infection, this ravager of whole *universes*, I might despoil your world from afar, thereby ripening it for conquest.
I want this *"virus."*
And what *I* want, *you* want, Parker Robbins.
Okay, so it's decided. We'll counter Talon's offer with fifty mil, going up to seventy-five if we have to.
What?

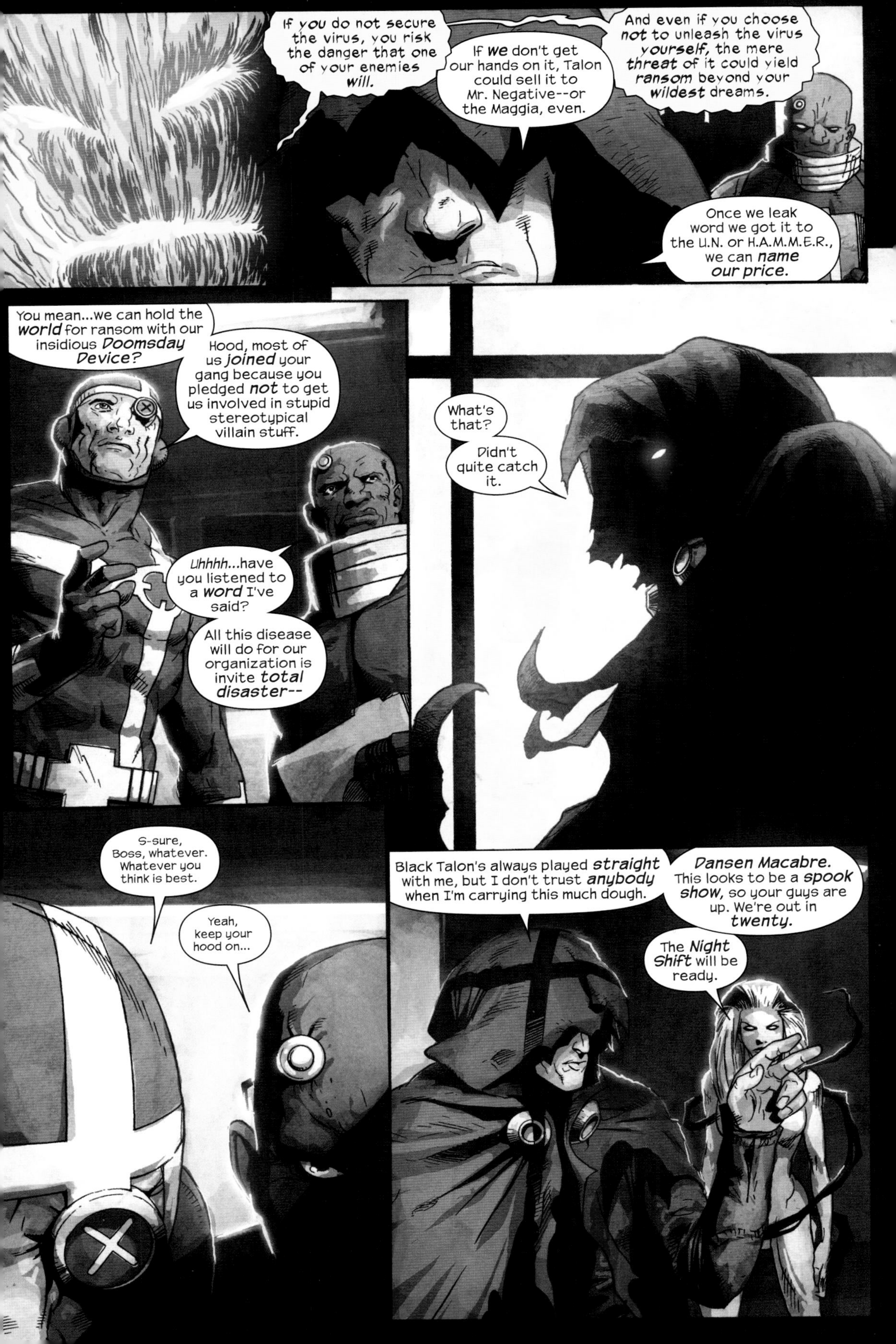

If *you* do not secure the virus, you risk the danger that one of your enemies *will.*
If *we* don't get our hands on it, Talon could sell it to Mr. Negative--or the Maggia, even.
And even if you choose *not* to unleash the virus *yourself,* the mere *threat* of it could yield *ransom* beyond your *wildest* dreams.
Once we leak word we got it to the U.N. or H.A.M.M.E.R., we can *name our price.*
You mean...we can hold the *world* for ransom with our insidious *Doomsday Device?*
Hood, most of us *joined* your gang because you pledged *not* to get us involved in stupid stereotypical villain stuff.
What's that?
Didn't quite catch it.
Uhhhh...have you listened to a *word* I've said?
All this disease will do for our organization is invite *total disaster--*
S-sure, Boss, whatever. Whatever you think is best.
Yeah, keep your hood on...
Black Talon's always played *straight* with me, but I don't trust *anybody* when I'm carrying this much dough.
Dansen Macabre. This looks to be a *spook show,* so your guys are up. We're out in *twenty.*
The *Night Shift* will be ready.

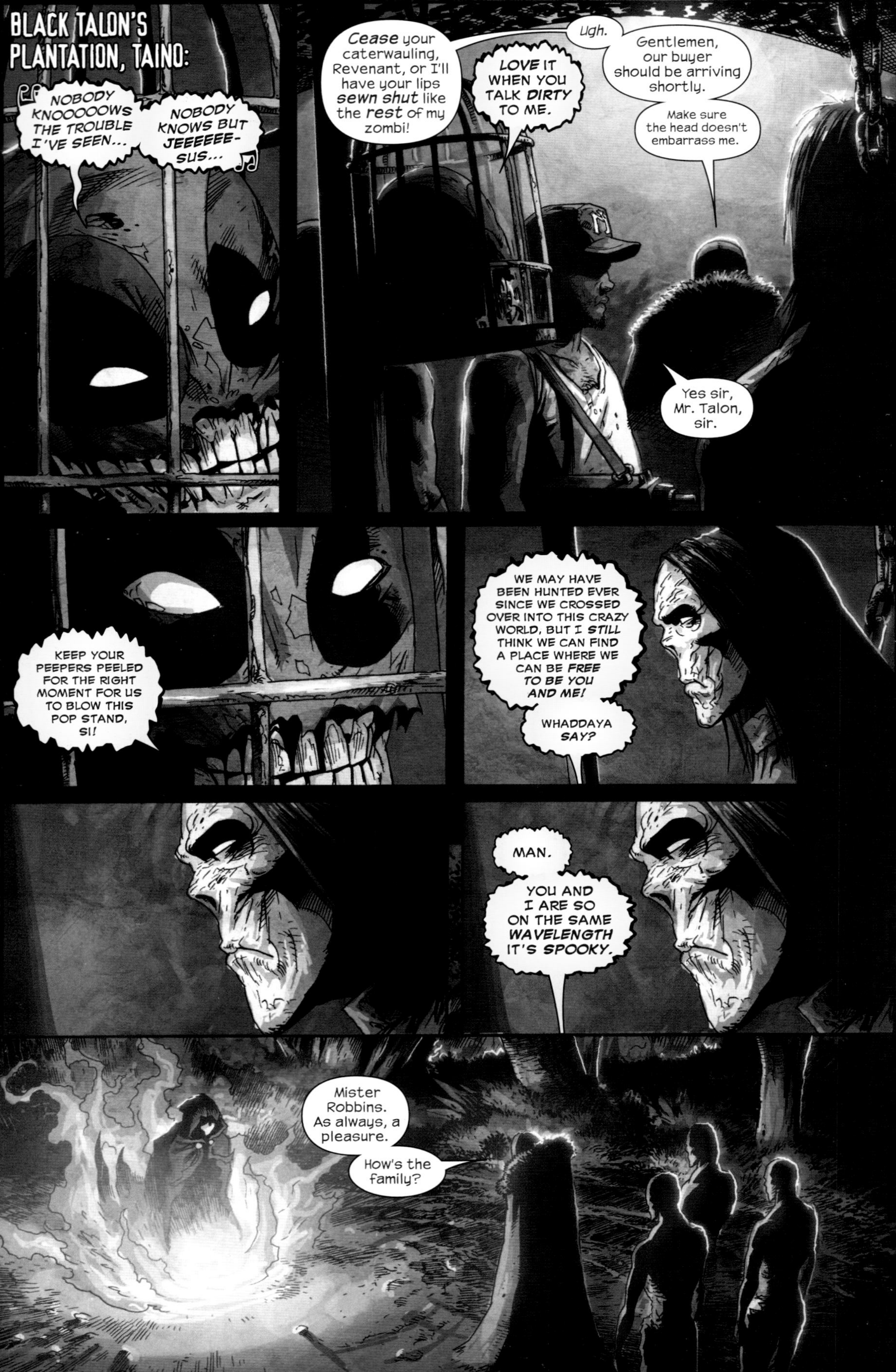
BLACK TALON'S PLANTATION, TAINO:
NOBODY KNOOOOOWS THE TROUBLE I'VE SEEN...
NOBODY KNOWS BUT JEEEEEE-SUS...
Cease your caterwauling, Revenant, or I'll have your lips sewn shut like the rest of my zombi!
LOVE IT WHEN YOU TALK DIRTY TO ME.
Ugh.
Gentlemen, our buyer should be arriving shortly.
Make sure the head doesn't embarrass me.
Yes sir, Mr. Talon, sir.
KEEP YOUR PEEPERS PEELED FOR THE RIGHT MOMENT FOR US TO BLOW THIS POP STAND, SI!
WE MAY HAVE BEEN HUNTED EVER SINCE WE CROSSED OVER INTO THIS CRAZY WORLD, BUT I STILL THINK WE CAN FIND A PLACE WHERE WE CAN BE FREE TO BE YOU AND ME!
WHADDAYA SAY?
MAN.
YOU AND I ARE SO ON THE SAME WAVELENGTH IT'S SPOOKY.
Mister Robbins. As always, a pleasure.
How's the family?

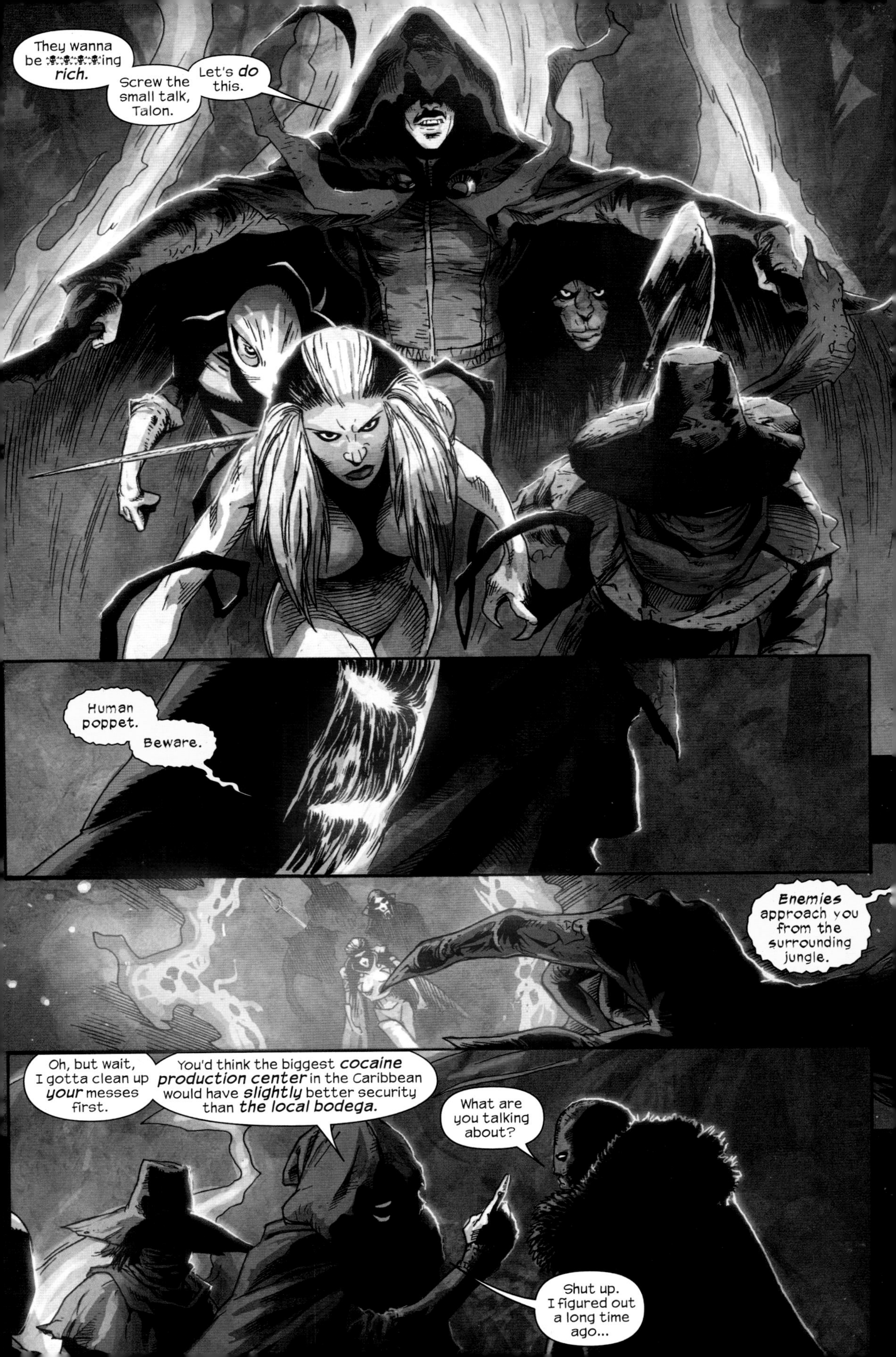
They wanna be ☠☠☠ing rich.
Screw the small talk, Talon.
Let's do this.
Human poppet.
Beware.
Enemies approach you from the surrounding jungle.
Oh, but wait, I gotta clean up your messes first.
You'd think the biggest cocaine production center in the Caribbean would have slightly better security than the local bodega.
What are you talking about?
Shut up. I figured out a long time ago...

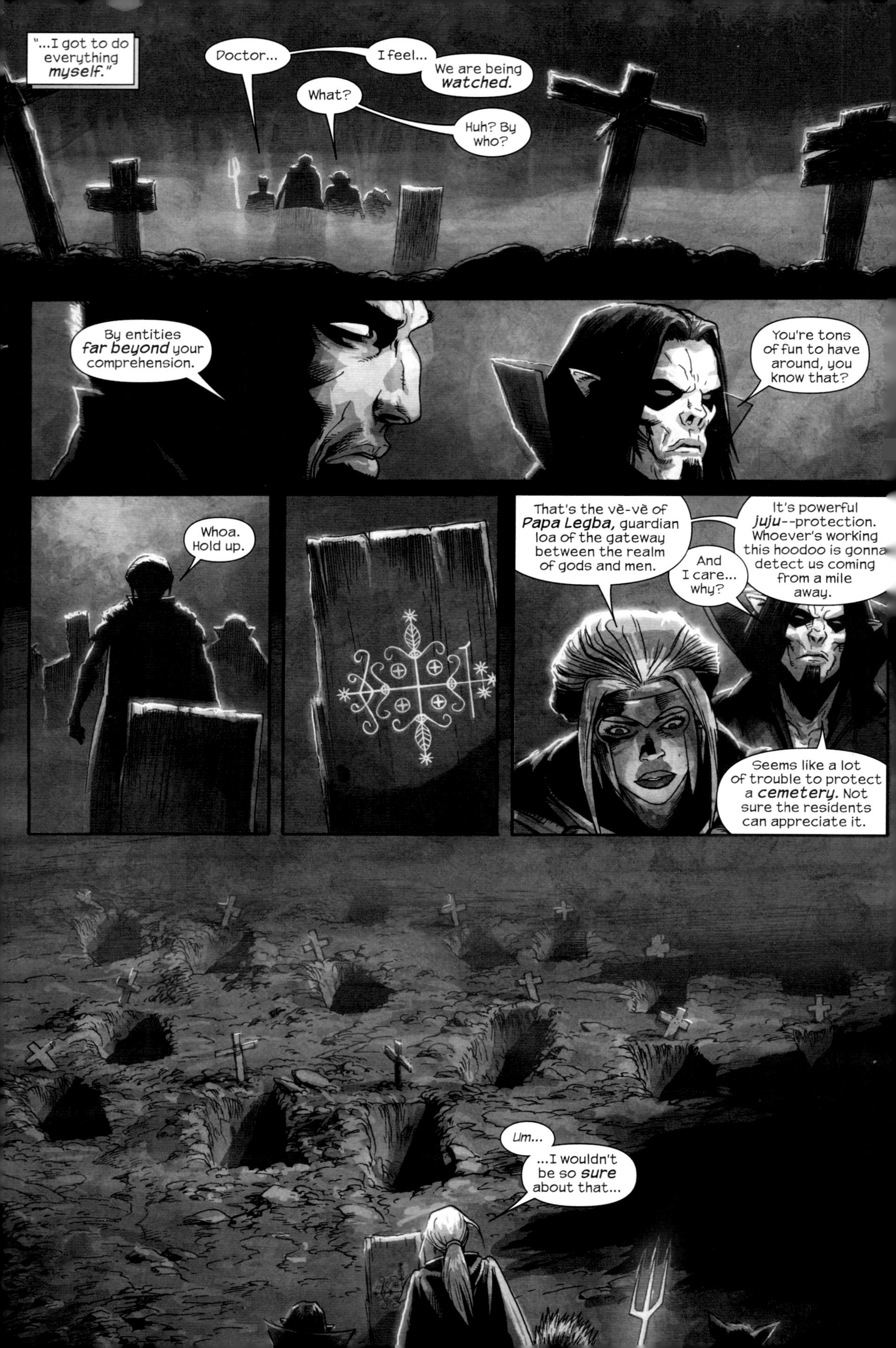
"...I got to do everything *myself.*"
Doctor...
I feel...
We are being *watched.*
What?
Huh? By who?
By entities *far beyond* your comprehension.
You're tons of fun to have around, you know that?
Whoa. Hold up.
That's the vē-vē of *Papa Legba,* guardian loa of the gateway between the realm of gods and men.
And I care... why?
It's powerful *juju*--protection. Whoever's working this hoodoo is gonna detect us coming from a mile away.
Seems like a lot of trouble to protect a *cemetery.* Not sure the residents can appreciate it.
Um...
...I wouldn't be so *sure* about that...

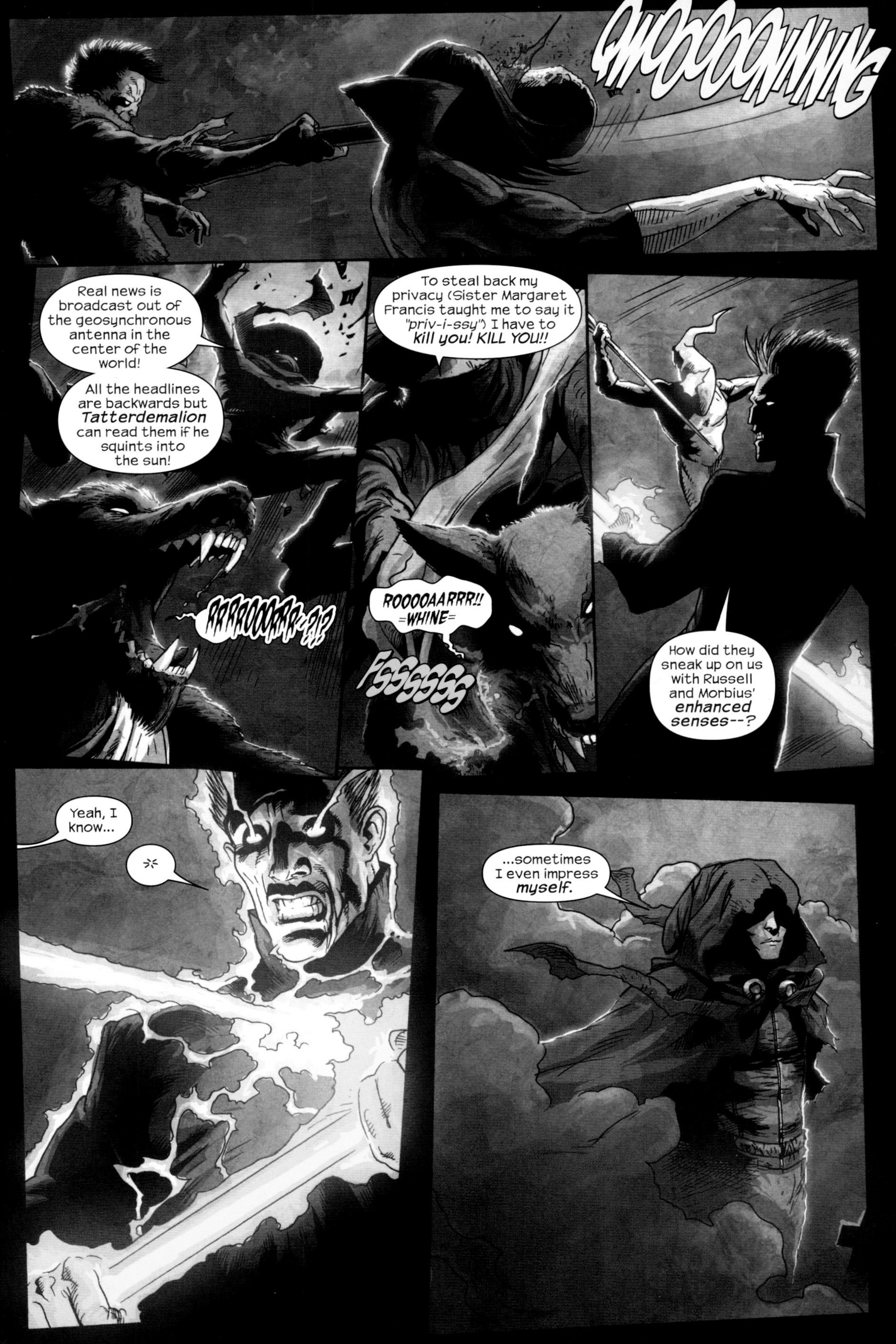

CHOOOOONNNNG
Real news is broadcast out of the geosynchronous antenna in the center of the world!
All the headlines are backwards but Tatterdemalion can read them if he squints into the sun!
ARRROOOARR-?!?
To steal back my privacy (Sister Margaret Francis taught me to say it "priv-i-ssy") I have to kill you! KILL YOU!!
ROOOOAARRR!! =WHINE=
FSSSSSS
How did they sneak up on us with Russell and Morbius' enhanced senses--?
Yeah, I know...
...sometimes I even impress myself.

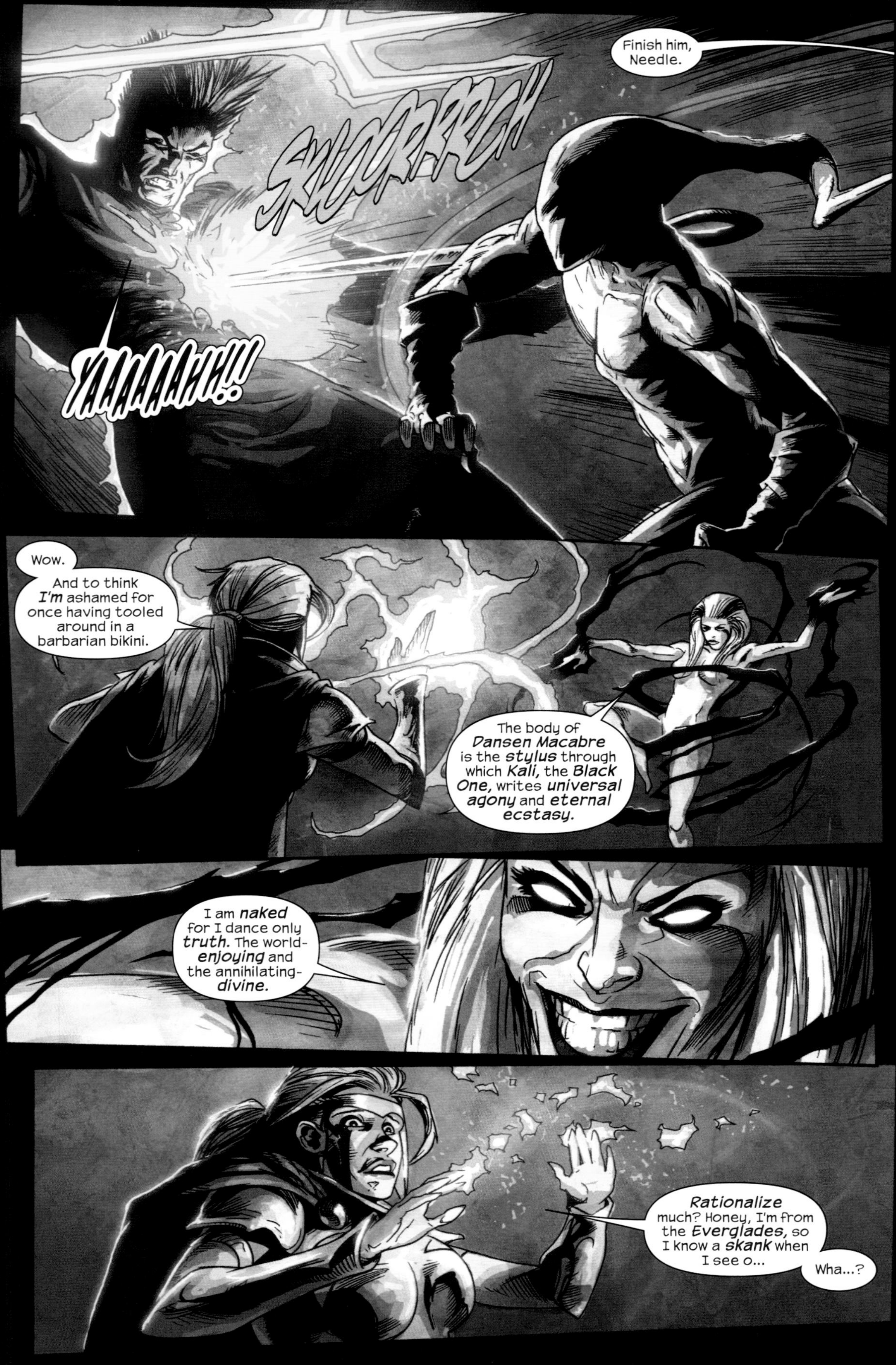
Finish him, Needle.
SKLUCRRRCH
YAAAAAAHH!!
Wow.
And to think *I'm* ashamed for once having tooled around in a barbarian bikini.
The body of *Dansen Macabre* is the *stylus* through which *Kali,* the *Black One,* writes *universal agony* and *eternal ecstasy.*
I am *naked* for I dance only *truth.* The world-*enjoying* and the annihilating-*divine.*
Rationalize much? Honey, I'm from the *Everglades,* so I know a *skank* when I see o...
Wha...?

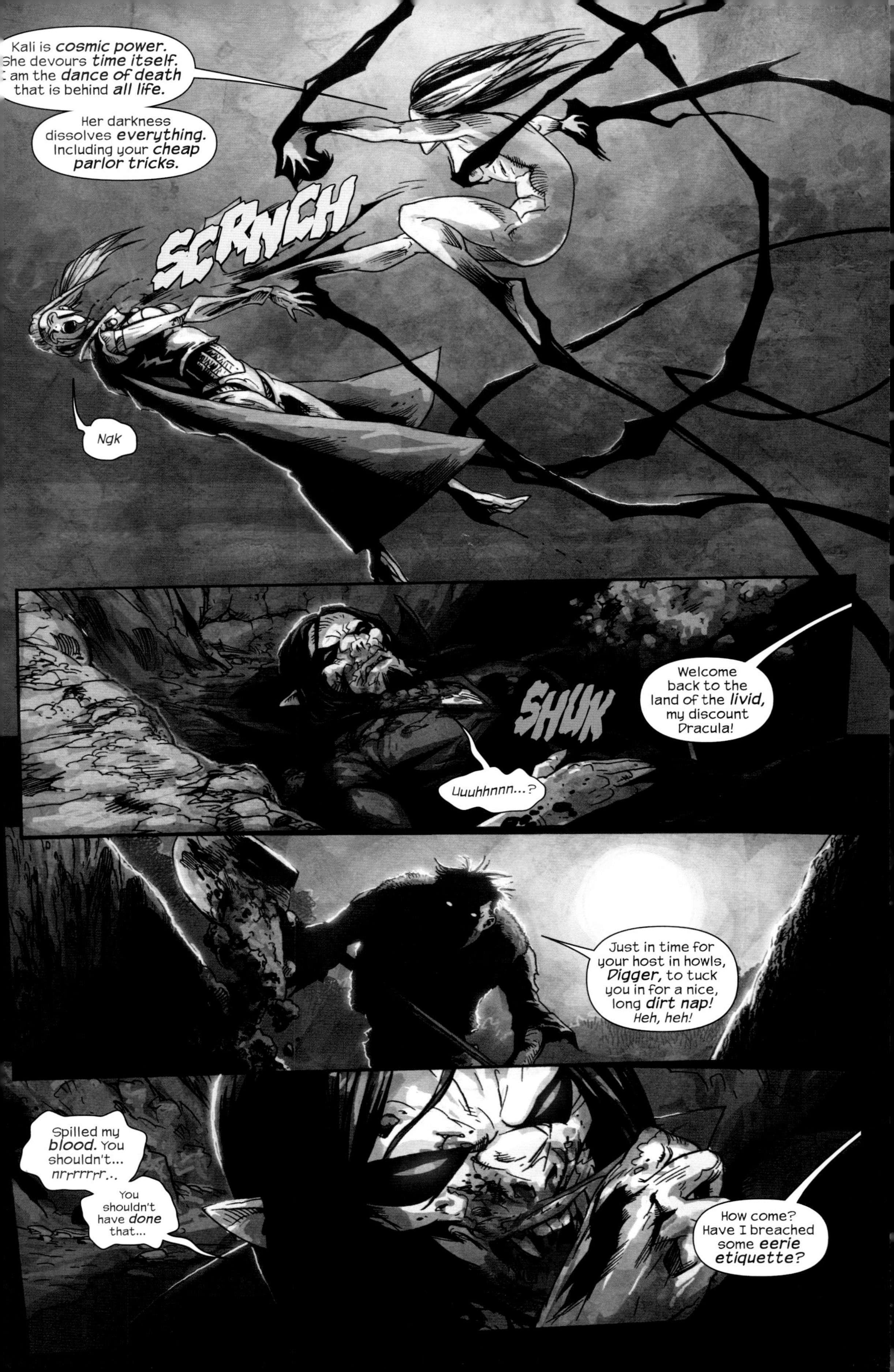
Kali is cosmic power. She devours time itself. I am the dance of death that is behind all life.
Her darkness dissolves everything. Including your cheap parlor tricks.
SCRNCH
Ngk
SHUK
Welcome back to the land of the livid, my discount Dracula!
Uuuhhnnn...?
Just in time for your host in howls, Digger, to tuck you in for a nice, long dirt nap! Heh, heh!
Spilled my blood. You shouldn't... nrrrrrr...
You shouldn't have done that...
How come? Have I breached some eerie etiquette?

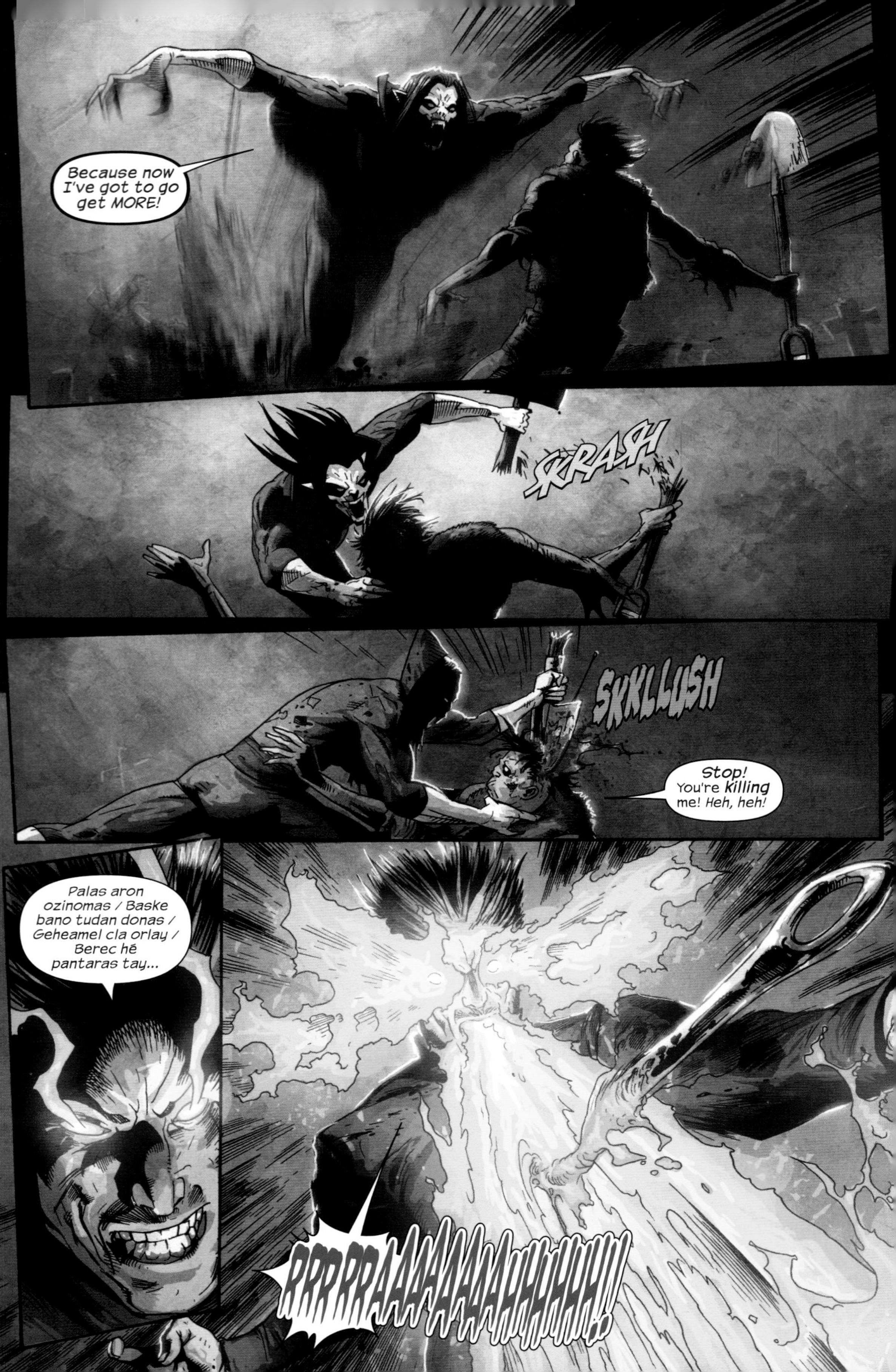
Because now I've got to go get MORE!
SKRASH
SKLLUSH
Stop! You're killing me! Heh, heh!
Palas aron ozinomas / Baske bano tudan donas / Geheamel cla orlay / Berec hẽ pantaras tay...
RRRRRAAAAAAAAHHHHHH!!

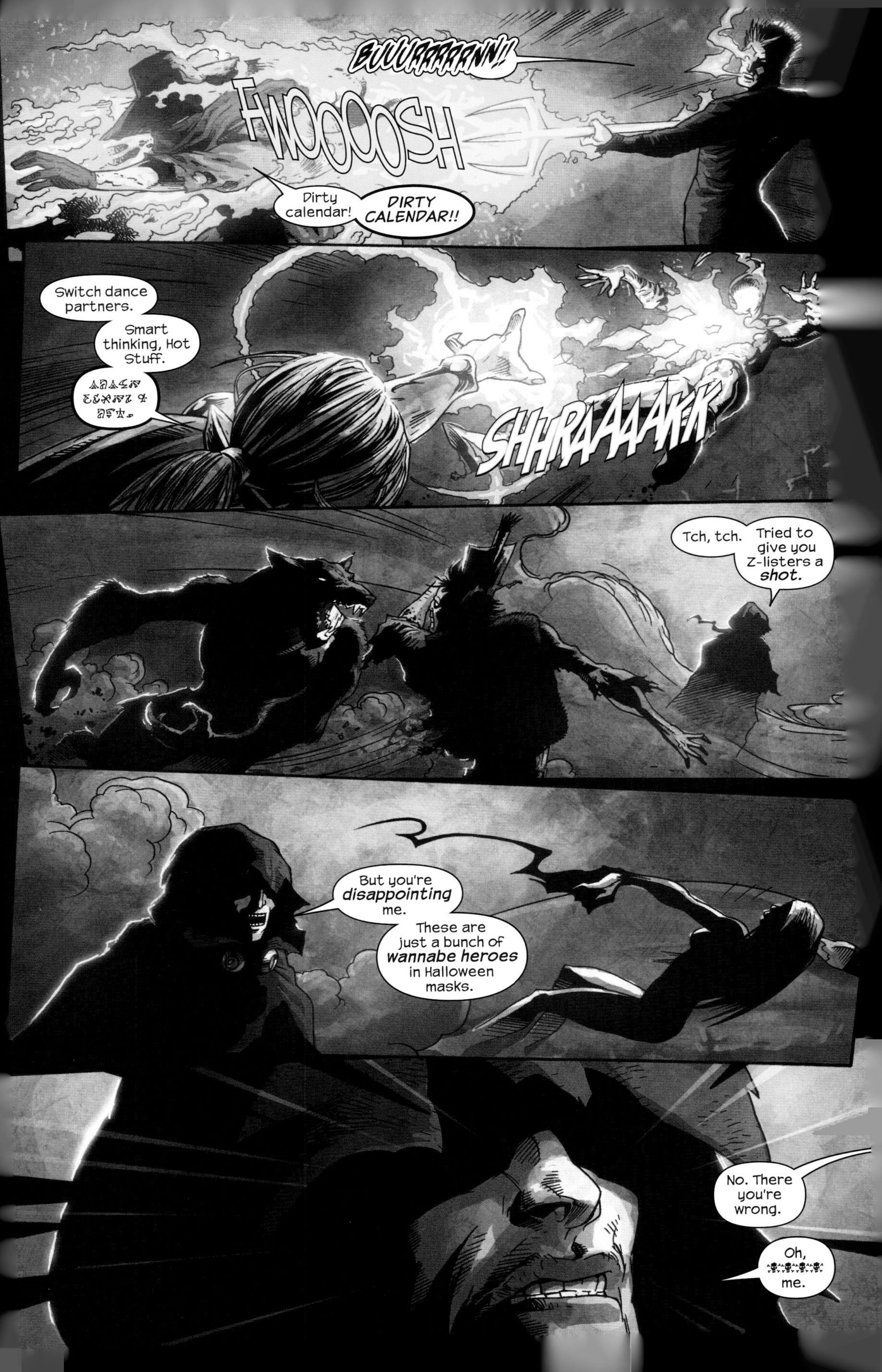
BUUURRRRRNN!!
FWOOOOSH
Dirty calendar!
DIRTY CALENDAR!!
Switch dance partners.
Smart thinking, Hot Stuff.
SHHRAAAAKK
Tch, tch.
Tried to give you Z-listers a shot.
But you're disappointing me.
These are just a bunch of wannabe heroes in Halloween masks.
No. There you're wrong.
Oh,
me.

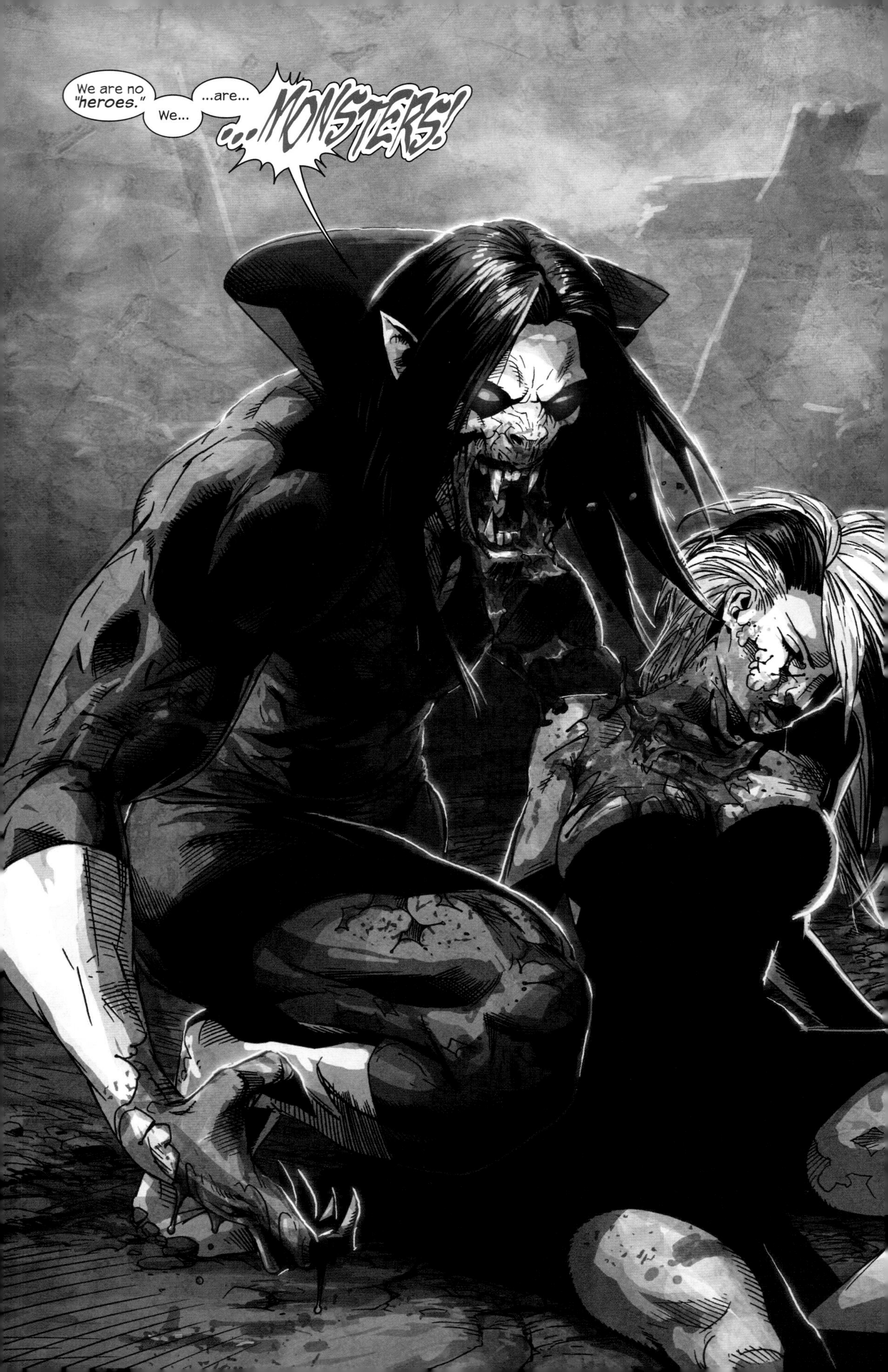
We are no "heroes."
We...
...are...
...MONSTERS!

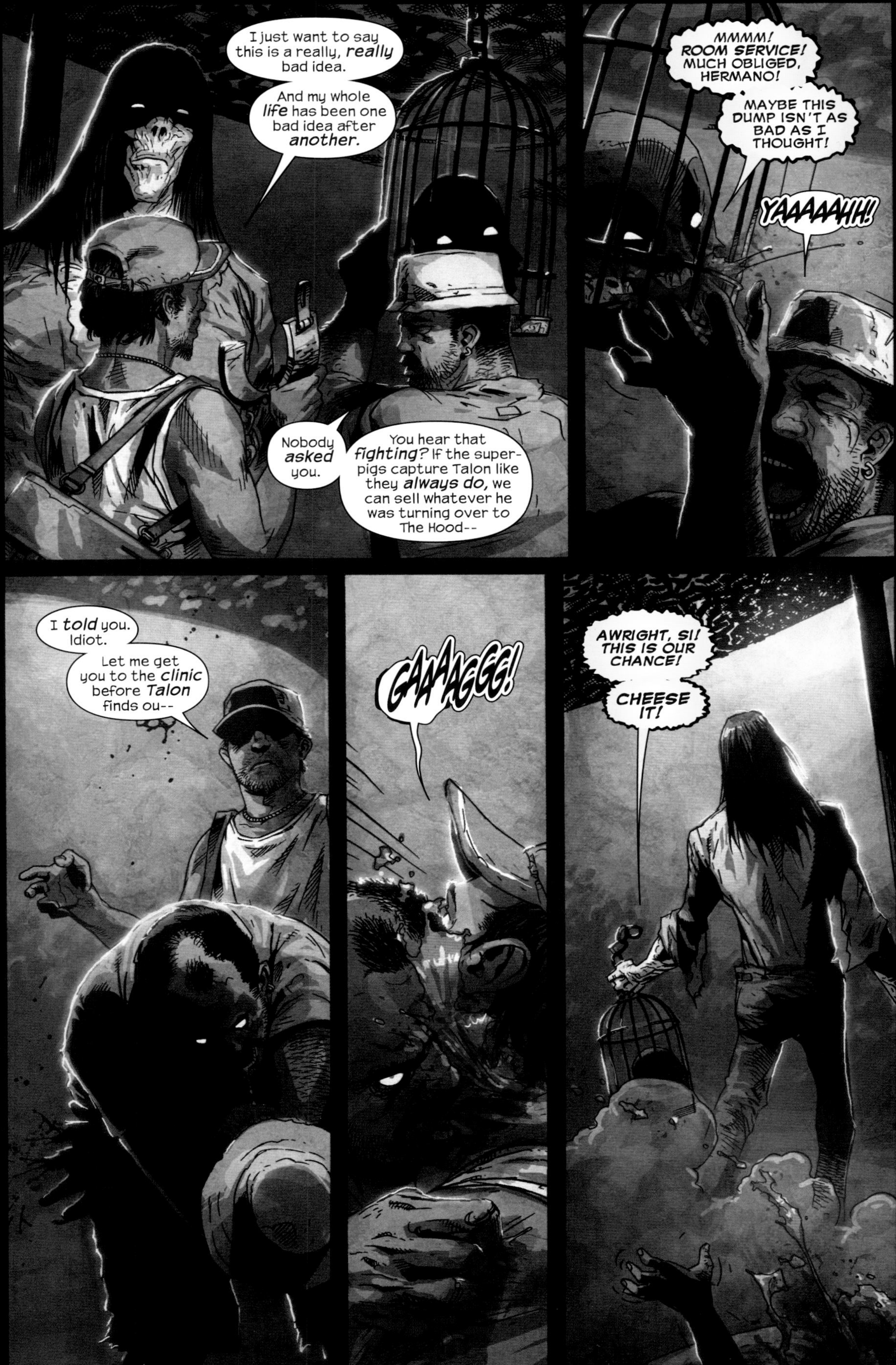
I just want to say this is a really, *really* bad idea.
And my whole *life* has been one bad idea after *another.*
Nobody *asked* you.
You hear that *fighting?* If the super-pigs capture Talon like they *always do,* we can sell whatever he was turning over to The Hood--
MMMM! ROOM SERVICE! MUCH OBLIGED, HERMANO!
MAYBE THIS DUMP ISN'T AS BAD AS I THOUGHT!
YAAAAAHH!
I *told* you. Idiot.
Let me get you to the *clinic* before *Talon* finds ou--
GAAAAGGG!
AWRIGHT, SI! THIS IS OUR CHANCE!
CHEESE IT!

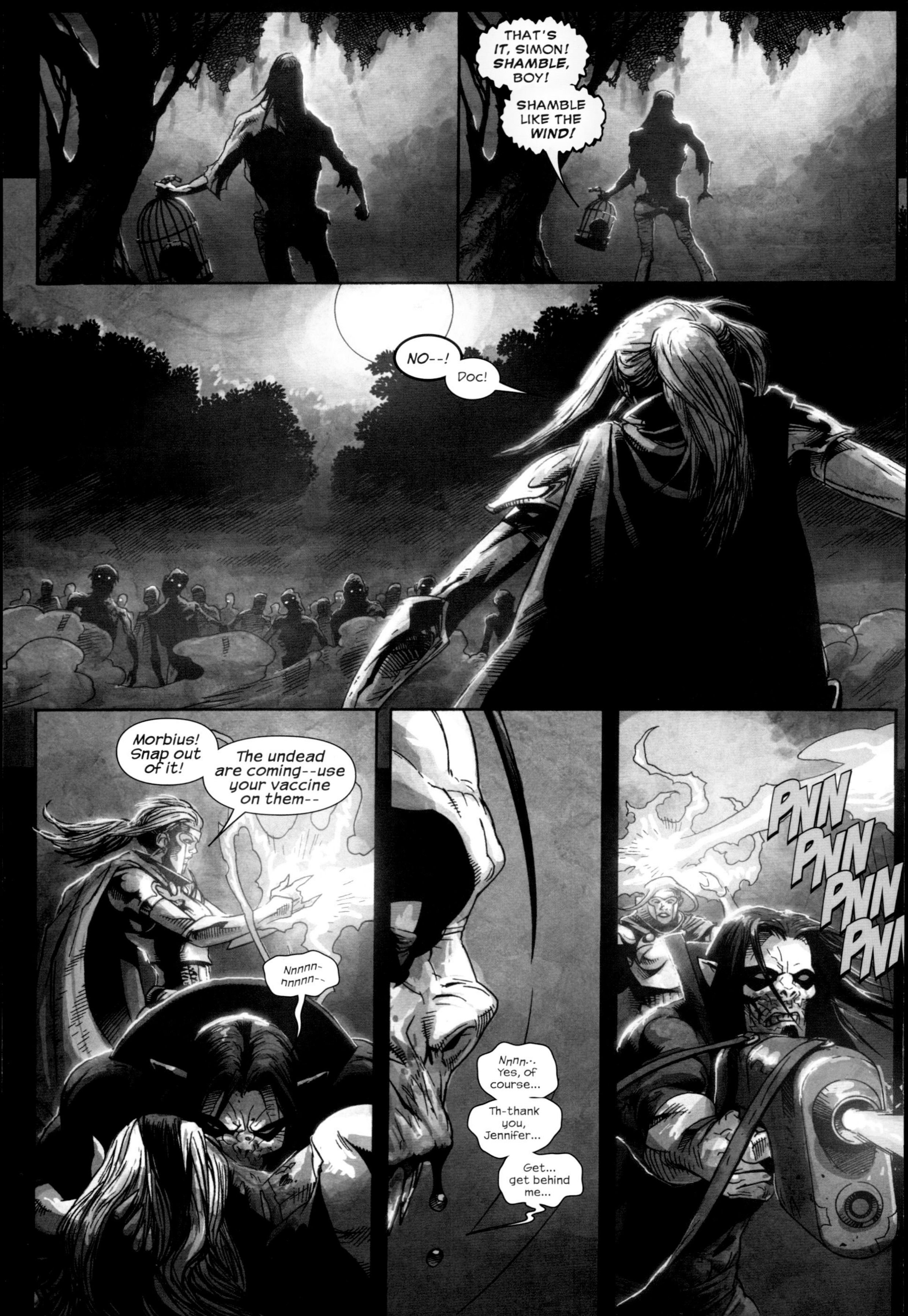

THAT'S IT, SIMON! SHAMBLE, BOY!
SHAMBLE LIKE THE WIND!
NO--!
Doc!
Morbius! Snap out of it!
The undead are coming--use your vaccine on them--
Nnnnn-nnnnn--
Nnnn... Yes, of course...
Th-thank you, Jennifer...
Get... get behind me...
PNN PNN PNN PNN

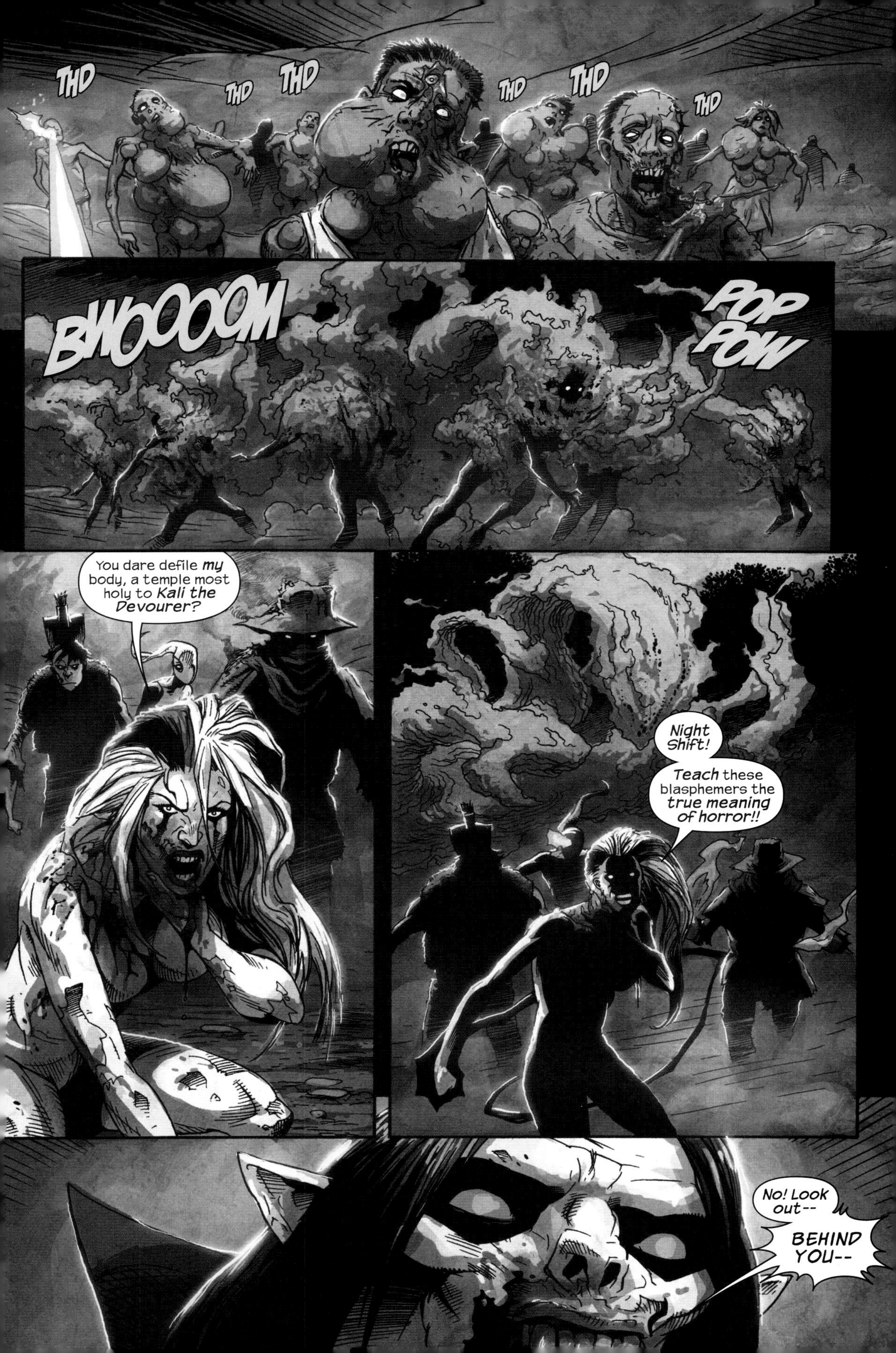
THD
THD
THD
THD
THD
THD
BWOOOOM
POP POW
You dare defile my body, a temple most holy to Kali the Devourer?
Night Shift!
Teach these blasphemers the true meaning of horror!!
No! Look out--
BEHIND YOU--

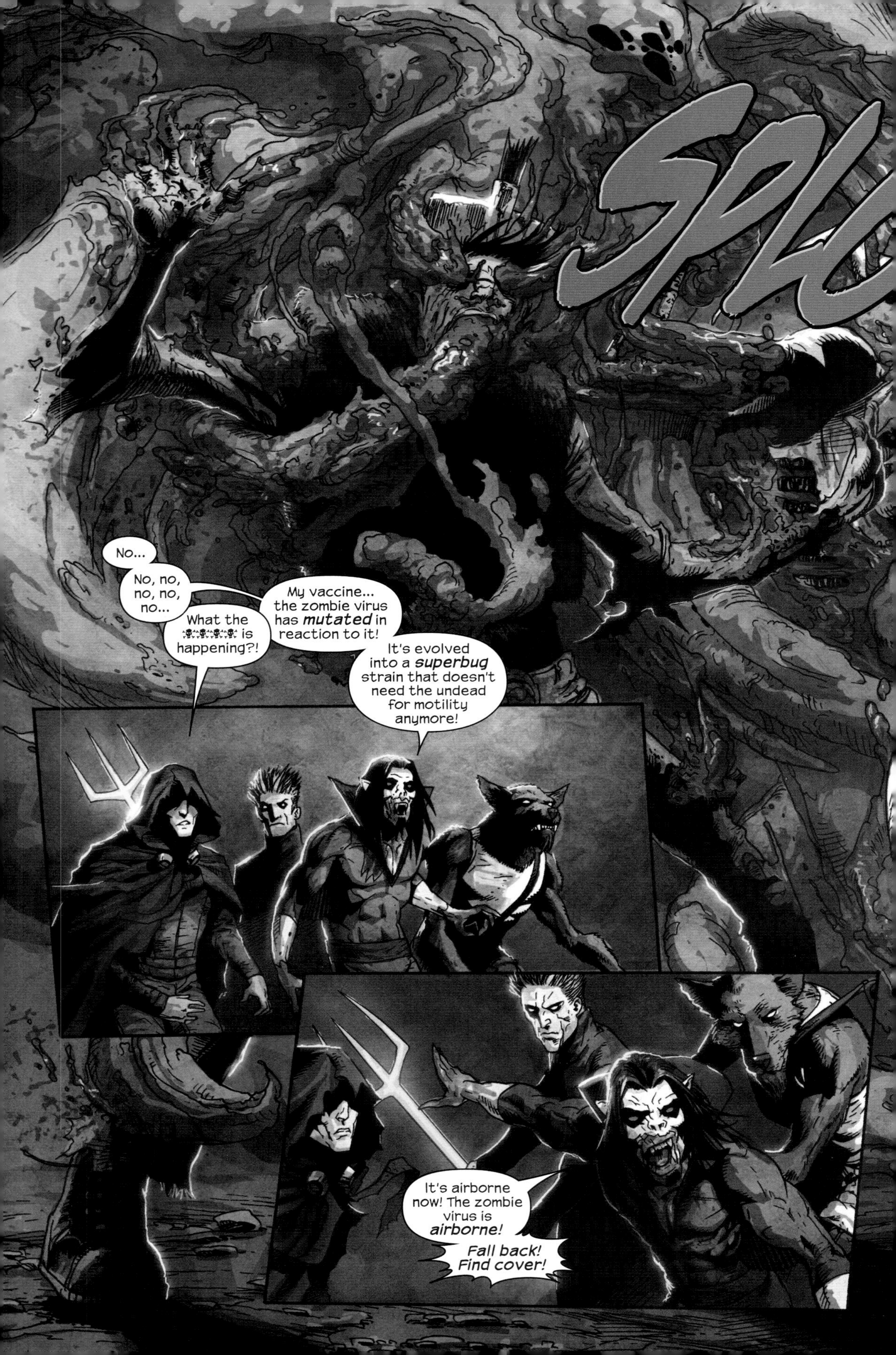
SPLU
No...
No, no, no, no, no...
My vaccine... the zombie virus has *mutated* in reaction to it!
What the ☠☠☠☠ is happening?!
It's evolved into a *superbug* strain that doesn't need the undead for motility anymore!
It's airborne now! The zombie virus is *airborne!*
Fall back! Find cover!

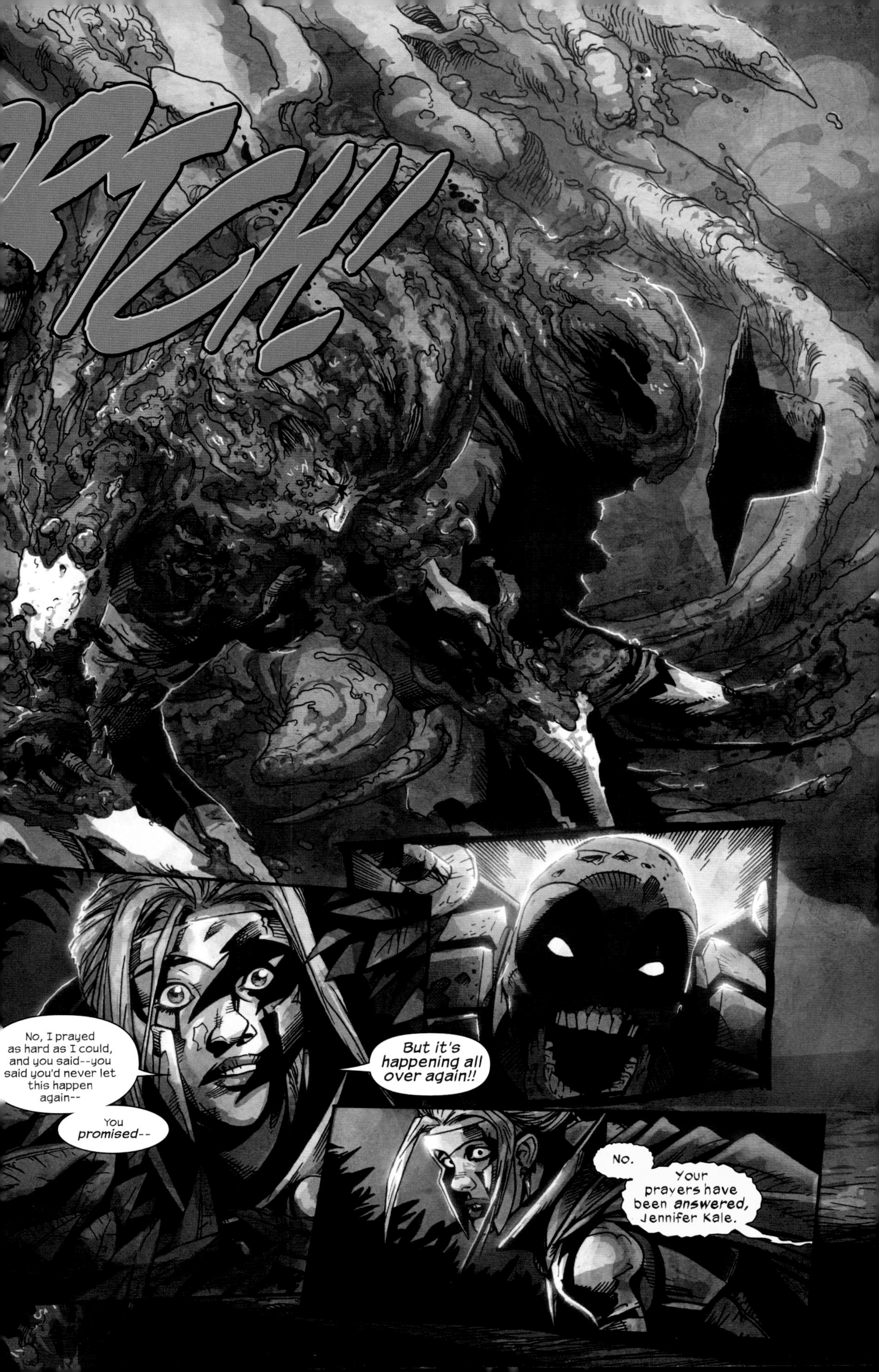

RRTCH!!
No, I prayed as hard as I could, and you said--you said you'd never let this happen again--
You *promised*--
But it's happening all over again!!
No.
Your prayers have been *answered*, Jennifer Kale.

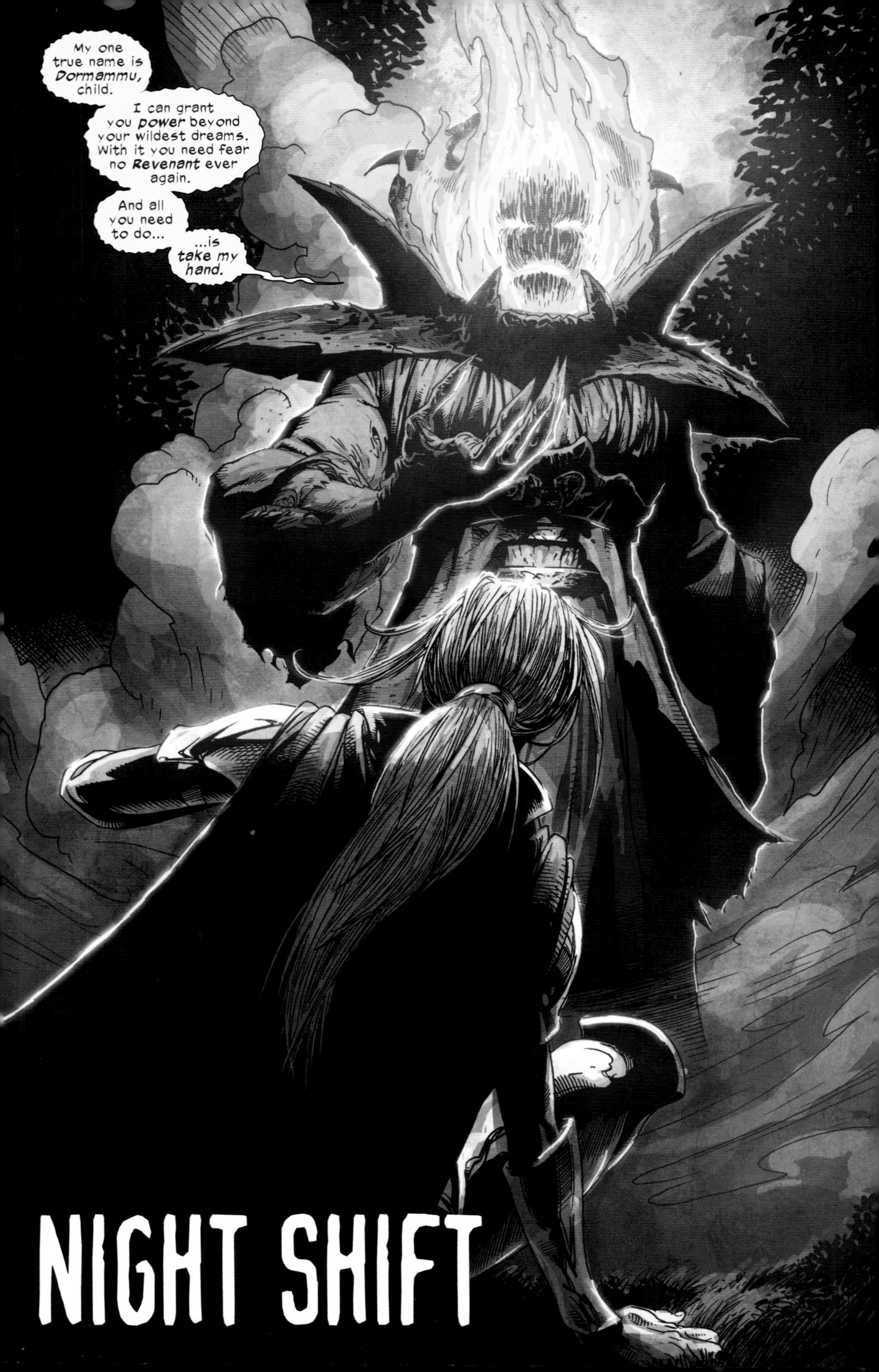
My one true name is *Dormammu*, child.
I can grant you **power** beyond your wildest dreams. With it you need fear no **Revenant** ever again.
And all you need to do...
...is *take my hand.*
NIGHT SHIFT

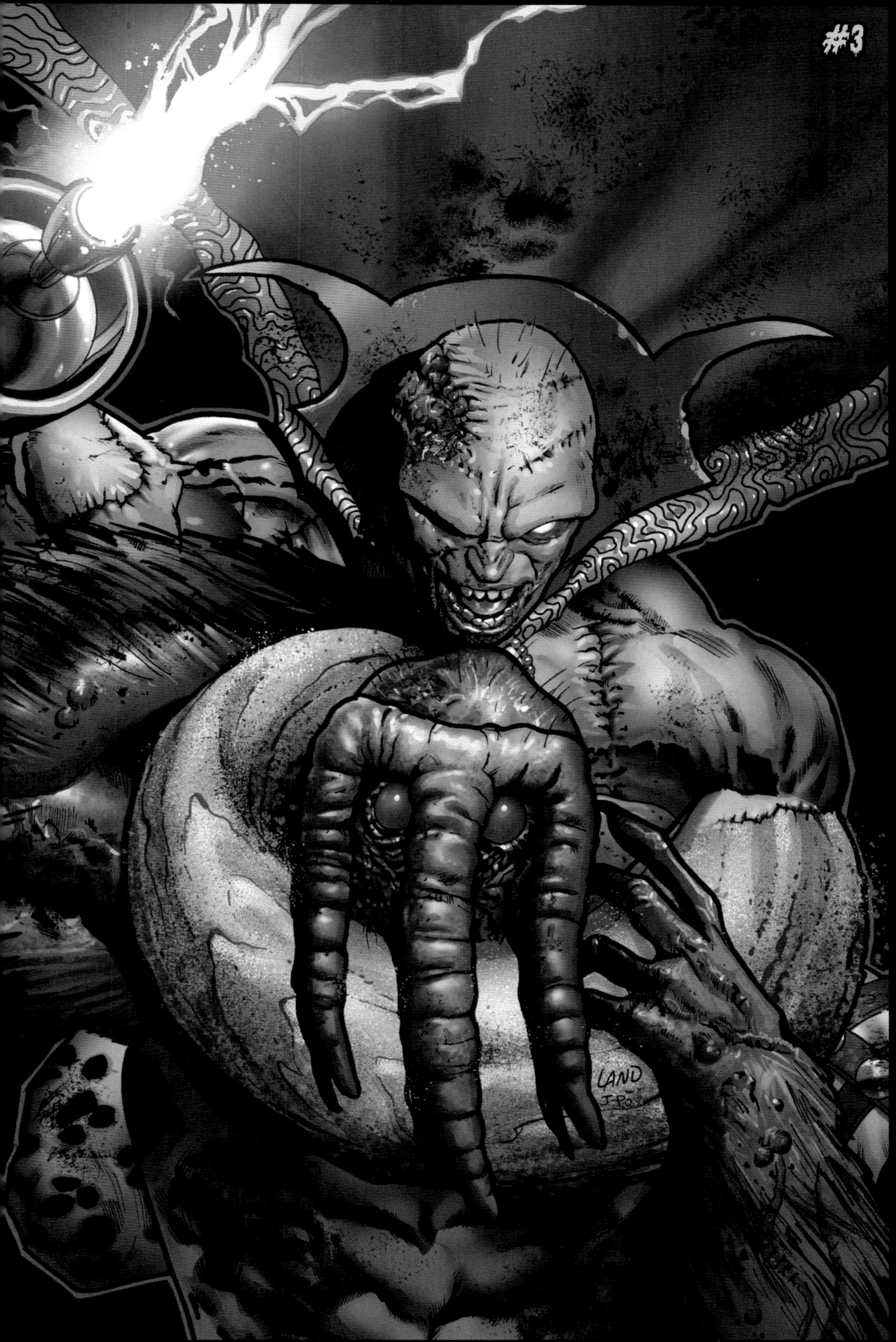
#3
LAND
J-Po

#3 '80S VARIANT BY MIKE PERKINS

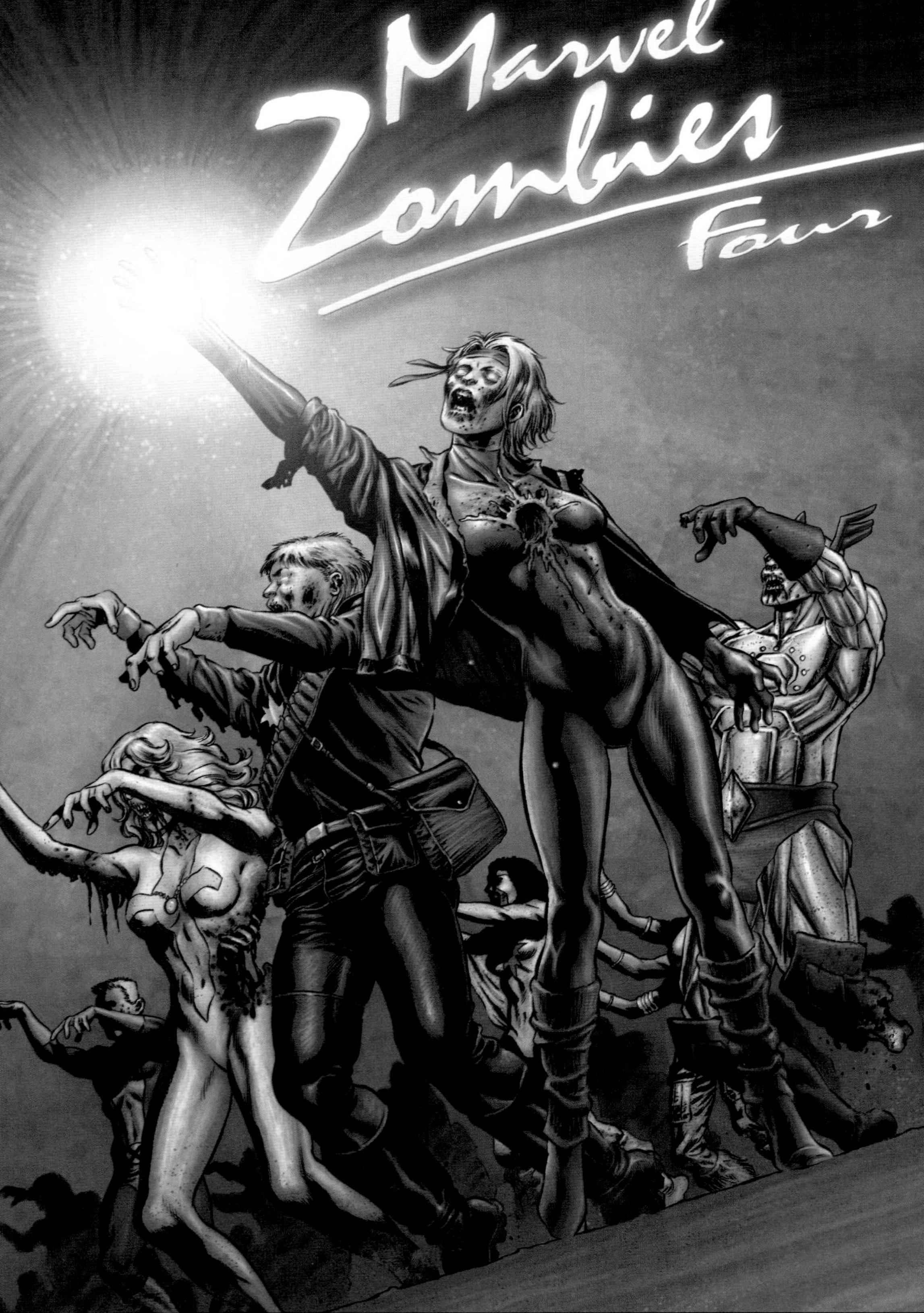
Marvel
Zombies
Four

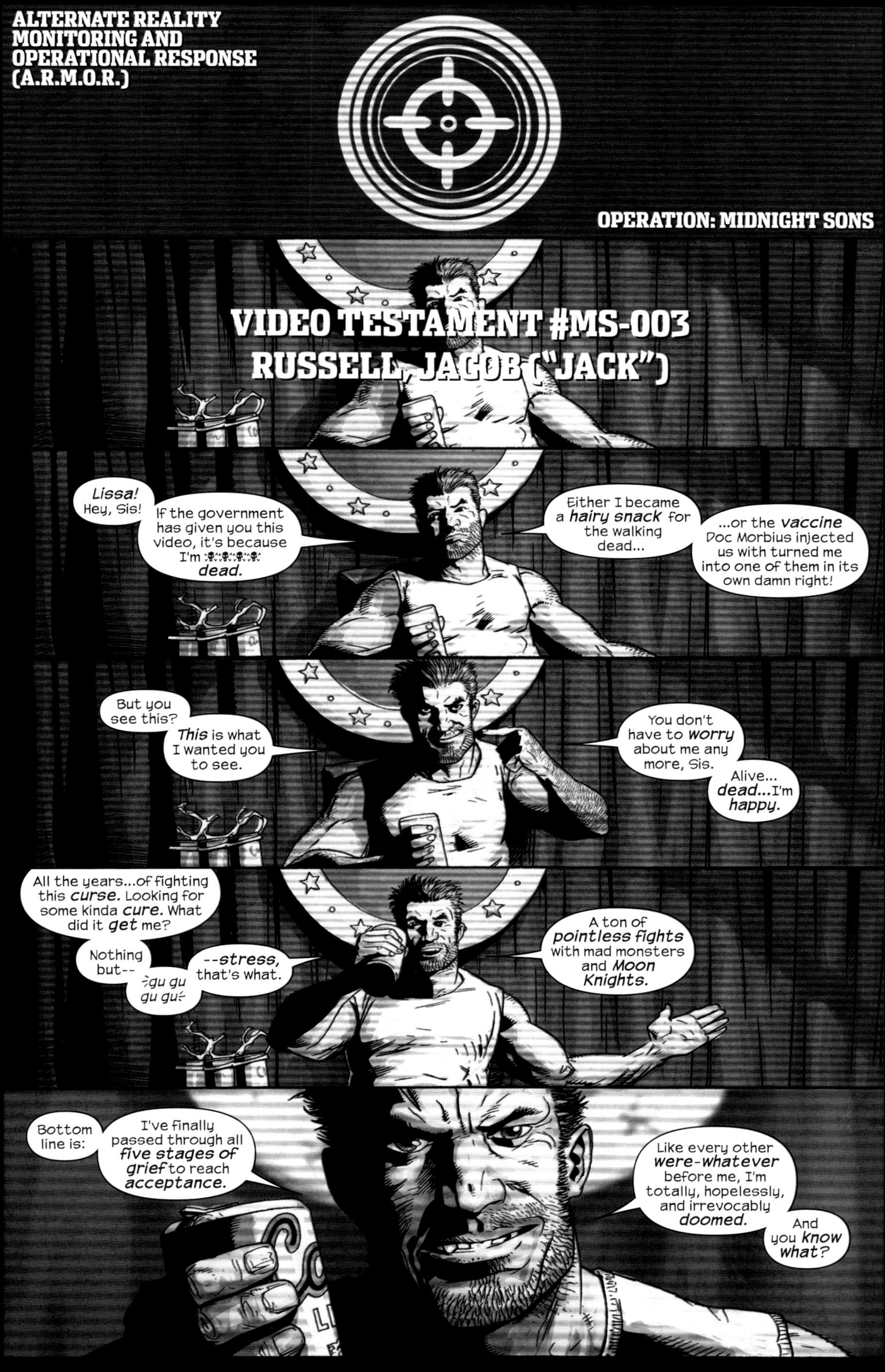
ALTERNATE REALITY MONITORING AND OPERATIONAL RESPONSE (A.R.M.O.R.)
OPERATION: MIDNIGHT SONS
VIDEO TESTAMENT #MS-003
RUSSELL, JACOB ("JACK")
Lissa! Hey, Sis!
If the government has given you this video, it's because I'm ☠☠☠☠ dead.
Either I became a hairy snack for the walking dead...
...or the vaccine Doc Morbius injected us with turned me into one of them in its own damn right!
But you see this?
This is what I wanted you to see.
You don't have to worry about me any more, Sis.
Alive... dead...I'm happy.
All the years...of fighting this curse. Looking for some kinda cure. What did it get me?
Nothing but--
gu gu gu gu
--stress, that's what.
A ton of pointless fights with mad monsters and Moon Knights.
Bottom line is:
I've finally passed through all five stages of grief to reach acceptance.
Like every other were-whatever before me, I'm totally, hopelessly, and irrevocably doomed.
And you know what?

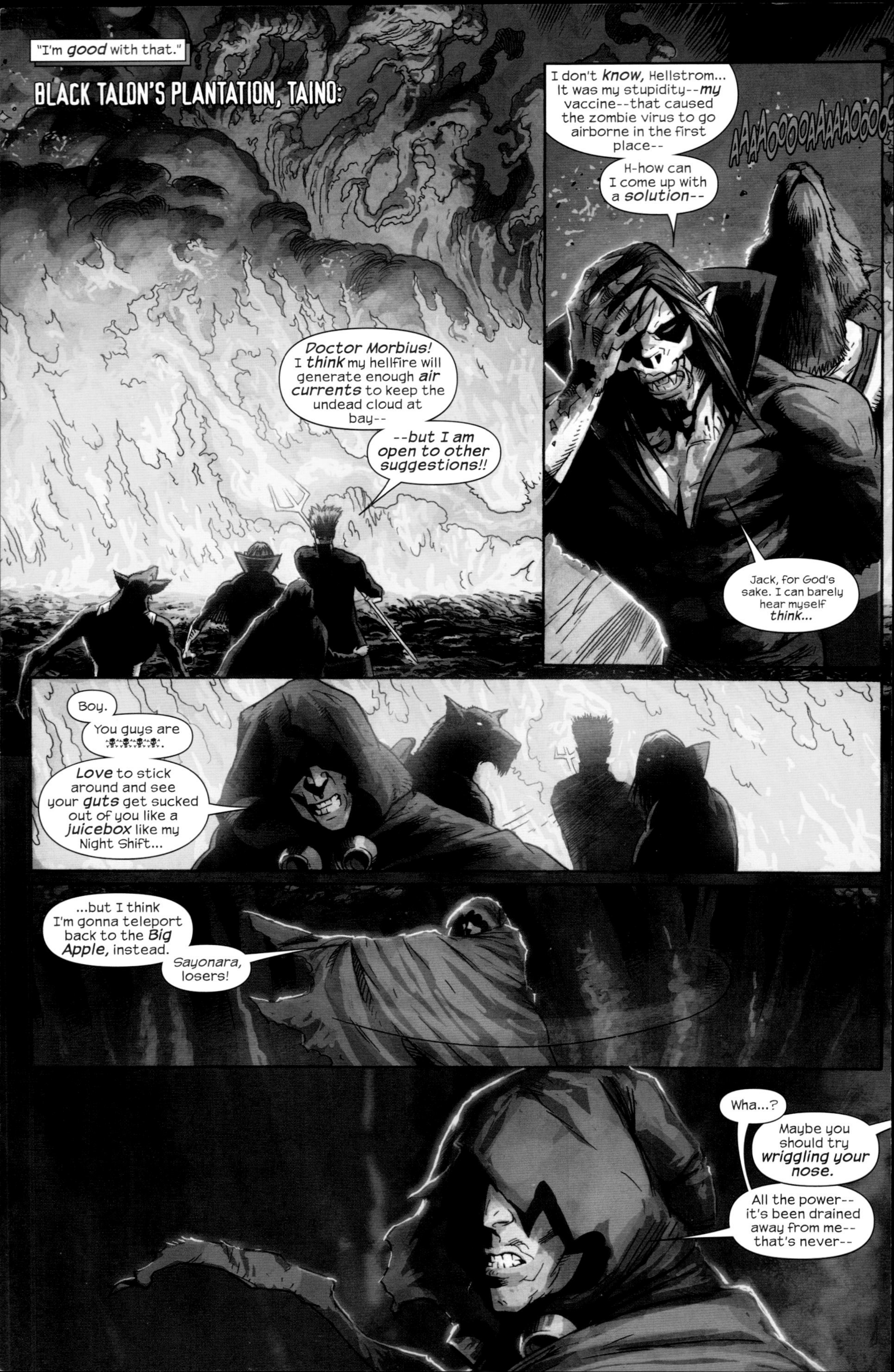
"I'm good with that."
BLACK TALON'S PLANTATION, TAINO:
Doctor Morbius! I think my hellfire will generate enough air currents to keep the undead cloud at bay--
--but I am open to other suggestions!!
I don't know, Hellstrom... It was my stupidity--my vaccine--that caused the zombie virus to go airborne in the first place--
H-how can I come up with a solution--
AAAAOOOOAAAAAOOOO
Jack, for God's sake. I can barely hear myself think...
Boy.
You guys are ☠☠☠☠.
Love to stick around and see your guts get sucked out of you like a juicebox like my Night Shift...
...but I think I'm gonna teleport back to the Big Apple, instead.
Sayonara, losers!
Wha...?
Maybe you should try wriggling your nose.
All the power-- it's been drained away from me-- that's never--

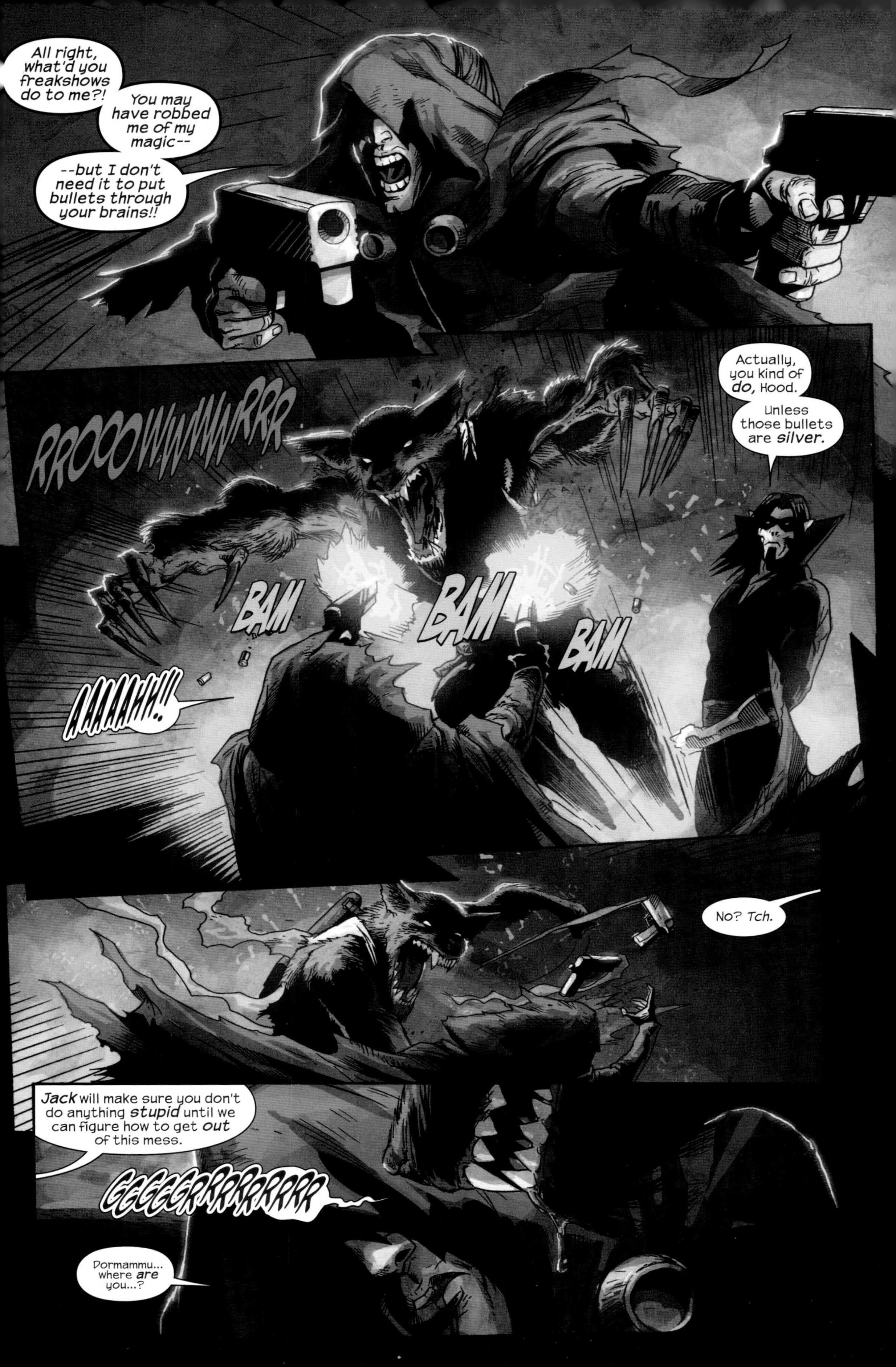

All right, what'd you freakshows do to me?!
You may have robbed me of my magic--
--but I don't need it to put bullets through your brains!!
Actually, you kind of *do*, Hood.
Unless those bullets are *silver.*
RROOOWWWWRRR
BAM
BAM
BAM
AAAAAHH!!
No? *Tch.*
Jack will make sure you don't do anything *stupid* until we can figure how to get *out* of this mess.
GGGGGRRRRRRRRR
Dormammu... where *are* you...?

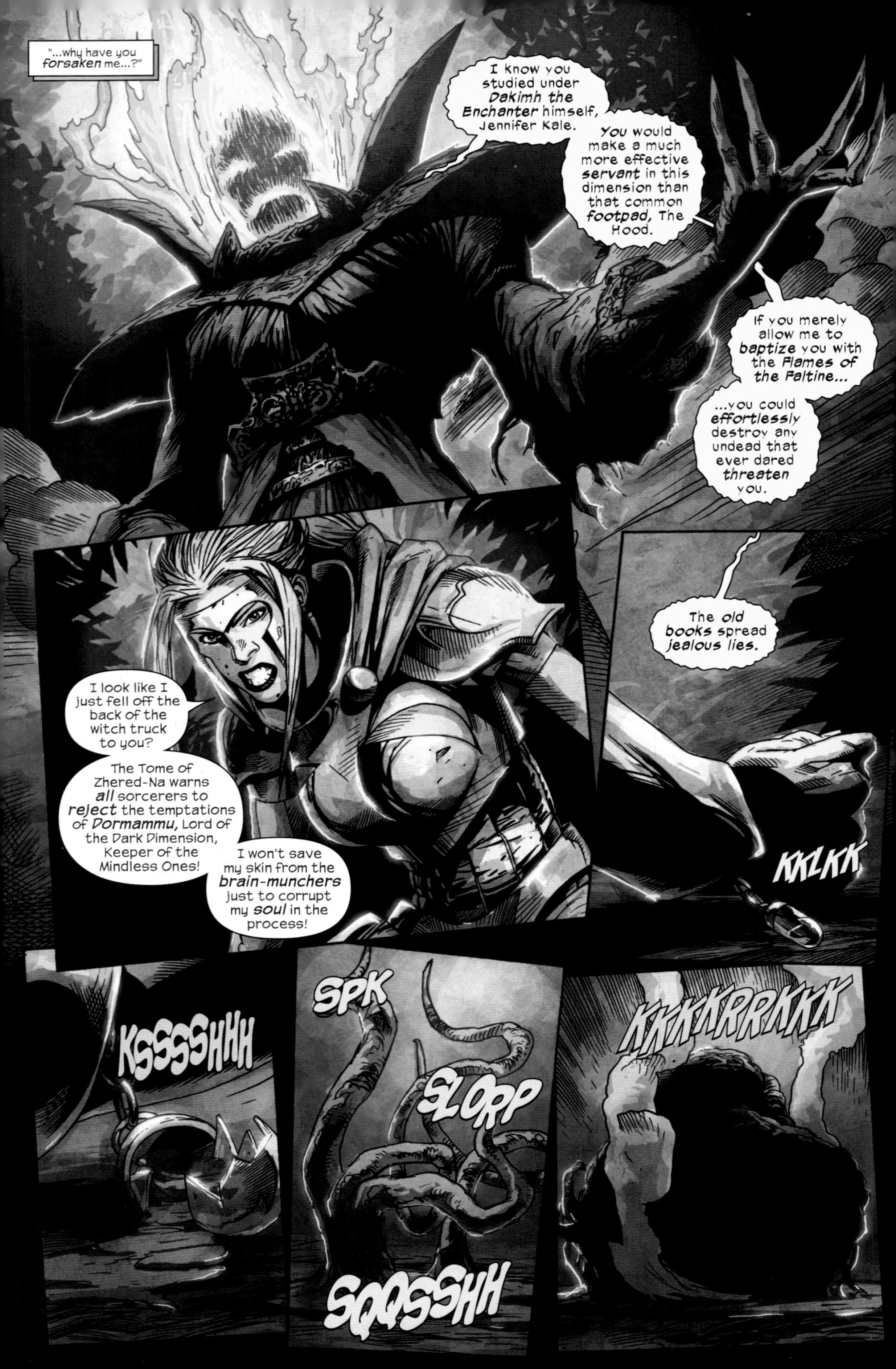
"...why have you forsaken me...?"
I know you studied under Dakimh the Enchanter himself, Jennifer Kale.
You would make a much more effective servant in this dimension than that common footpad, The Hood.
If you merely allow me to baptize you with the Flames of the Faltine...
...you could effortlessly destroy any undead that ever dared threaten you.
I look like I just fell off the back of the witch truck to you?
The Tome of Zhered-Na warns all sorcerers to reject the temptations of Dormammu, Lord of the Dark Dimension, Keeper of the Mindless Ones!
I won't save my skin from the brain-munchers just to corrupt my soul in the process!
The old books spread jealous lies.
KKLKK
KSSSSHHH
SPK
SLORP
SQQSSHH
KKKKRRRKKK

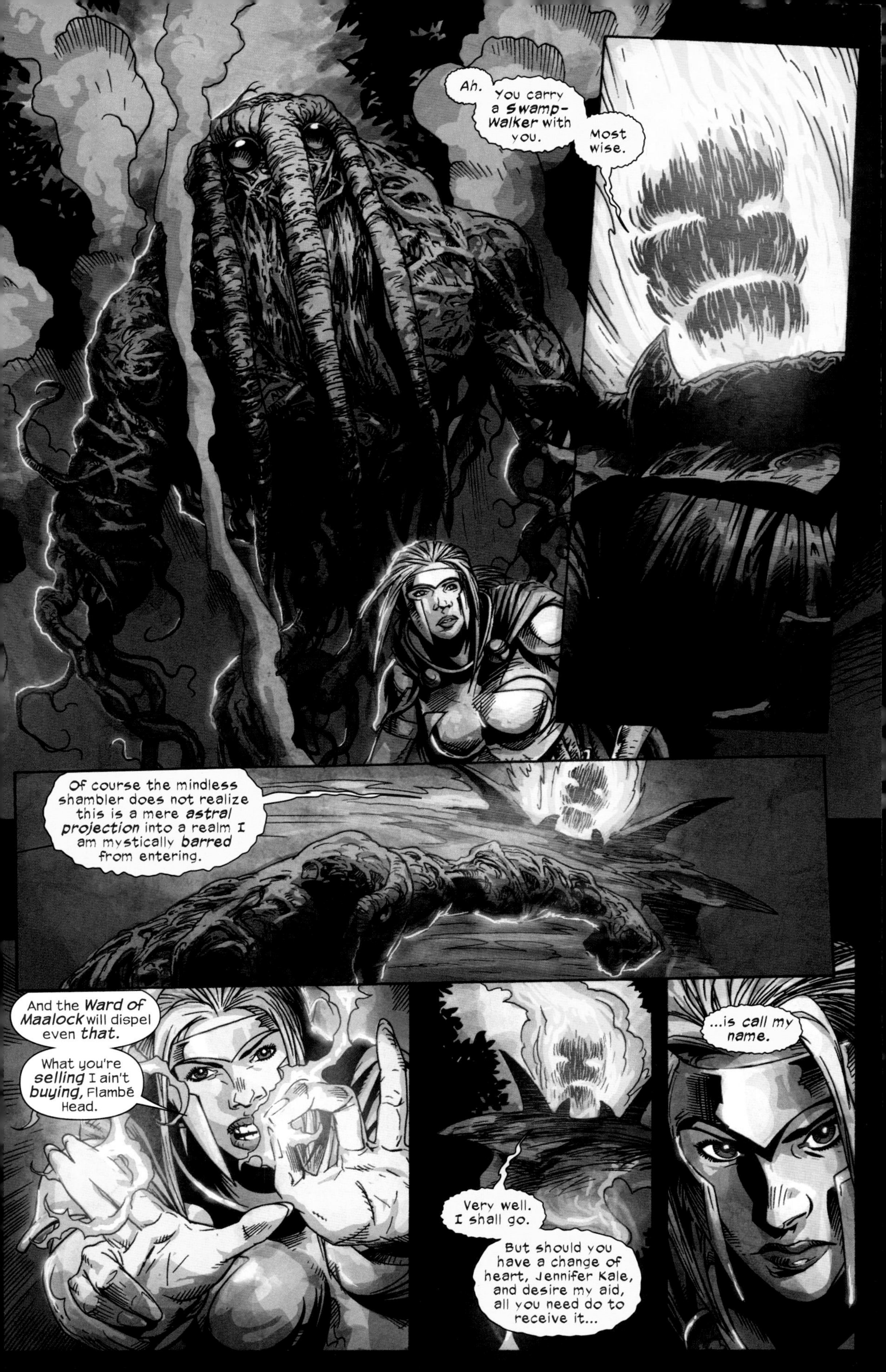

Ah.
You carry a Swamp-Walker with you.
Most wise.
Of course the mindless shambler does not realize this is a mere astral projection into a realm I am mystically barred from entering.
And the Ward of Maalock will dispel even that.
What you're selling I ain't buying, Flambé Head.
Very well. I shall go.
But should you have a change of heart, Jennifer Kale, and desire my aid, all you need do to receive it...
...is call my name.

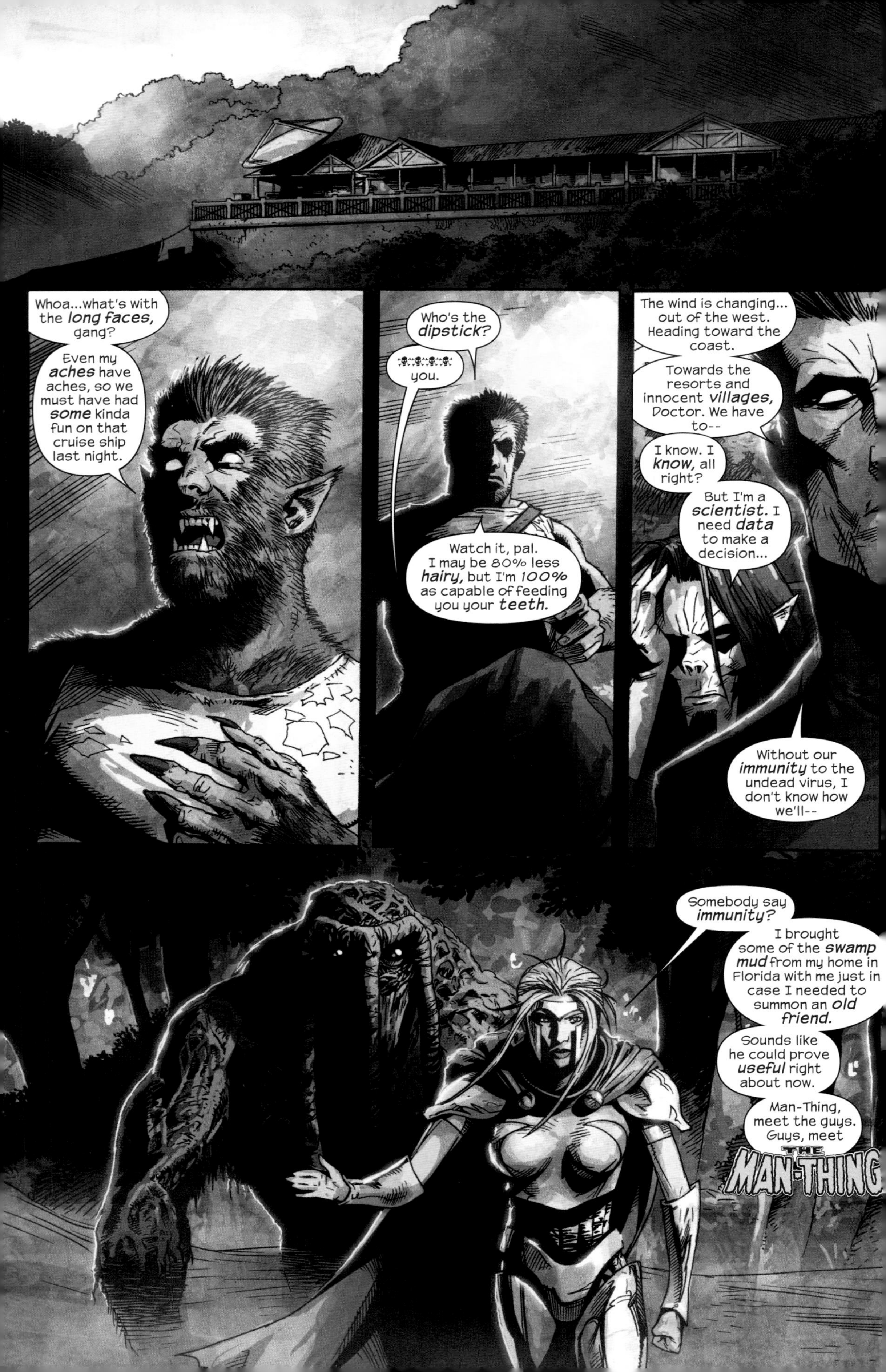
Whoa...what's with the long faces, gang?
Even my aches have aches, so we must have had some kinda fun on that cruise ship last night.
Who's the dipstick?
☠☠☠☠ you.
Watch it, pal. I may be 80% less hairy, but I'm 100% as capable of feeding you your teeth.
The wind is changing... out of the west. Heading toward the coast.
Towards the resorts and innocent villages, Doctor. We have to--
I know. I know, all right?
But I'm a scientist. I need data to make a decision...
Without our immunity to the undead virus, I don't know how we'll--
Somebody say immunity?
I brought some of the swamp mud from my home in Florida with me just in case I needed to summon an old friend.
Sounds like he could prove useful right about now.
Man-Thing, meet the guys. Guys, meet
THE MAN-THING

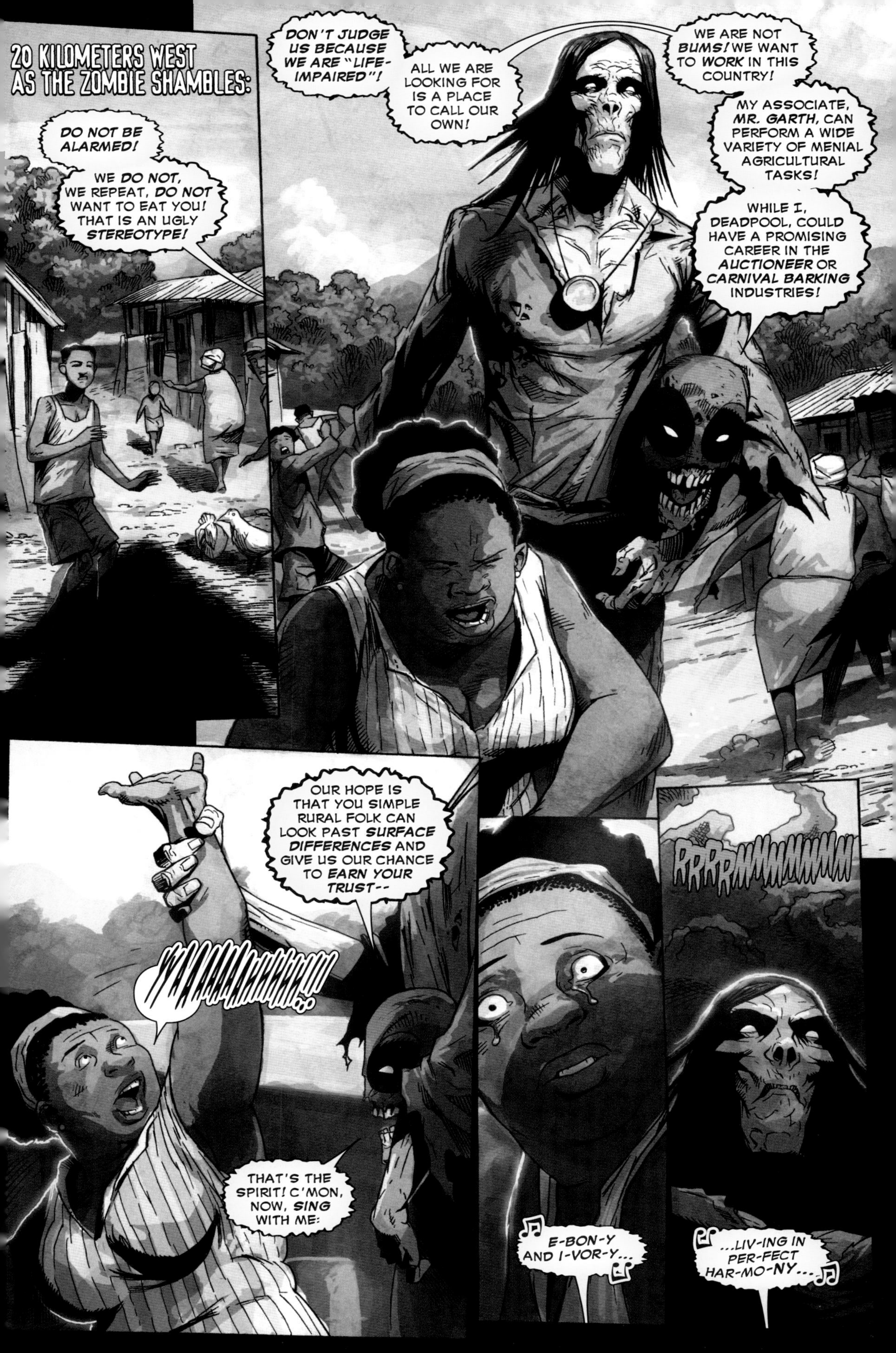
20 KILOMETERS WEST AS THE ZOMBIE SHAMBLES:
DO NOT BE ALARMED!
WE DO NOT, WE REPEAT, DO NOT WANT TO EAT YOU! THAT IS AN UGLY STEREOTYPE!
DON'T JUDGE US BECAUSE WE ARE "LIFE-IMPAIRED"!
ALL WE ARE LOOKING FOR IS A PLACE TO CALL OUR OWN!
WE ARE NOT BUMS! WE WANT TO WORK IN THIS COUNTRY!
MY ASSOCIATE, MR. GARTH, CAN PERFORM A WIDE VARIETY OF MENIAL AGRICULTURAL TASKS!
WHILE I, DEADPOOL, COULD HAVE A PROMISING CAREER IN THE AUCTIONEER OR CARNIVAL BARKING INDUSTRIES!
OUR HOPE IS THAT YOU SIMPLE RURAL FOLK CAN LOOK PAST SURFACE DIFFERENCES AND GIVE US OUR CHANCE TO EARN YOUR TRUST--
YAAAAAAAHHHHHH!!!
THAT'S THE SPIRIT! C'MON, NOW, SING WITH ME:
RRRRNNMMMMMM
E-BON-Y AND I-VOR-Y...
...LIV-ING IN PER-FECT HAR-MO-NY...

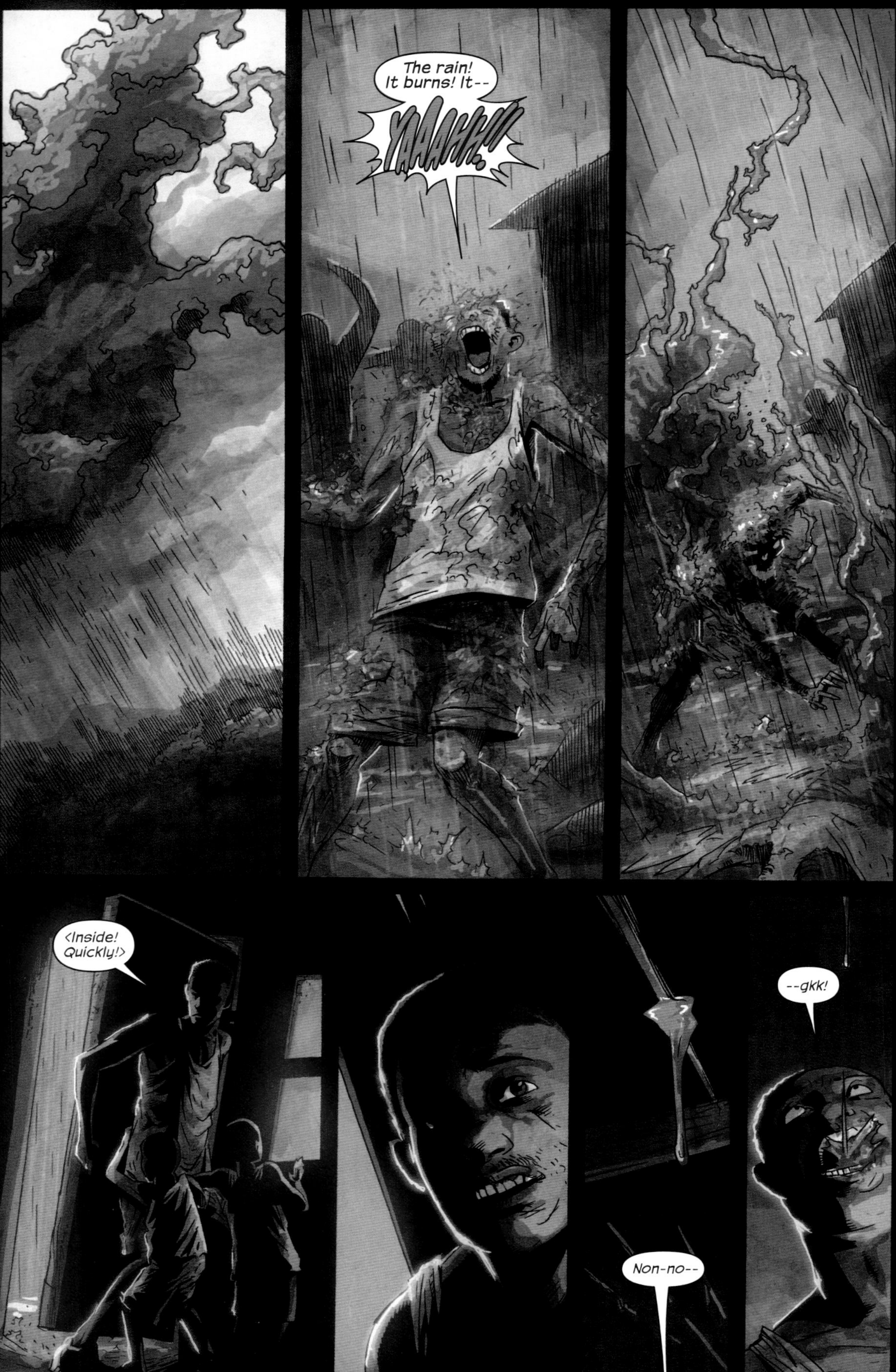

The rain! It burns! It--
YAAAHH!!
<Inside! Quickly!>
Non-no--
--gkk!

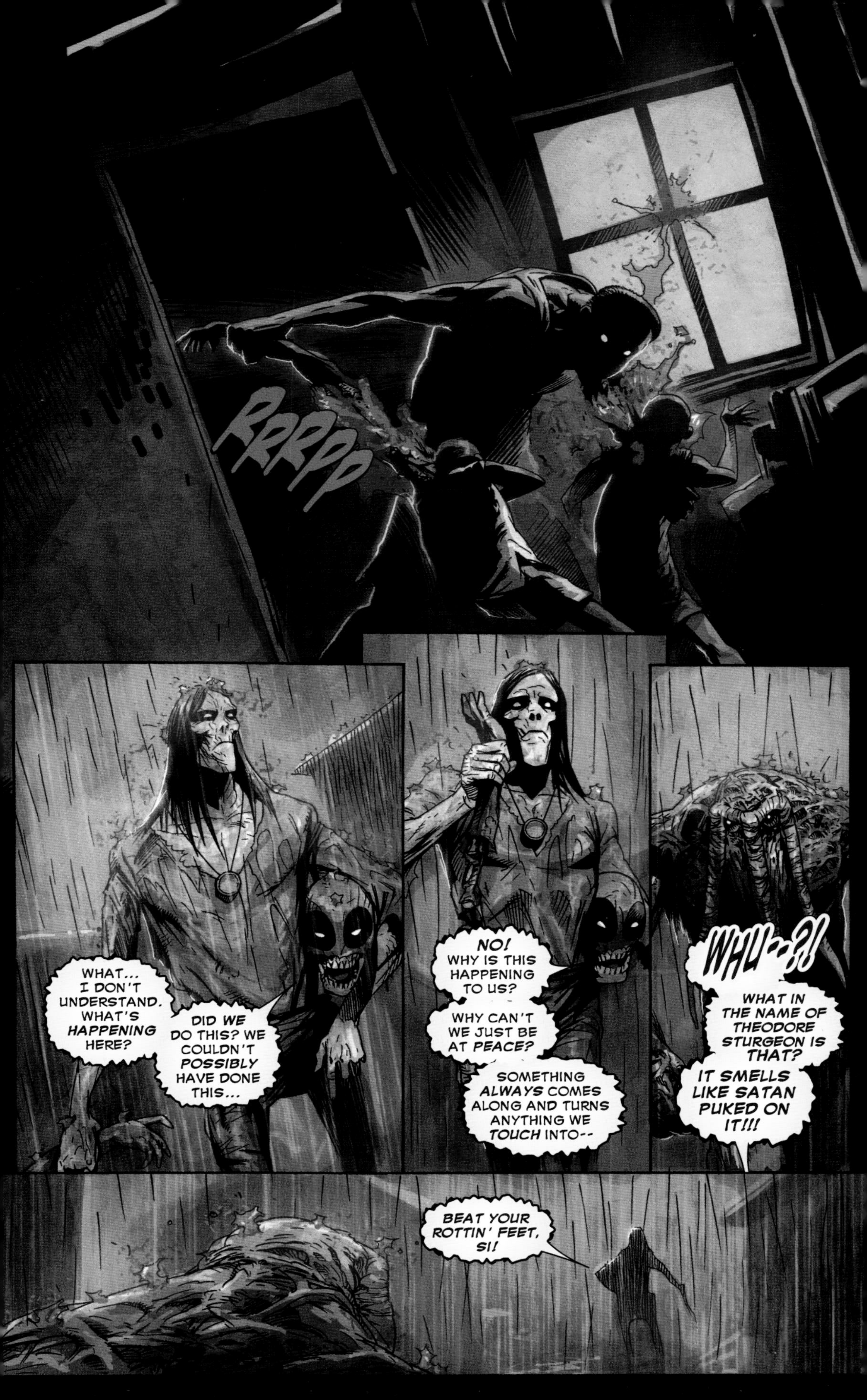
RRRPP
WHAT... I DON'T UNDERSTAND. WHAT'S HAPPENING HERE?
DID WE DO THIS? WE COULDN'T POSSIBLY HAVE DONE THIS...
NO! WHY IS THIS HAPPENING TO US?
WHY CAN'T WE JUST BE AT PEACE?
SOMETHING ALWAYS COMES ALONG AND TURNS ANYTHING WE TOUCH INTO--
WHU--?!
WHAT IN THE NAME OF THEODORE STURGEON IS THAT?
IT SMELLS LIKE SATAN PUKED ON IT!!!
BEAT YOUR ROTTIN' FEET, SI!

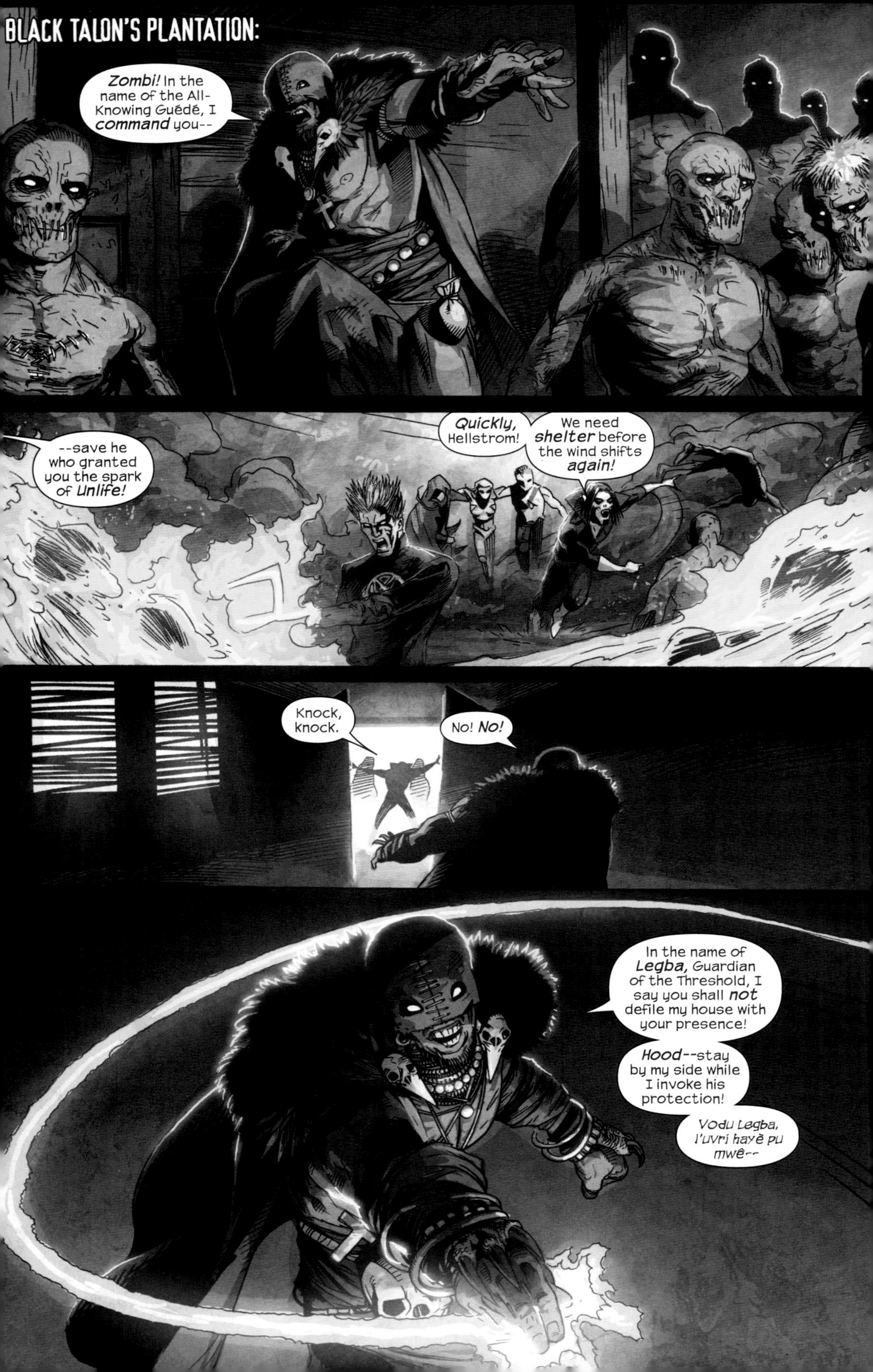

BLACK TALON'S PLANTATION:
Zombi! In the name of the All-Knowing Guédé, I command you--
--save he who granted you the spark of Unlife!
Quickly, Hellstrom!
We need shelter before the wind shifts again!
Knock, knock.
No! No!
In the name of Legba, Guardian of the Threshold, I say you shall not defile my house with your presence!
Hood--stay by my side while I invoke his protection!
Vodu Legba, l'uvri hayê pu mwê--

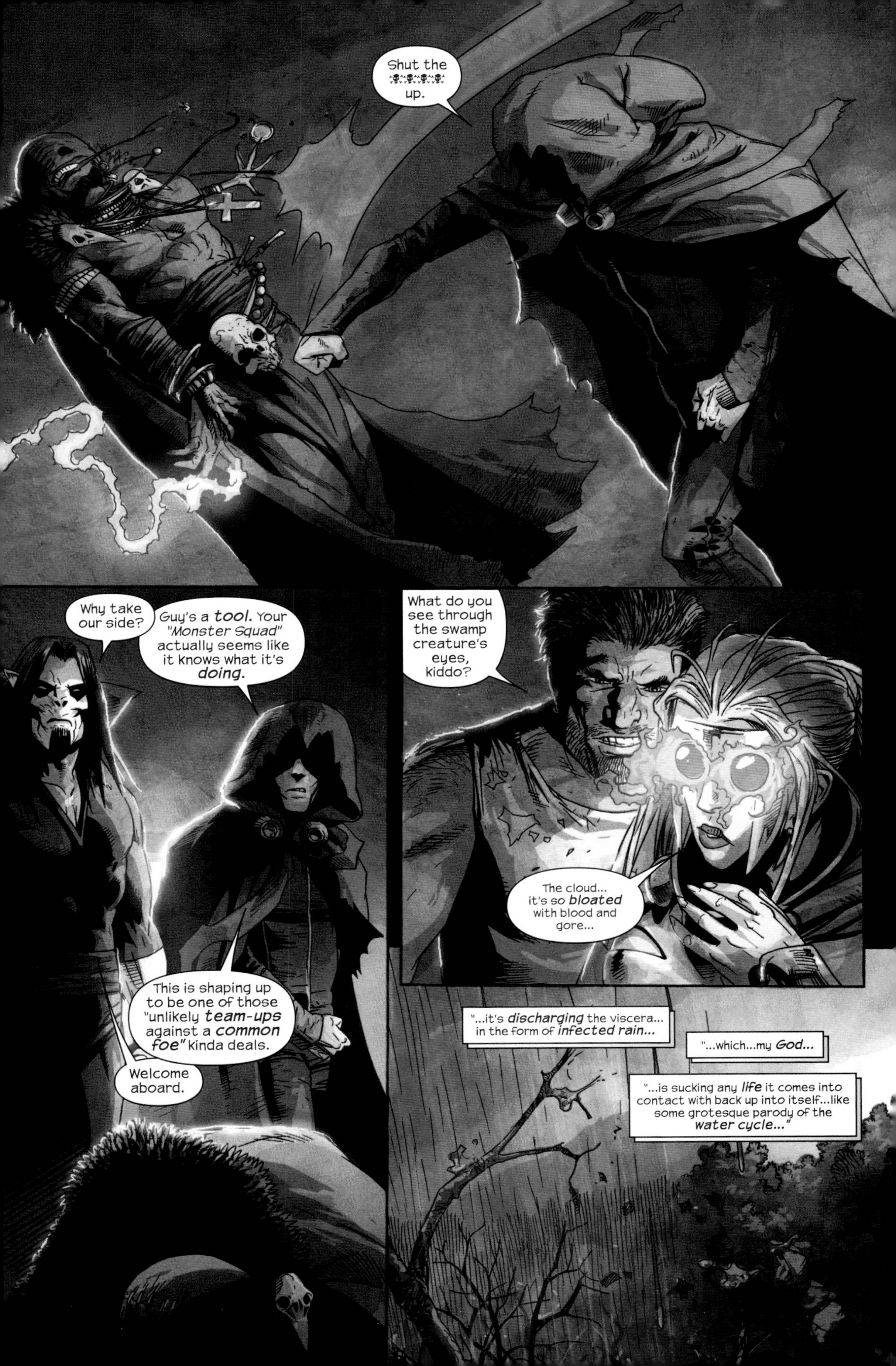
Shut the ☠☠☠☠ up.
Why take our side?
Guy's a ***tool.*** Your *"Monster Squad"* actually seems like it knows what it's ***doing.***
This is shaping up to be one of those "unlikely ***team-ups*** against a ***common foe"*** kinda deals.
Welcome aboard.
What do you see through the swamp creature's eyes, kiddo?
The cloud... it's so ***bloated*** with blood and gore...
"...it's ***discharging*** the viscera... in the form of ***infected rain...***
"...which...my ***God...***
"...is sucking any ***life*** it comes into contact with back up into itself...like some grotesque parody of the ***water cycle..."***

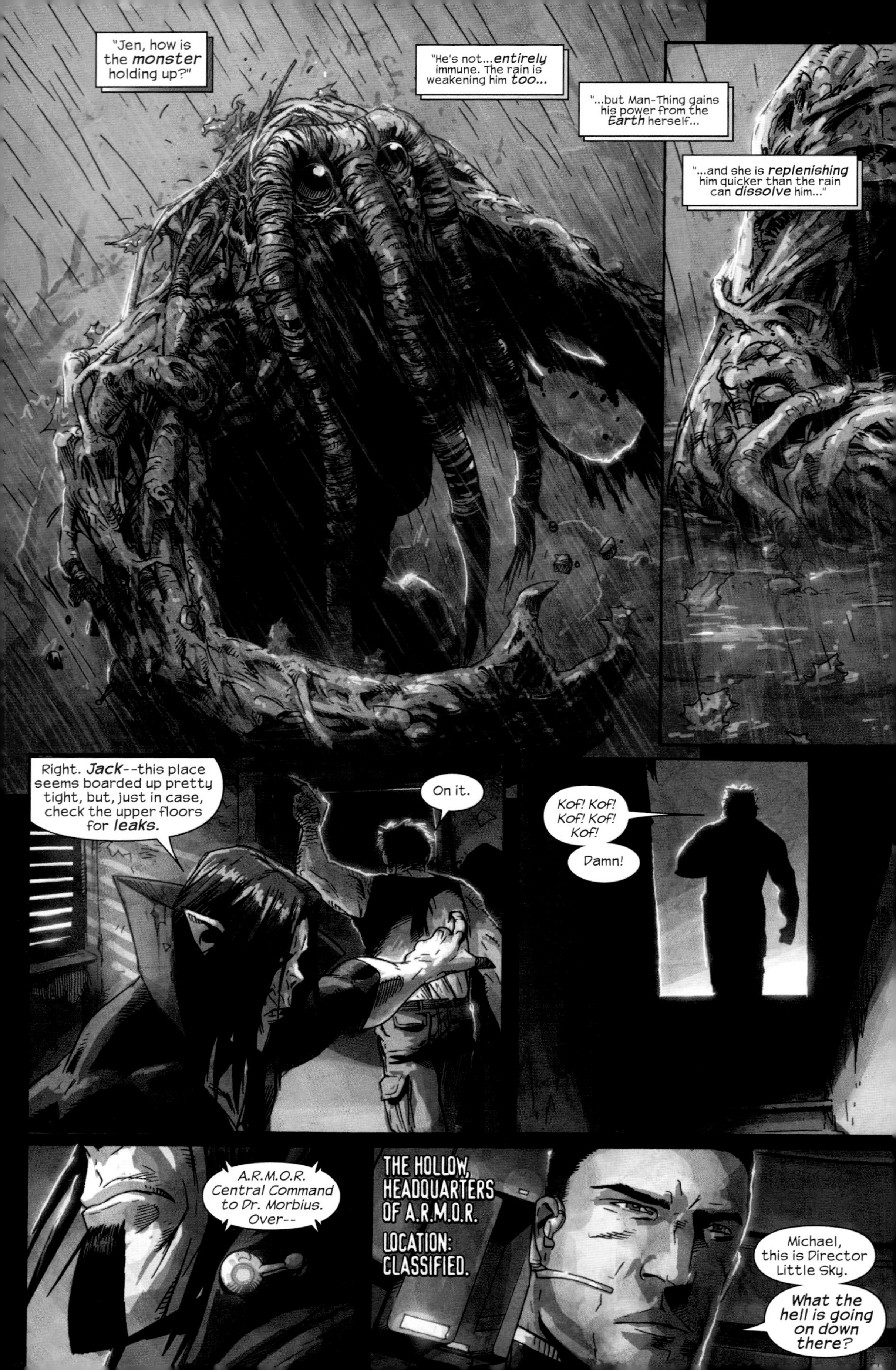

"Jen, how is the monster holding up?"
"He's not...entirely immune. The rain is weakening him too...
"...but Man-Thing gains his power from the Earth herself...
"...and she is replenishing him quicker than the rain can dissolve him..."
Right. Jack--this place seems boarded up pretty tight, but, just in case, check the upper floors for leaks.
On it.
Kof! Kof! Kof! Kof! Kof!
Damn!
A.R.M.O.R. Central Command to Dr. Morbius. Over--
THE HOLLOW, HEADQUARTERS OF A.R.M.O.R.
LOCATION: CLASSIFIED.
Michael, this is Director Little Sky.
What the hell is going on down there?

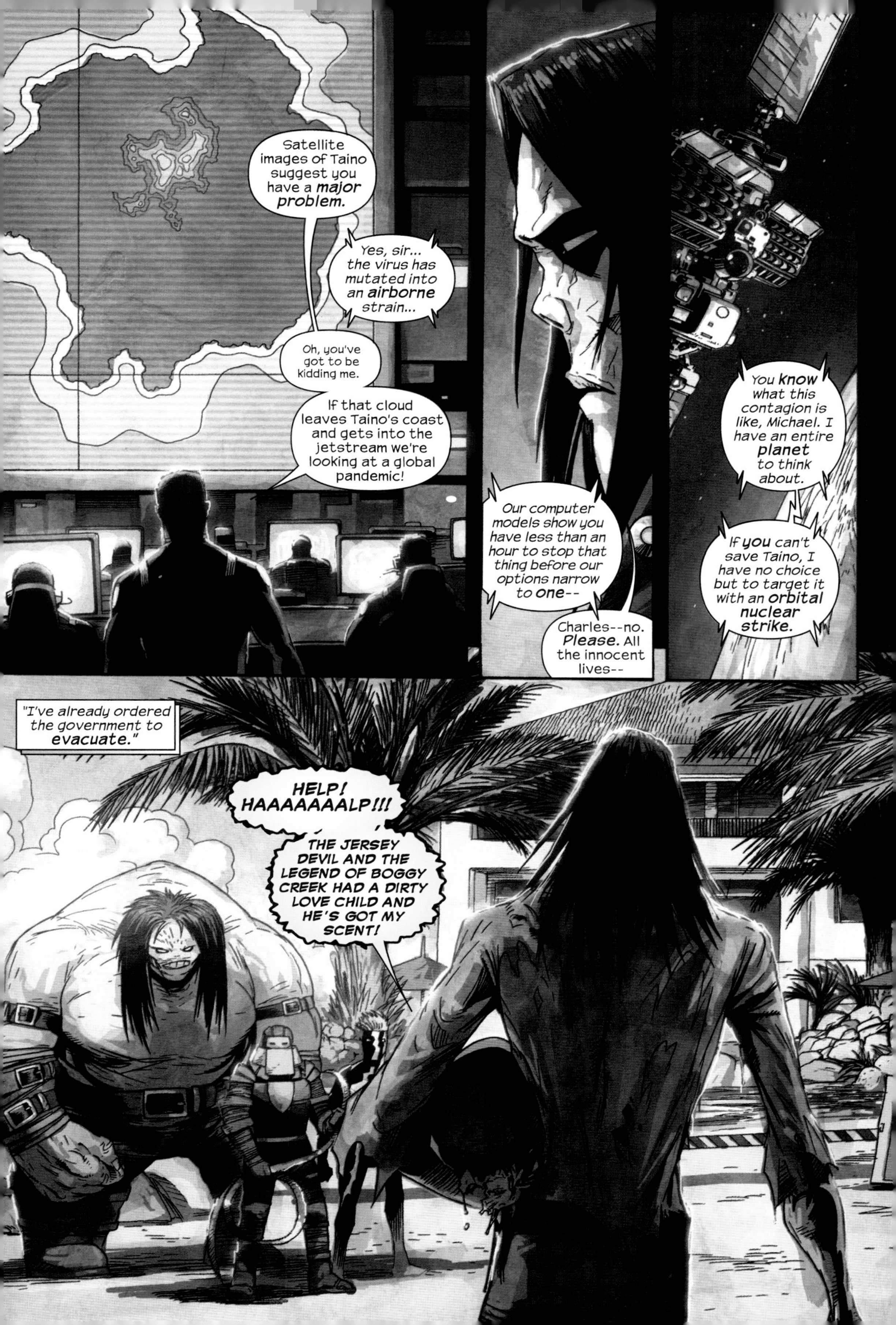
Satellite images of Taino suggest you have a major problem.
Yes, sir... the virus has mutated into an airborne strain...
Oh, you've got to be kidding me.
If that cloud leaves Taino's coast and gets into the jetstream we're looking at a global pandemic!
Our computer models show you have less than an hour to stop that thing before our options narrow to one--
Charles--no. Please. All the innocent lives--
You know what this contagion is like, Michael. I have an entire planet to think about.
If you can't save Taino, I have no choice but to target it with an orbital nuclear strike.
"I've already ordered the government to evacuate."
HELP! HAAAAAAALP!!!
THE JERSEY DEVIL AND THE LEGEND OF BOGGY CREEK HAD A DIRTY LOVE CHILD AND HE'S GOT MY SCENT!

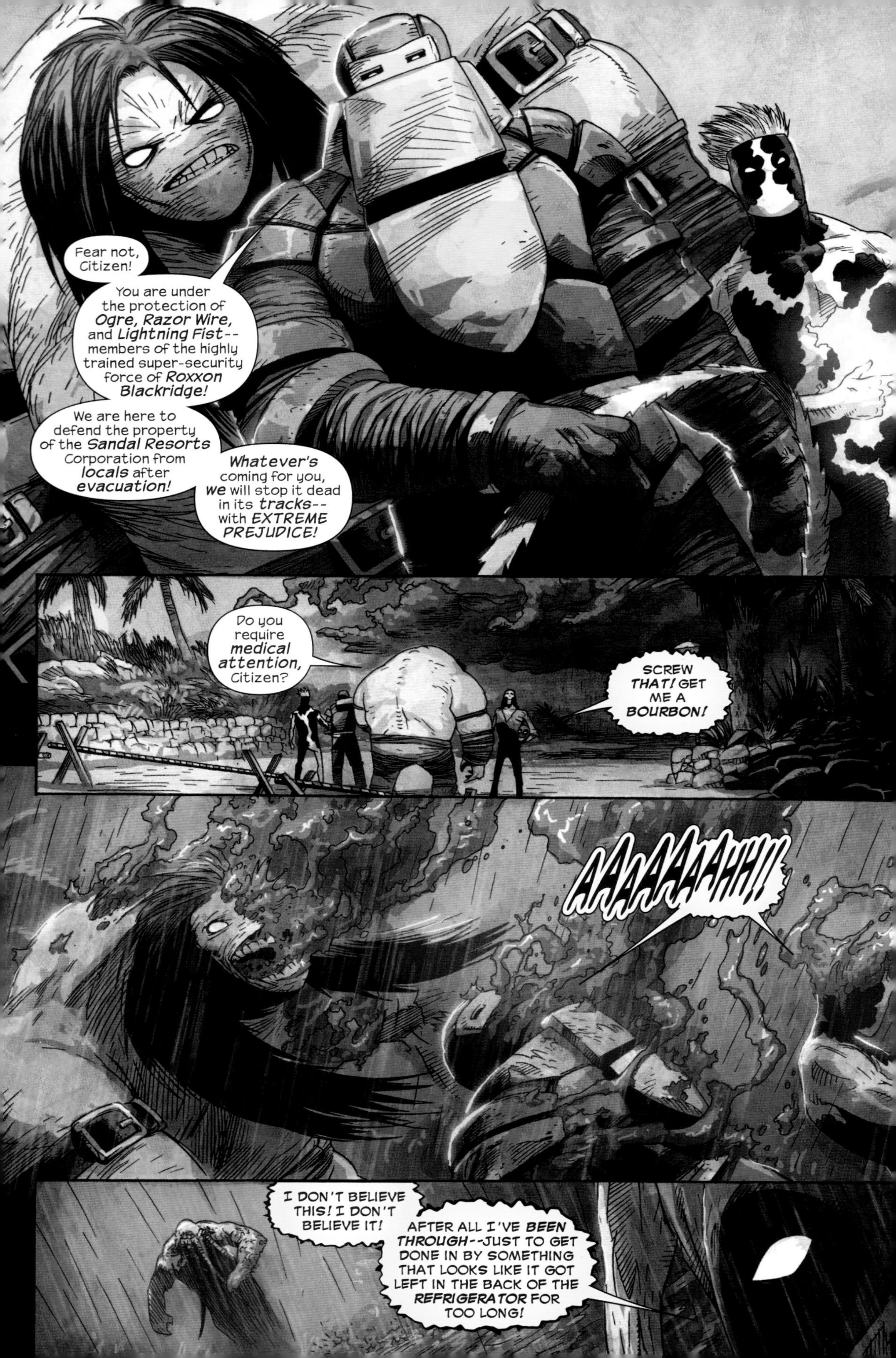
Fear not, Citizen!
You are under the protection of Ogre, Razor Wire, and Lightning Fist--members of the highly trained super-security force of Roxxon Blackridge!
We are here to defend the property of the Sandal Resorts Corporation from locals after evacuation!
Whatever's coming for you, we will stop it dead in its tracks--with EXTREME PREJUDICE!
Do you require medical attention, Citizen?
SCREW THAT! GET ME A BOURBON!
AAAAAAAHH!!
I DON'T BELIEVE THIS! I DON'T BELIEVE IT!
AFTER ALL I'VE BEEN THROUGH--JUST TO GET DONE IN BY SOMETHING THAT LOOKS LIKE IT GOT LEFT IN THE BACK OF THE REFRIGERATOR FOR TOO LONG!

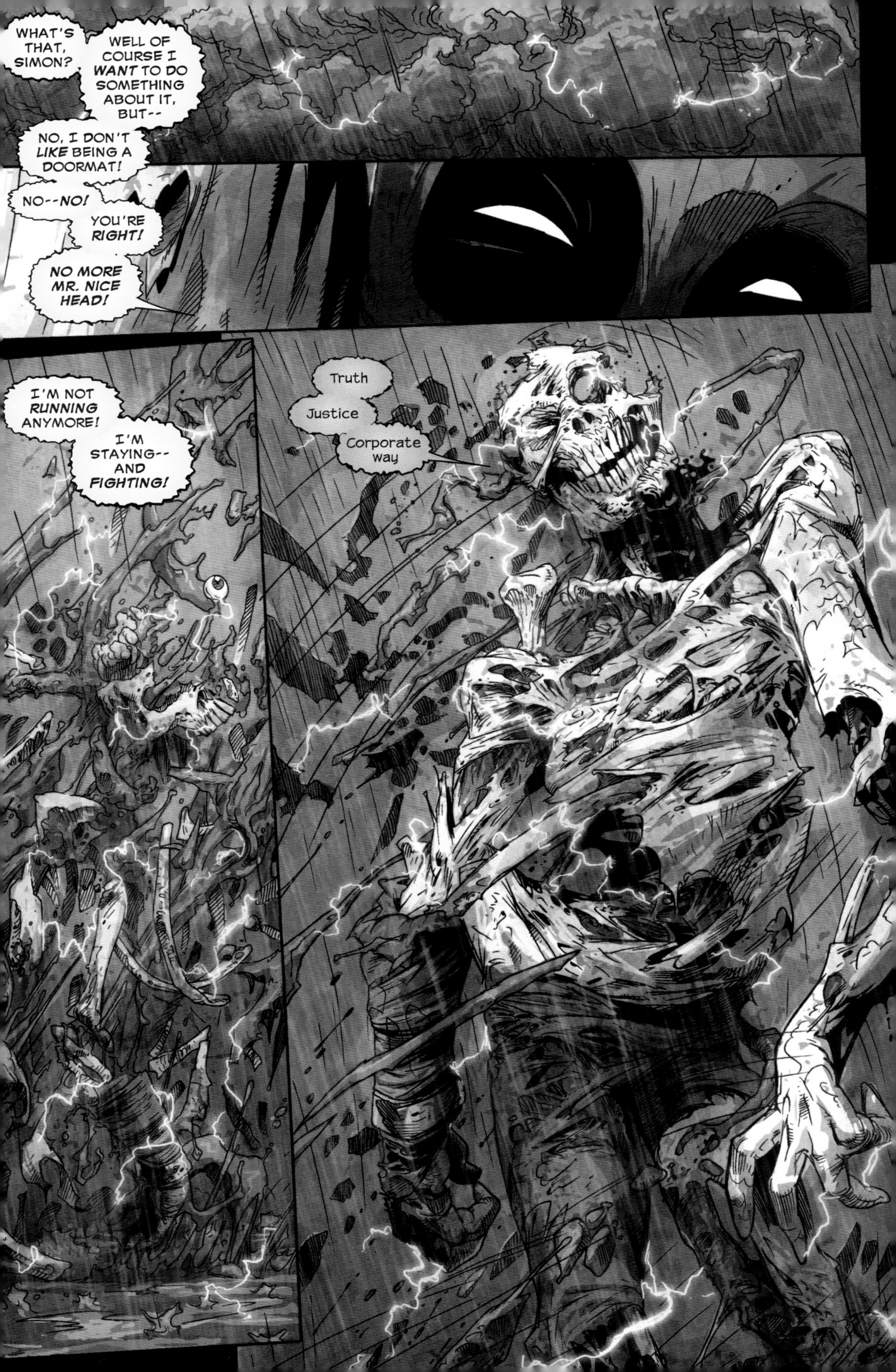
WHAT'S THAT, SIMON?
WELL OF COURSE I *WANT* TO DO SOMETHING ABOUT IT, BUT--
NO, I DON'T *LIKE* BEING A DOORMAT!
NO--*NO!*
YOU'RE *RIGHT!*
NO MORE MR. NICE HEAD!
I'M NOT *RUNNING* ANYMORE!
I'M STAYING--AND *FIGHTING!*
Truth
Justice
Corporate way

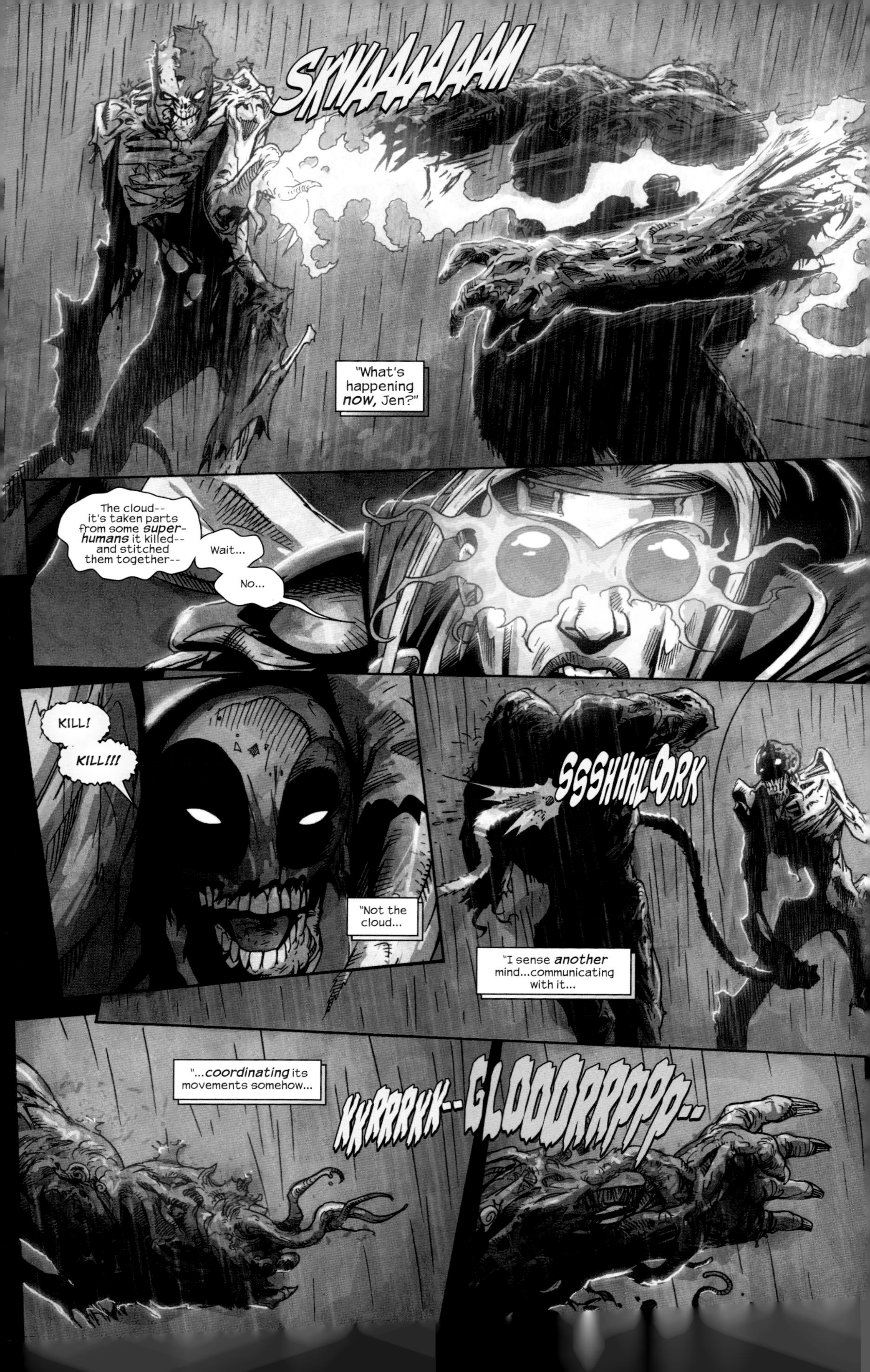
SKWAAAAAAM
"What's happening *now,* Jen?"
The cloud-- it's taken parts from some *super-humans* it killed-- and stitched them together--
Wait...
No...
KILL!
KILL!!!
"Not the cloud...
SSSHHHLOORK
"I sense *another* mind...communicating with it...
"...*coordinating* its movements somehow...
KKRRRKK--GLOOORRPPP--

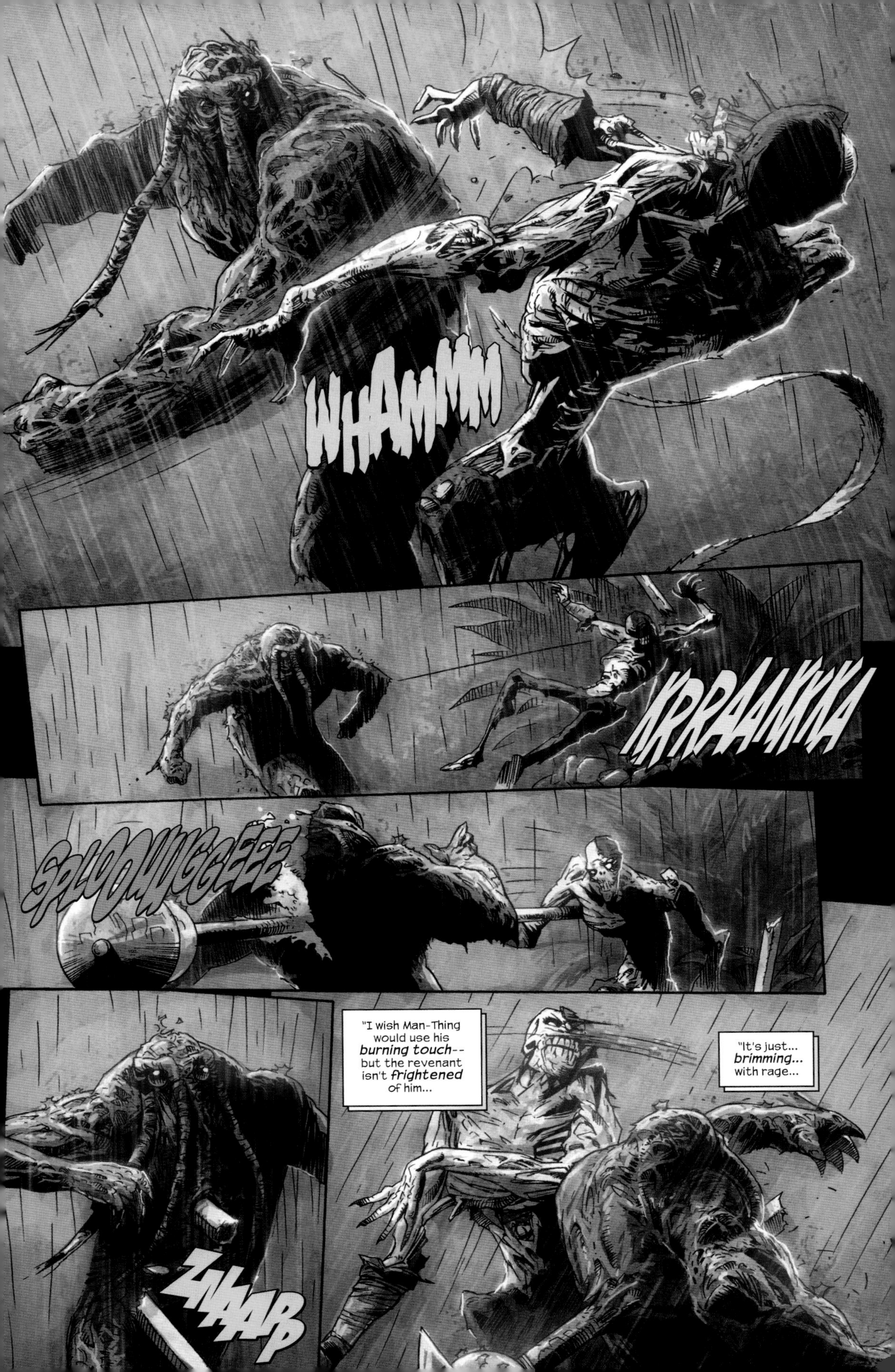
WHAMMM
KRRAAKKA
SPLOOMUGGLEEE
"I wish Man-Thing would use his *burning touch*-- but the revenant isn't *frightened* of him...
"It's just... *brimming...* with rage...
ZHAAP

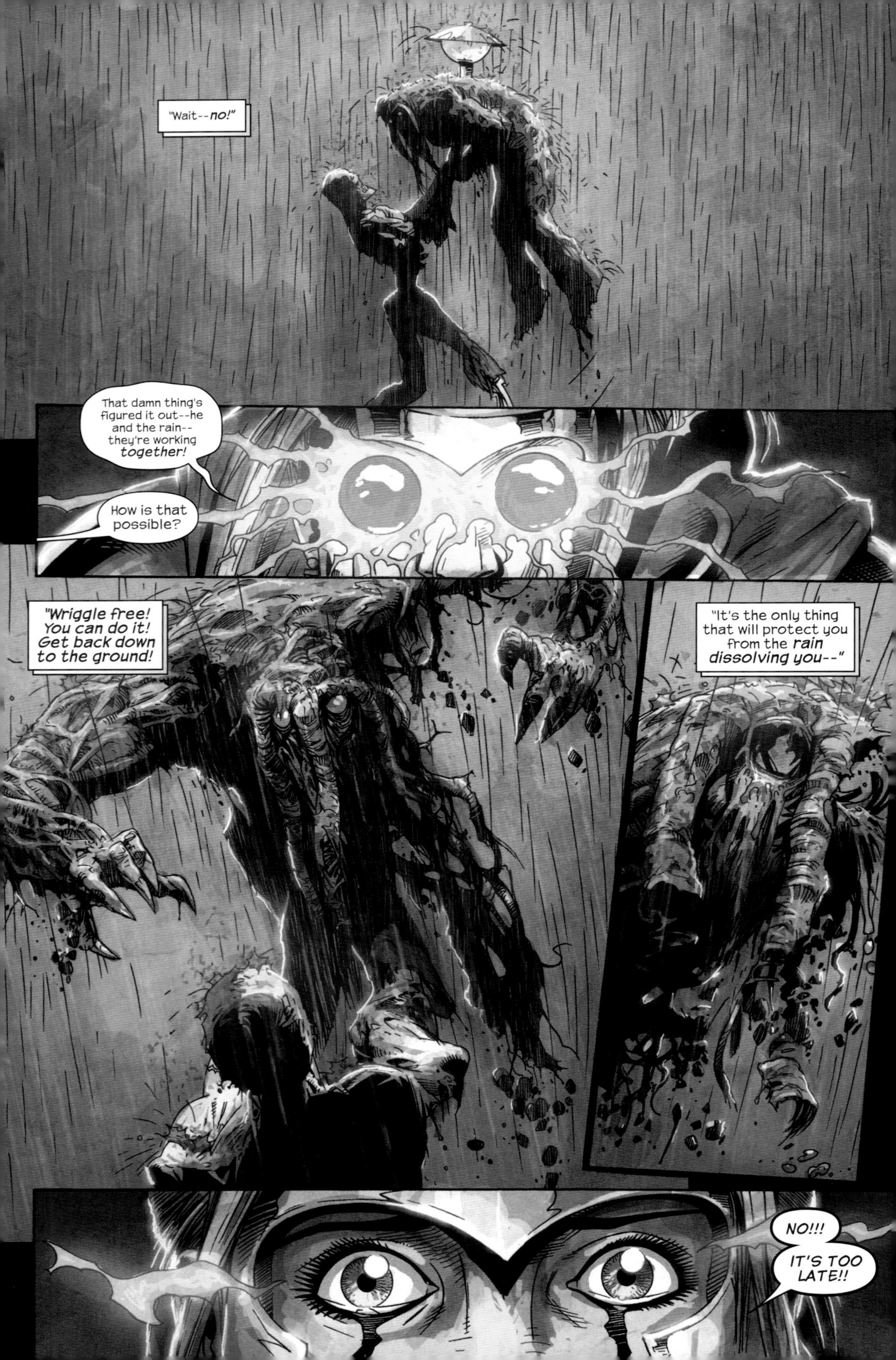
"Wait--*no!*"
That damn thing's figured it out--he and the rain--they're working *together!*
How is that possible?
"Wriggle free! You can do it! Get back down to the ground!
"It's the only thing that will protect you from the *rain dissolving you--"*
NO!!!
IT'S TOO LATE!!

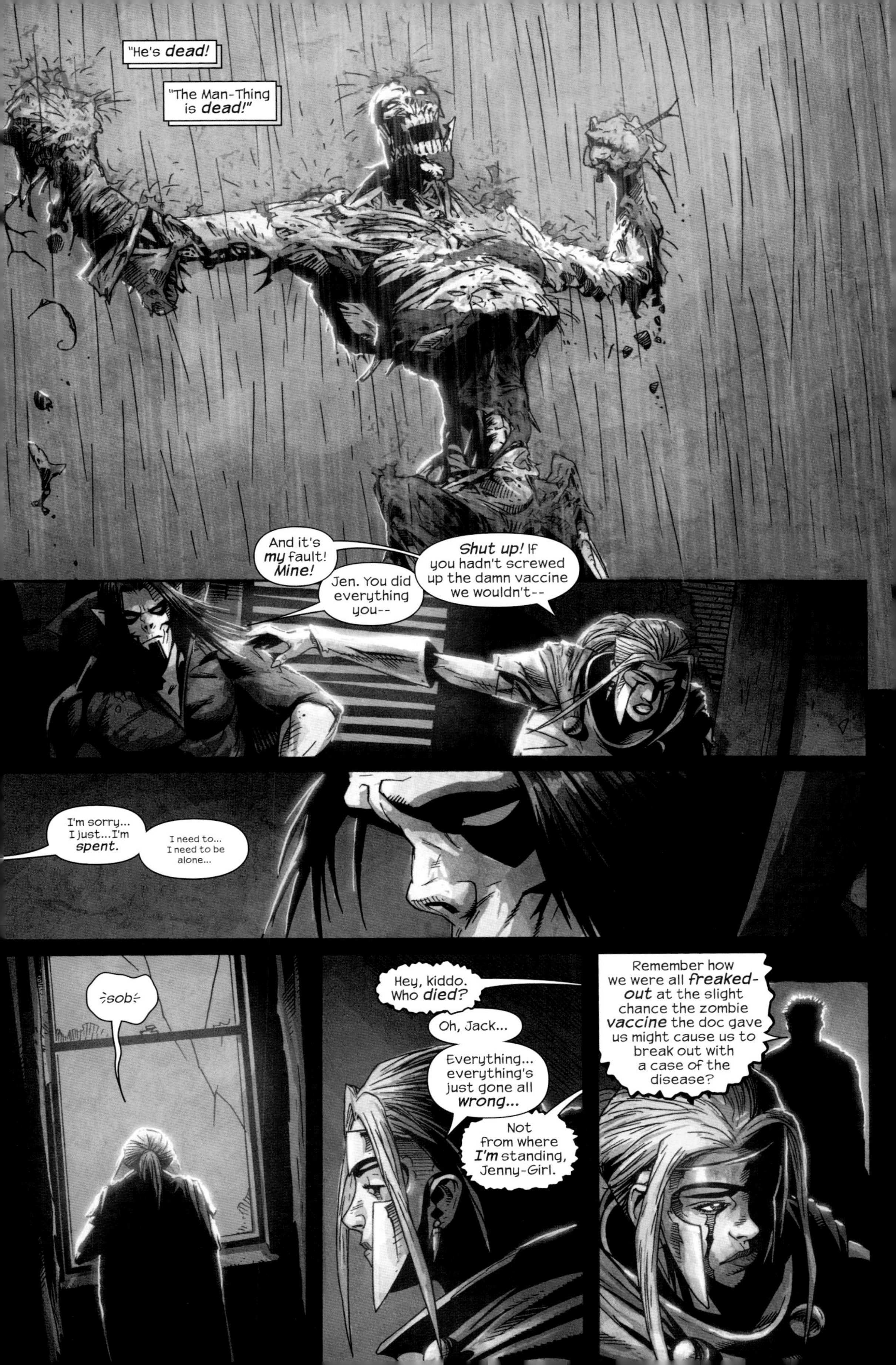
"He's *dead!*
"The Man-Thing is *dead!*"
And it's *my* fault! *Mine!*
Jen. You did everything you--
Shut up! If you hadn't screwed up the damn vaccine we wouldn't--
I'm sorry... I just...I'm *spent.*
I need to... I need to be alone...
sob
Hey, kiddo. Who *died?*
Oh, Jack...
Everything... everything's just gone all *wrong...*
Not from where *I'm* standing, Jenny-Girl.
Remember how we were all *freaked-out* at the slight chance the zombie *vaccine* the doc gave us might cause us to break out with a case of the disease?

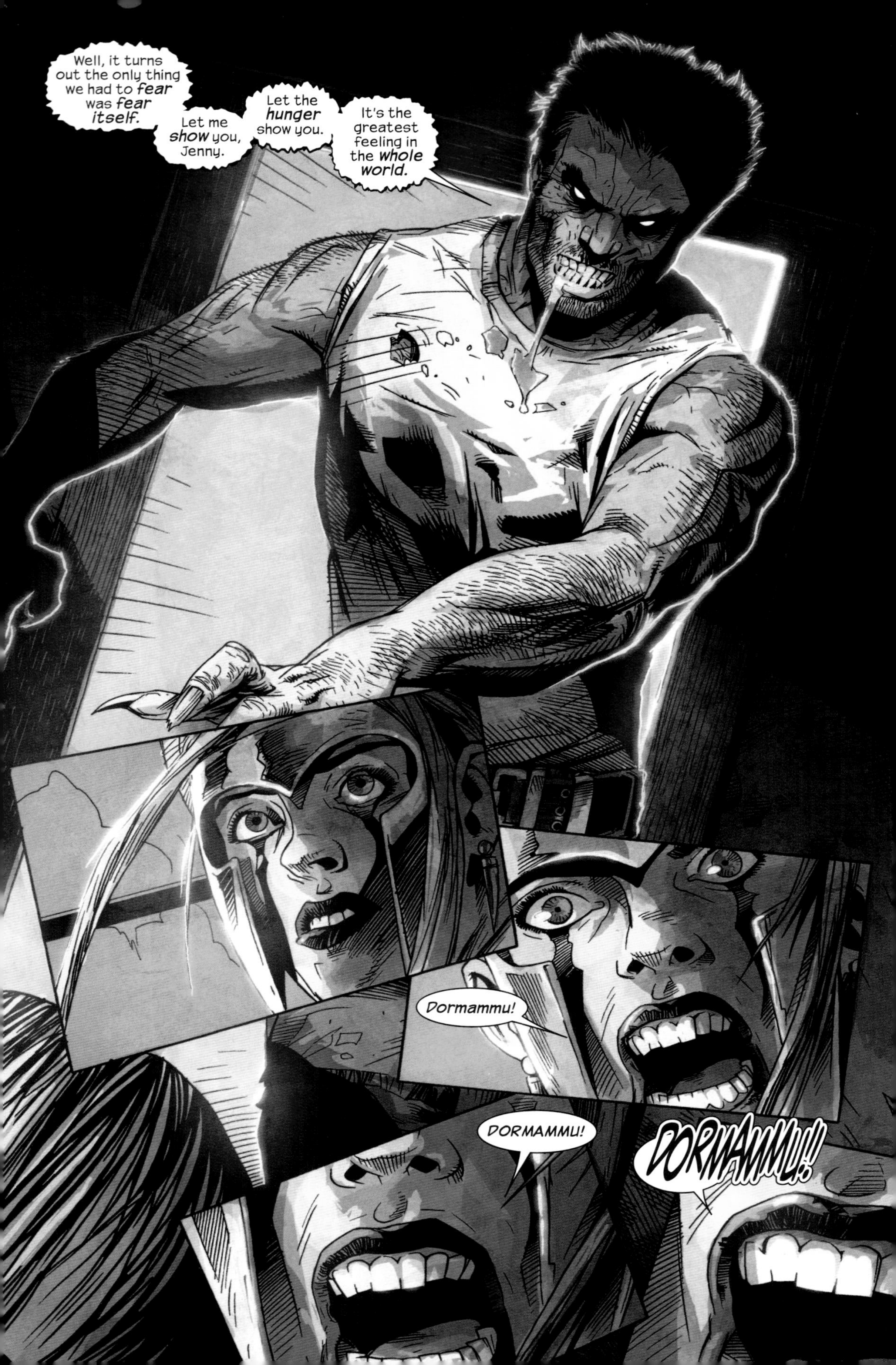

Well, it turns out the only thing we had to fear was fear itself.
Let me show you, Jenny.
Let the hunger show you.
It's the greatest feeling in the whole world.
Dormammu!
DORMAMMU!
DORMAMMU!!

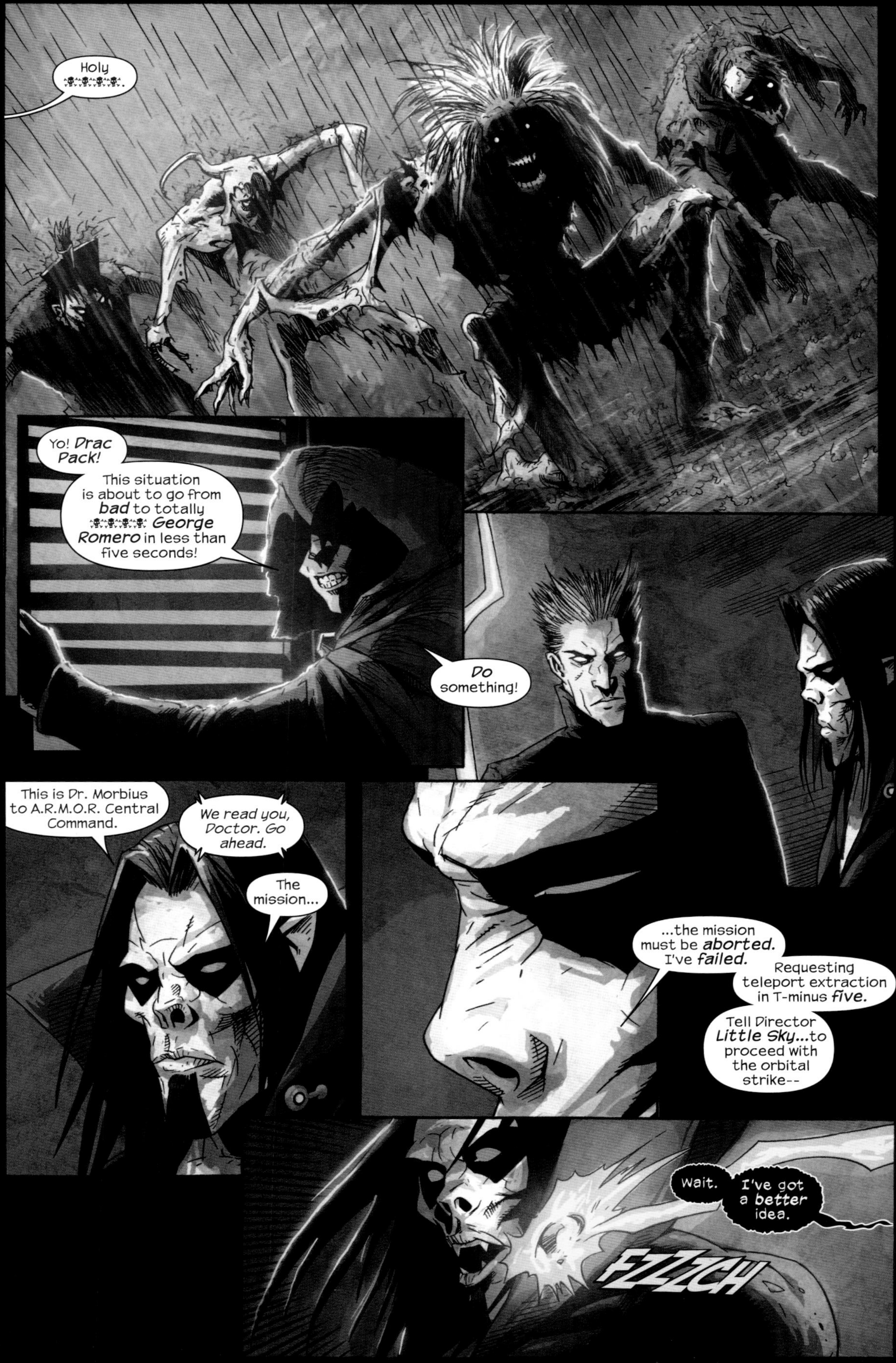

Holy ☠☠☠☠.
Yo! Drac Pack!
This situation is about to go from bad to totally ☠☠☠☠ George Romero in less than five seconds!
Do something!
This is Dr. Morbius to A.R.M.O.R. Central Command.
We read you, Doctor. Go ahead.
The mission...
...the mission must be aborted. I've failed.
Requesting teleport extraction in T-minus five.
Tell Director Little Sky...to proceed with the orbital strike--
Wait.
I've got a better idea.
FZZZCH

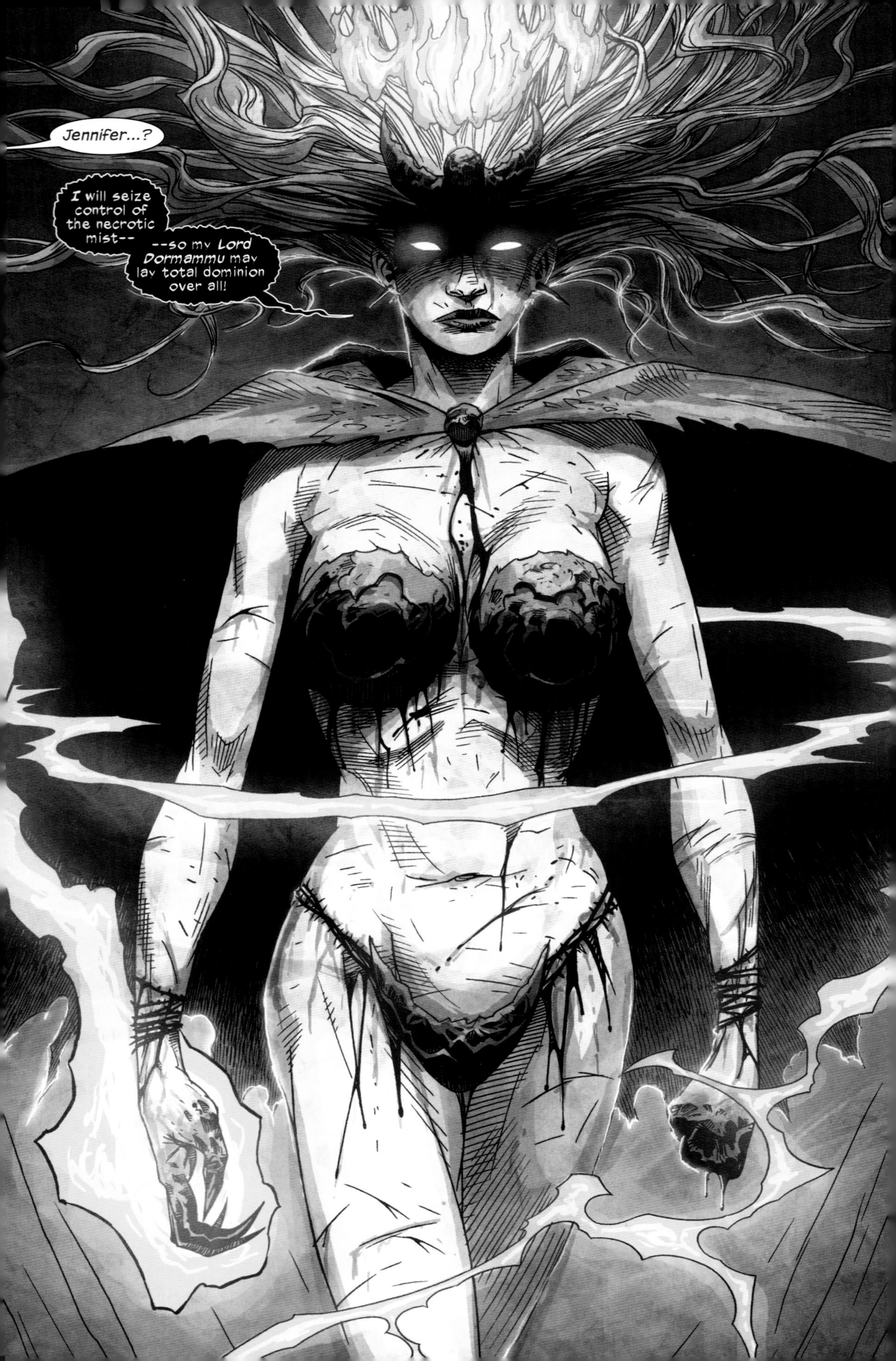
Jennifer...?
I will seize control of the necrotic mist--
--so my Lord Dormammu may lay total dominion over all!

#4

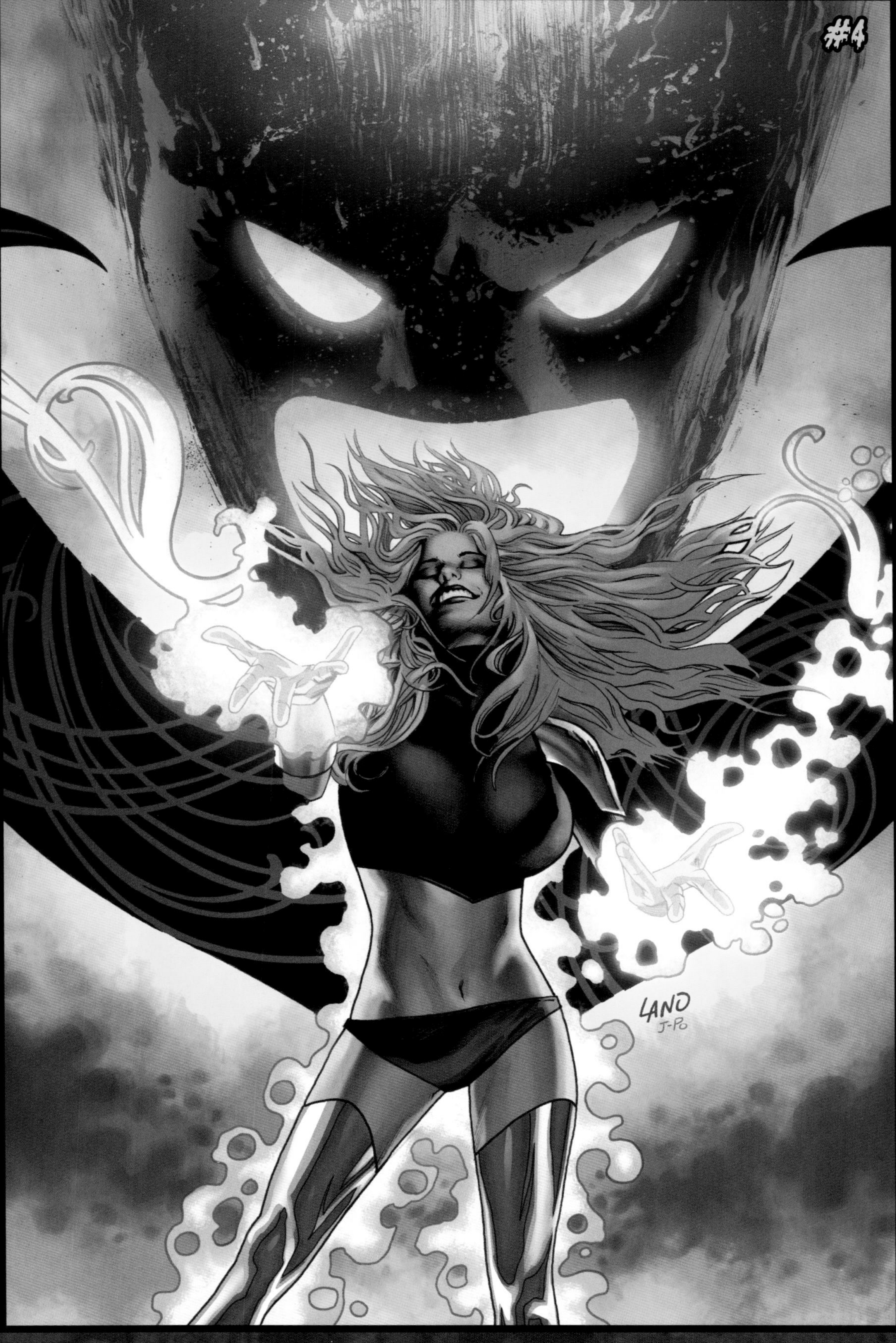
LAND
J-Po

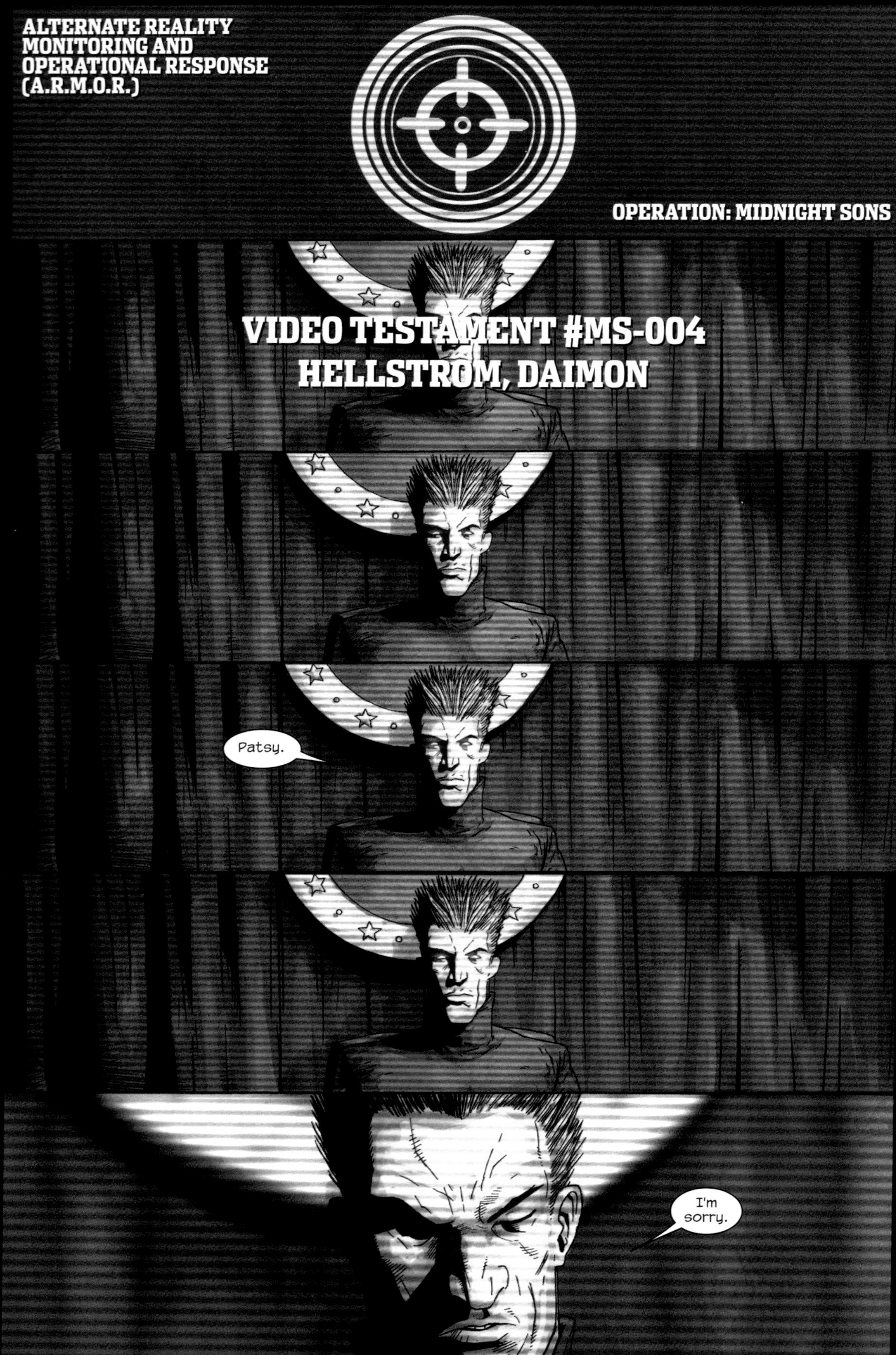
ALTERNATE REALITY MONITORING AND OPERATIONAL RESPONSE (A.R.M.O.R.)
OPERATION: MIDNIGHT SONS
VIDEO TESTAMENT #MS-004
HELLSTROM, DAIMON
Patsy.
I'm sorry.

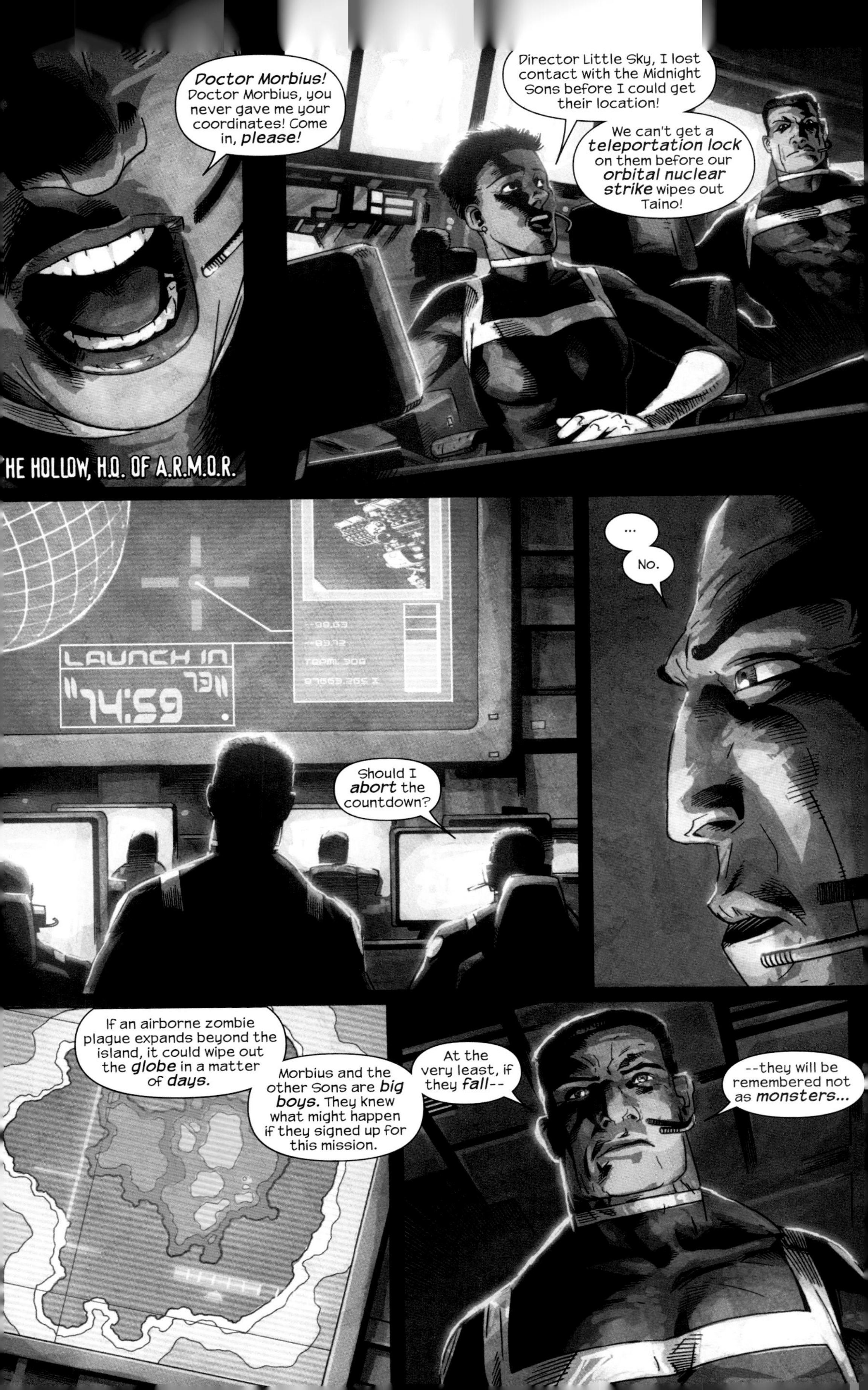
HE HOLLOW, H.Q. OF A.R.M.O.R.
Doctor Morbius! Doctor Morbius, you never gave me your coordinates! Come in, please!
Director Little Sky, I lost contact with the Midnight Sons before I could get their location!
We can't get a teleportation lock on them before our orbital nuclear strike wipes out Taino!
LAUNCH IN
14:59
...
No.
Should I abort the countdown?
If an airborne zombie plague expands beyond the island, it could wipe out the globe in a matter of days.
Morbius and the other Sons are big boys. They knew what might happen if they signed up for this mission.
At the very least, if they fall--
--they will be remembered not as monsters...

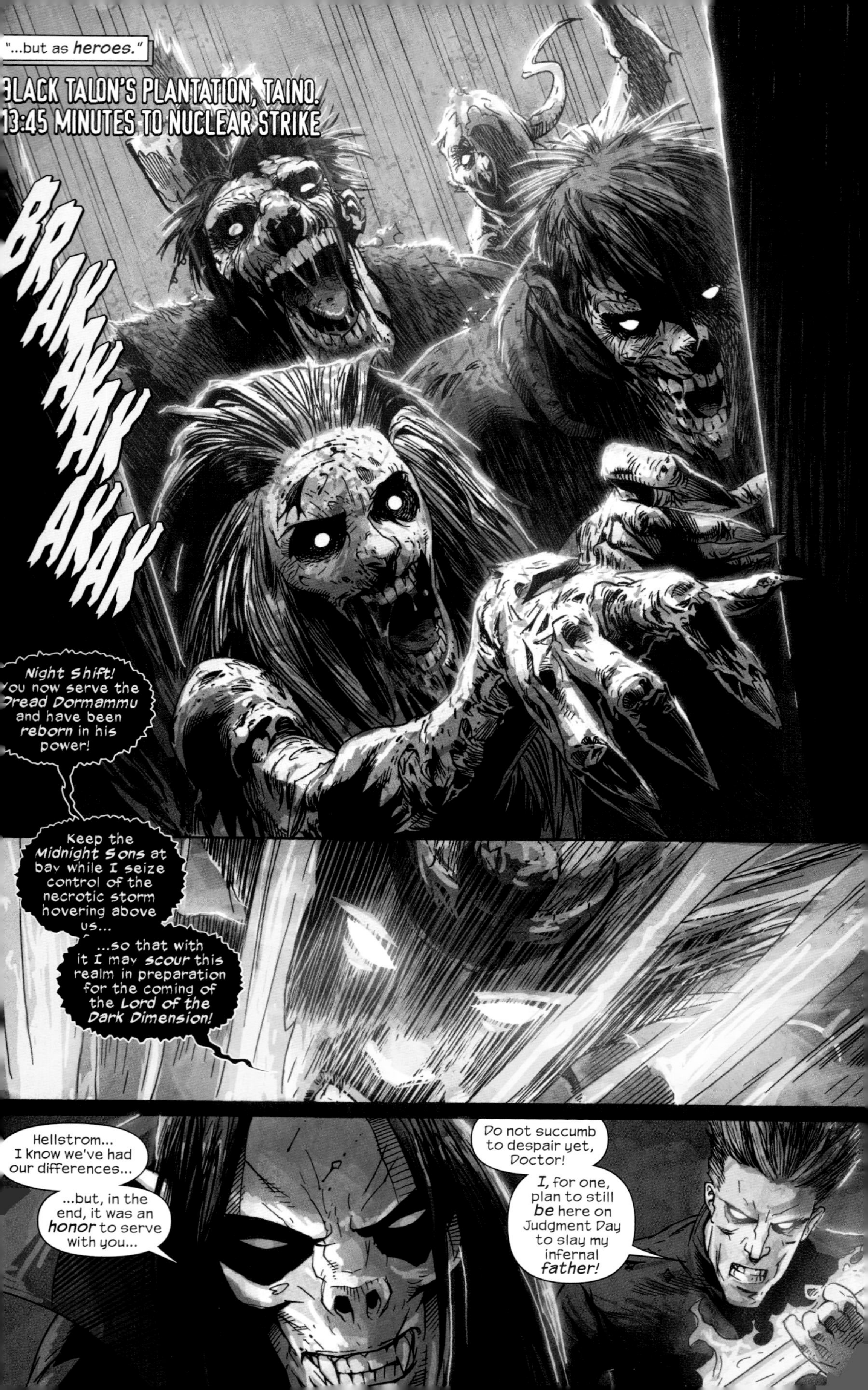

"...but as heroes."
BLACK TALON'S PLANTATION, TAINO.
13:45 MINUTES TO NUCLEAR STRIKE
BRAKAKAKAKAK
Night Shift! You now serve the Dread Dormammu and have been reborn in his power!
Keep the Midnight Sons at bay while I seize control of the necrotic storm hovering above us...
...so that with it I may scour this realm in preparation for the coming of the Lord of the Dark Dimension!
Hellstrom... I know we've had our differences...
...but, in the end, it was an honor to serve with you...
Do not succumb to despair yet, Doctor!
I, for one, plan to still be here on Judgment Day to slay my infernal father!

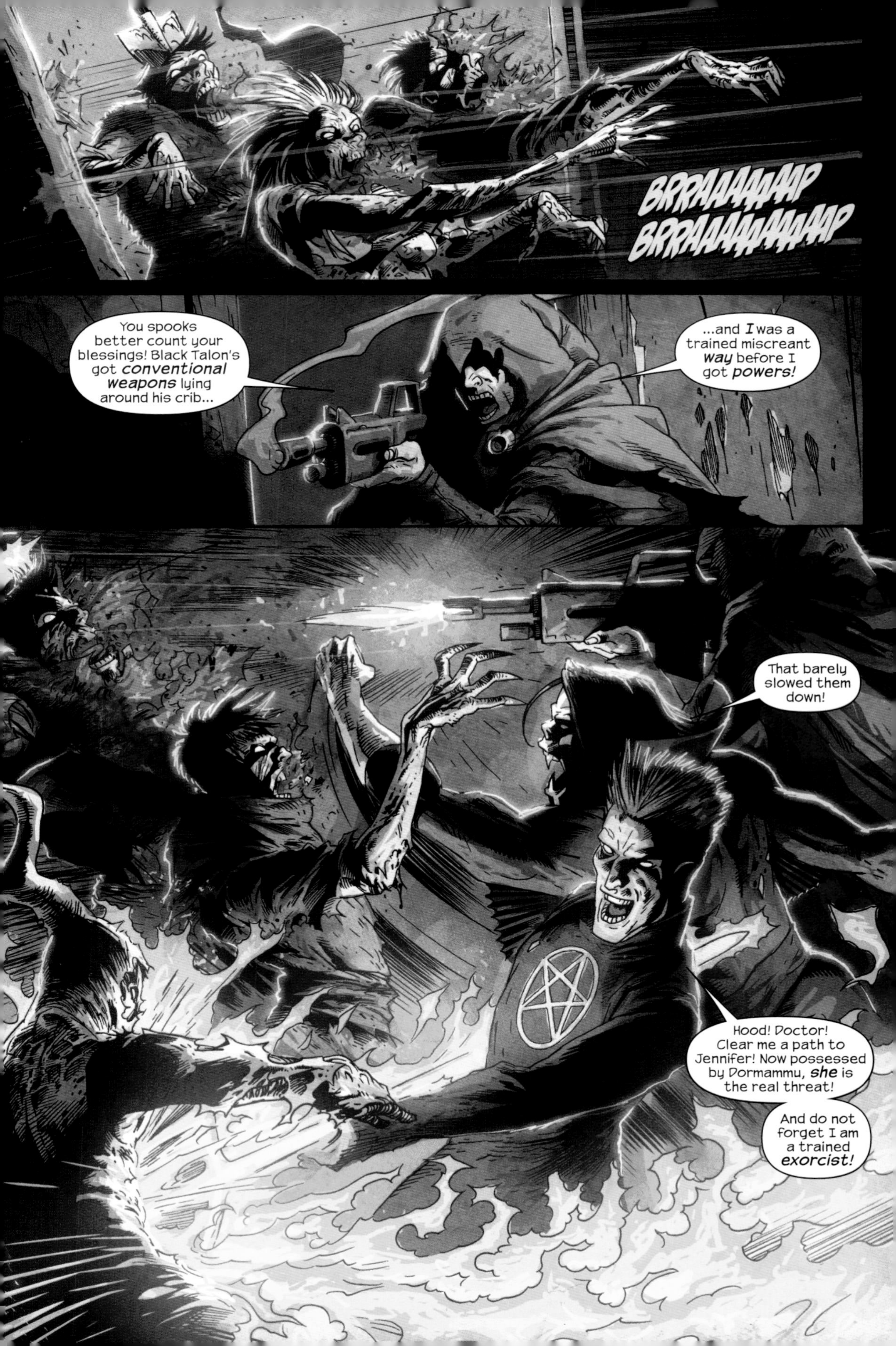
BRRAAAAAAAP
BRRAAAAAAAAAP
You spooks better count your blessings! Black Talon's got *conventional weapons* lying around his crib...
...and *I* was a trained miscreant *way* before I got *powers!*
That barely slowed them down!
Hood! Doctor! Clear me a path to Jennifer! Now possessed by Dormammu, *she* is the real threat!
And do not forget I am a trained *exorcist!*

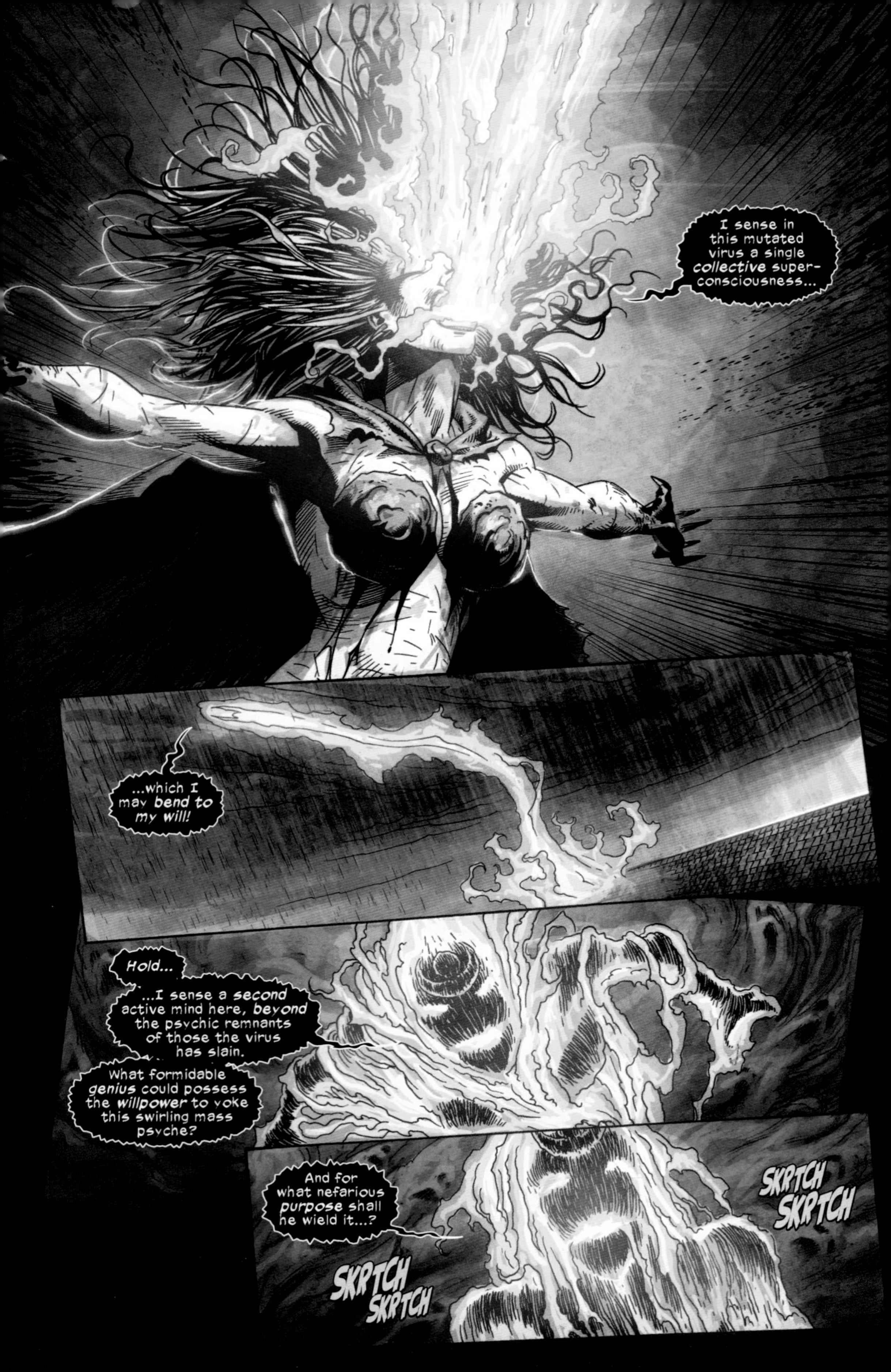
I sense in this mutated virus a single collective super-consciousness...
...which I may bend to my will!
Hold...
...I sense a second active mind here, beyond the psychic remnants of those the virus has slain.
What formidable genius could possess the willpower to yoke this swirling mass psyche?
And for what nefarious purpose shall he wield it...?
SKRTCH SKRTCH
SKRTCH SKRTCH

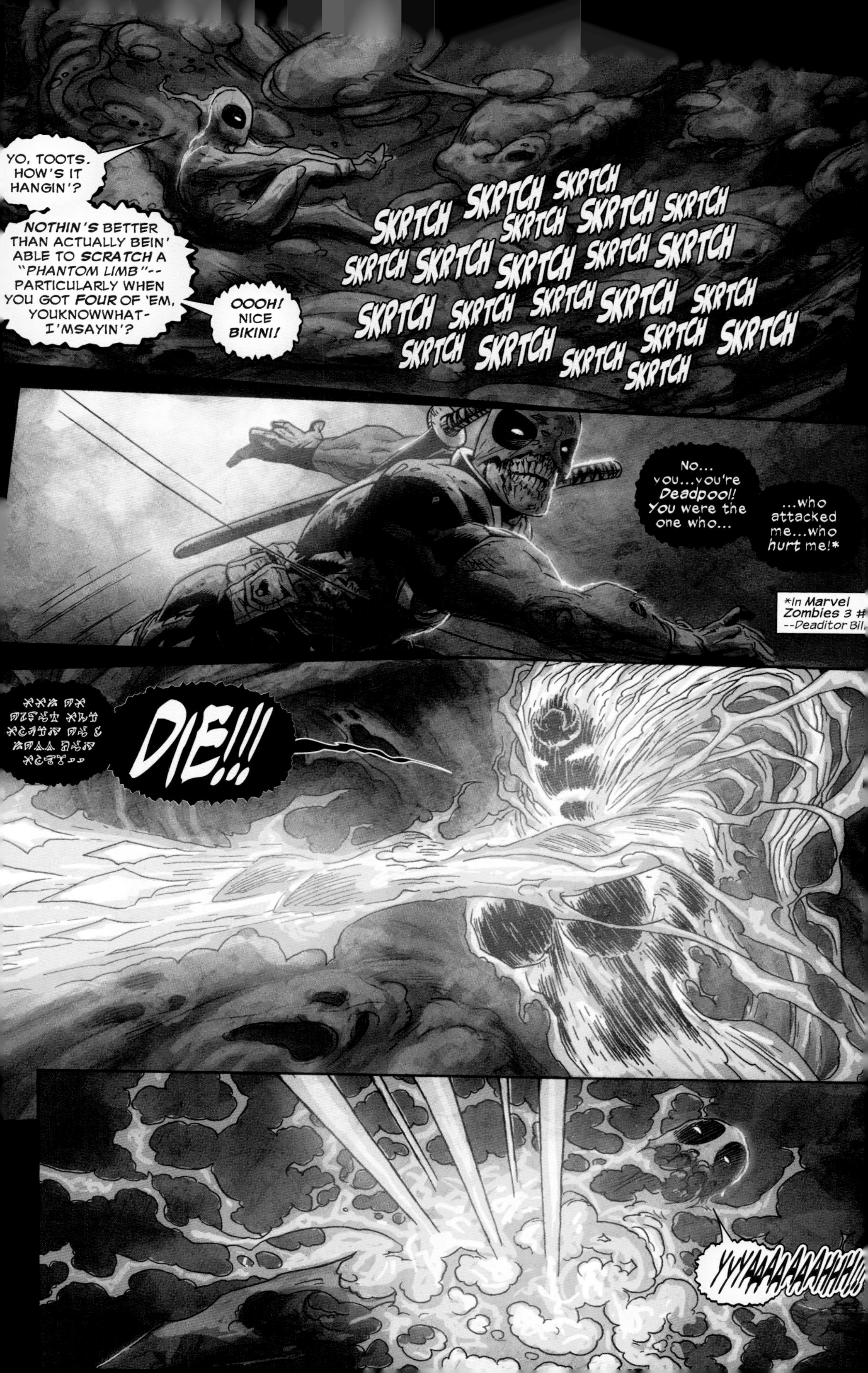

YO, TOOTS. HOW'S IT HANGIN'?
NOTHIN'S BETTER THAN ACTUALLY BEIN' ABLE TO SCRATCH A "PHANTOM LIMB"-- PARTICULARLY WHEN YOU GOT FOUR OF 'EM, YOUKNOWWHAT-I'MSAYIN'?
OOOH! NICE BIKINI!
SKRTCH SKRTCH
No... you...you're Deadpool! You were the one who...
...who attacked me...who hurt me!*
*In Marvel Zombies 3 # --Deaditor Bil
DIE!!!
YYYAAAAAAAHHH!!

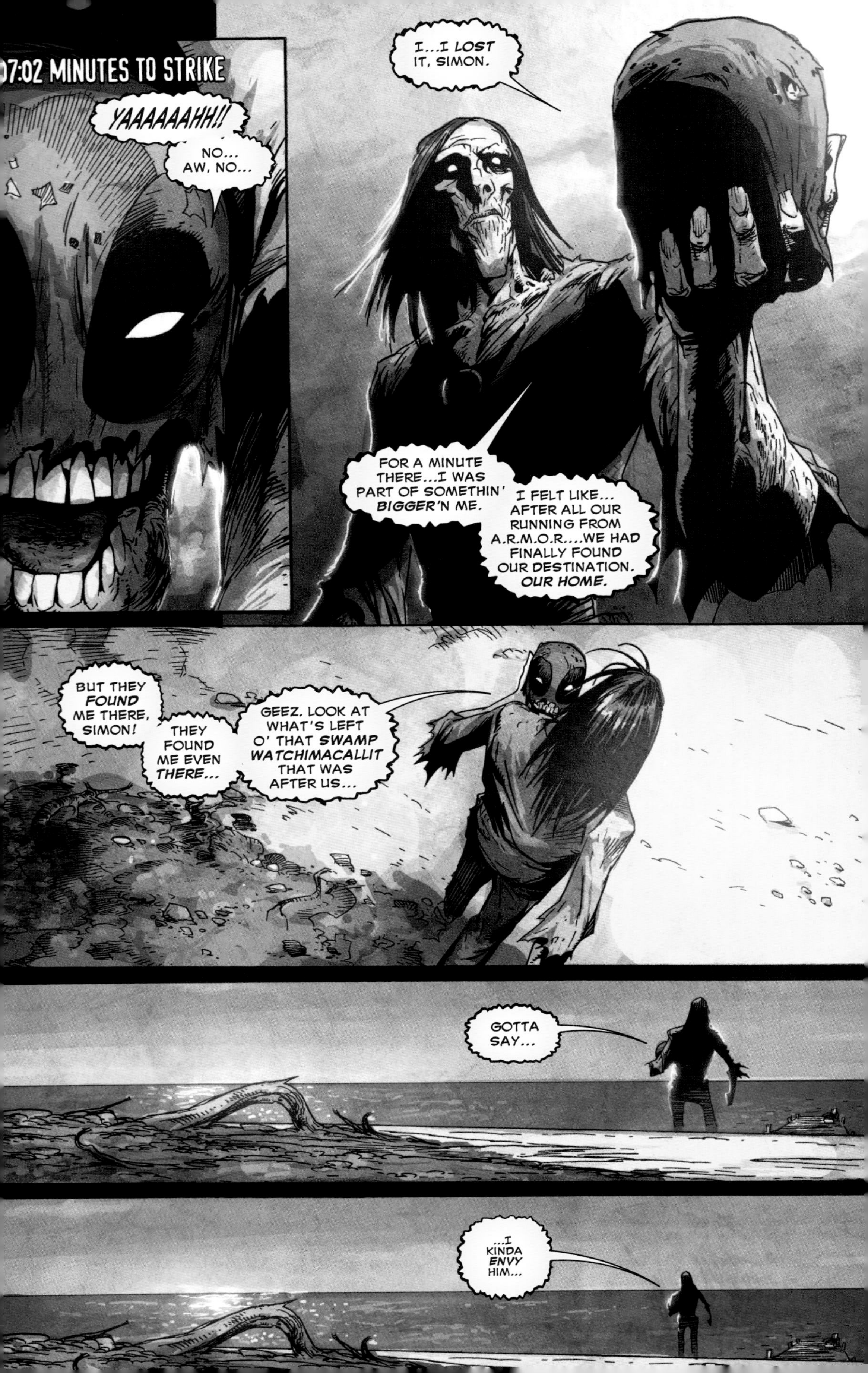
07:02 MINUTES TO STRIKE
YAAAAAAHH!!
NO... AW, NO...
I...I LOST IT, SIMON.
FOR A MINUTE THERE...I WAS PART OF SOMETHIN' BIGGER'N ME.
I FELT LIKE... AFTER ALL OUR RUNNING FROM A.R.M.O.R....WE HAD FINALLY FOUND OUR DESTINATION. OUR HOME.
BUT THEY FOUND ME THERE, SIMON!
THEY FOUND ME EVEN THERE...
GEEZ. LOOK AT WHAT'S LEFT O' THAT SWAMP WATCHIMACALLIT THAT WAS AFTER US...
GOTTA SAY...
...I KINDA ENVY HIM...

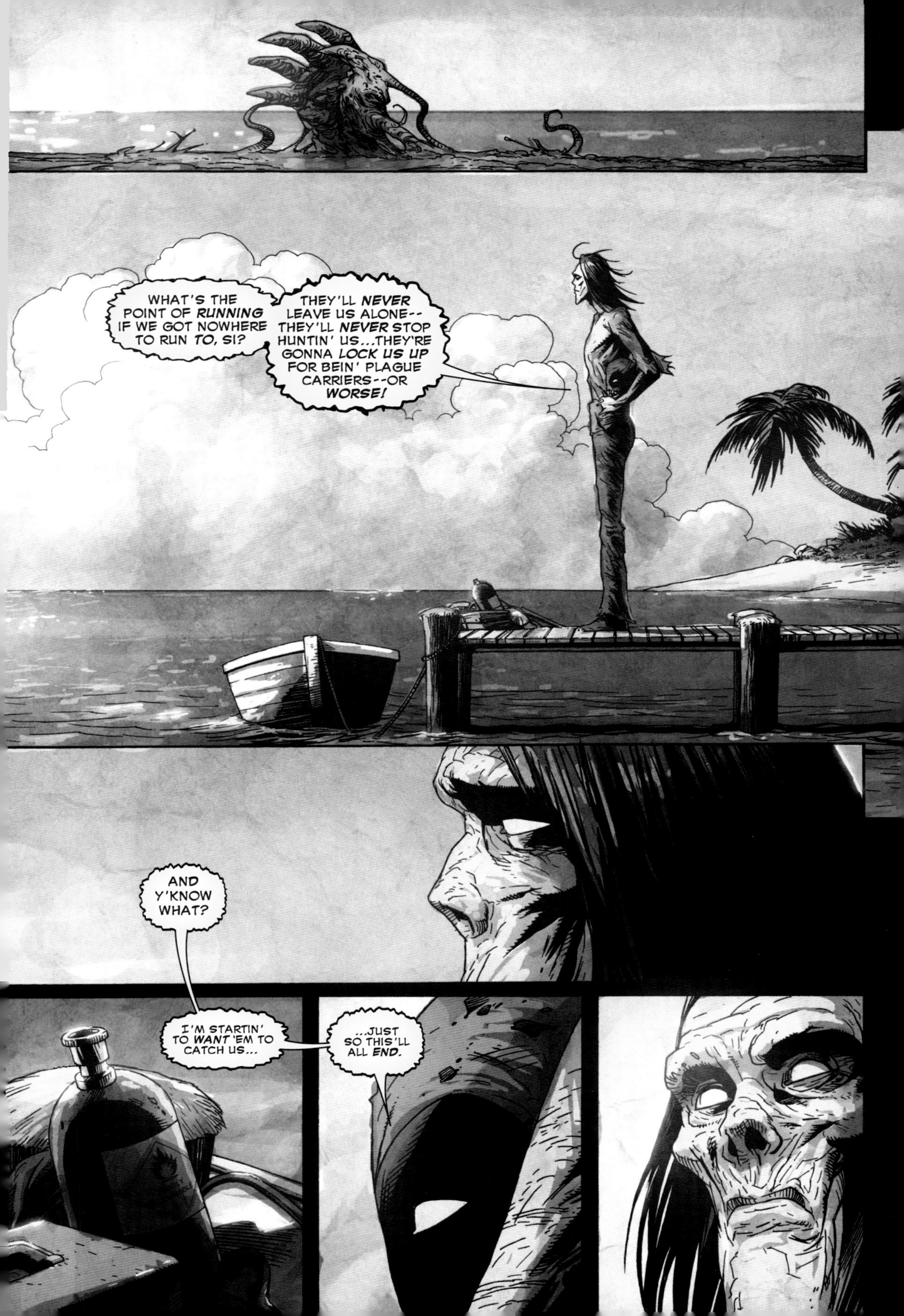
WHAT'S THE POINT OF RUNNING IF WE GOT NOWHERE TO RUN TO, SI?
THEY'LL NEVER LEAVE US ALONE-- THEY'LL NEVER STOP HUNTIN' US...THEY'RE GONNA LOCK US UP FOR BEIN' PLAGUE CARRIERS--OR WORSE!
AND Y'KNOW WHAT?
I'M STARTIN' TO WANT 'EM TO CATCH US...
...JUST SO THIS'LL ALL END.

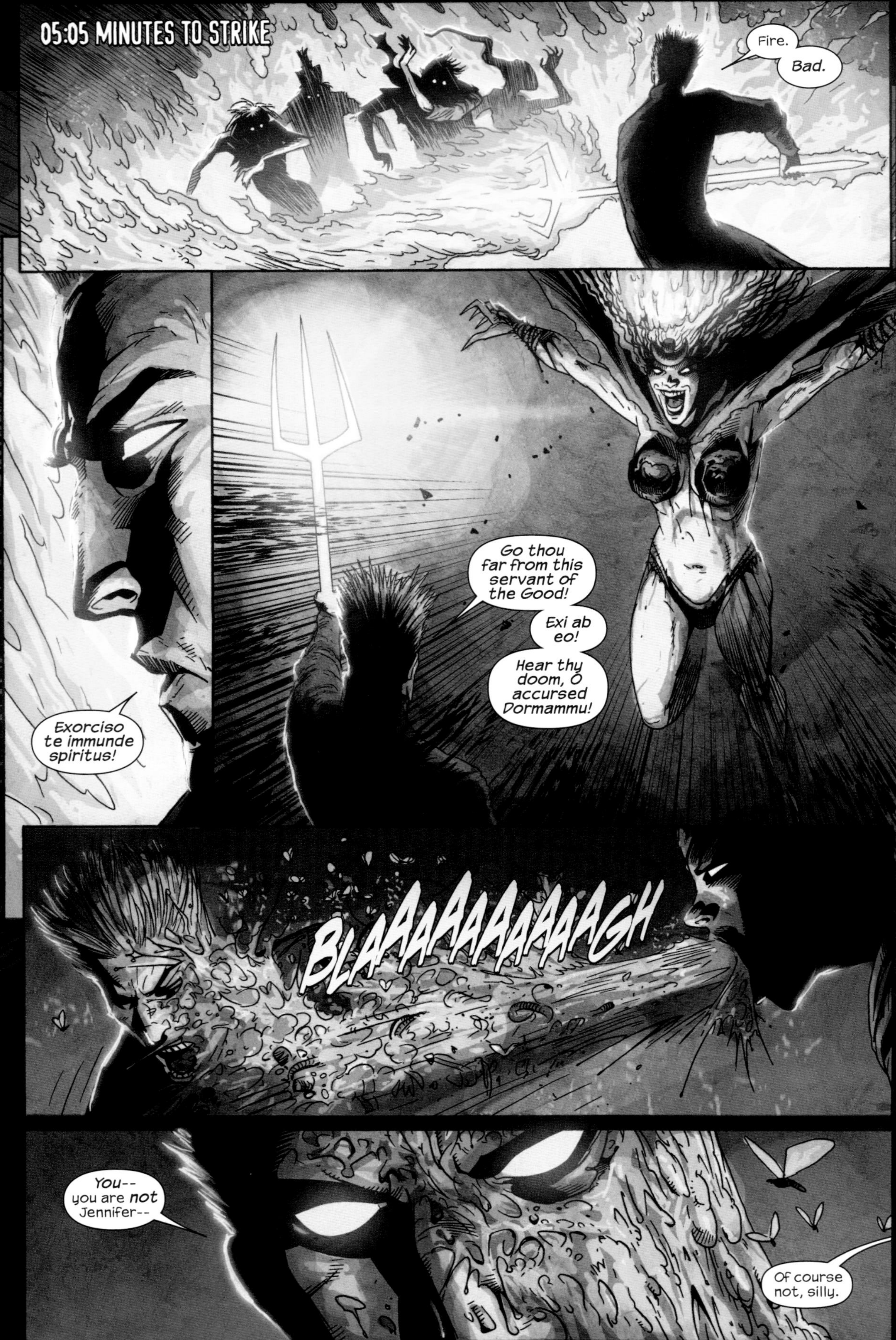
05:05 MINUTES TO STRIKE
Fire.
Bad.
Exorciso te immunde spiritus!
Go thou far from this servant of the Good!
Exi ab eo!
Hear thy doom, O accursed Dormammu!
BLAAAAAAAAAAAGH
You-- you are *not* Jennifer--
Of course not, silly.

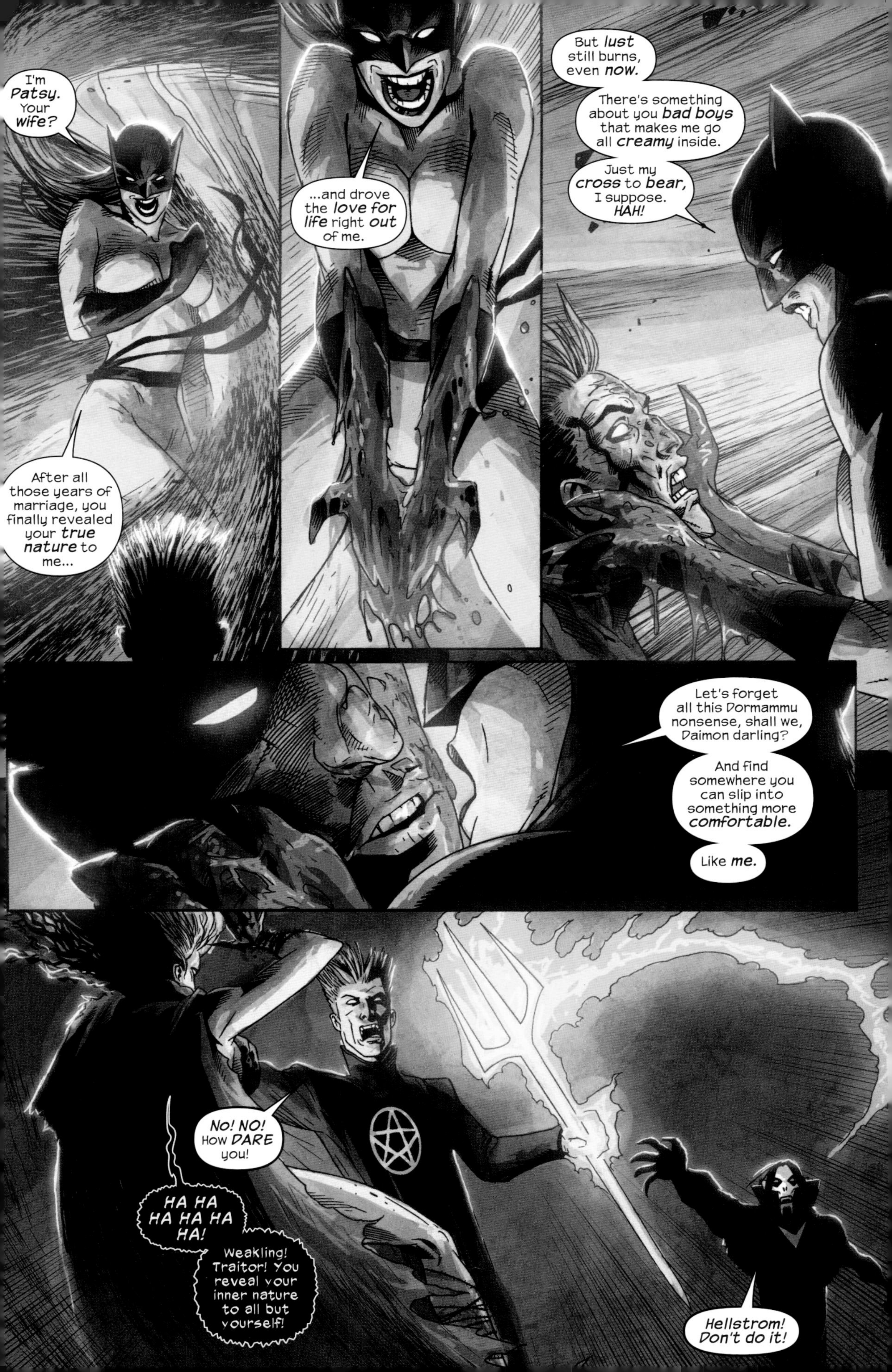
I'm Patsy. Your wife?
After all those years of marriage, you finally revealed your true nature to me...
...and drove the love for life right out of me.
But lust still burns, even now.
There's something about you bad boys that makes me go all creamy inside.
Just my cross to bear, I suppose. HAH!
Let's forget all this Dormammu nonsense, shall we, Daimon darling?
And find somewhere you can slip into something more comfortable.
Like me.
No! NO! How DARE you!
HA HA HA HA HA HA!
Weakling! Traitor! You reveal your inner nature to all but yourself!
Hellstrom! Don't do it!

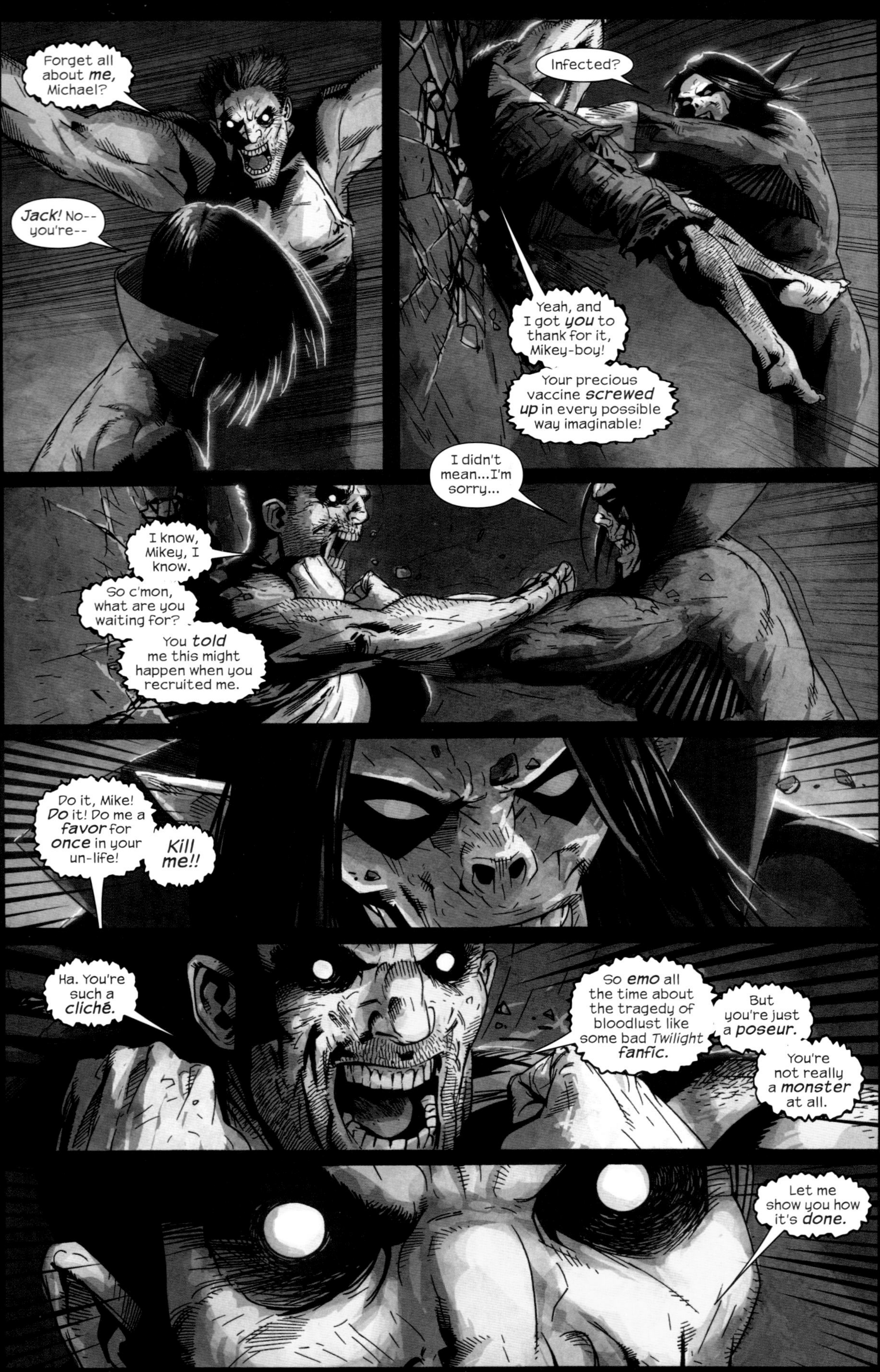
Forget all about me, Michael?
Jack! No-- you're--
Infected?
Yeah, and I got you to thank for it, Mikey-boy!
Your precious vaccine screwed up in every possible way imaginable!
I didn't mean...I'm sorry...
I know, Mikey, I know.
So c'mon, what are you waiting for?
You told me this might happen when you recruited me.
Do it, Mike! Do it! Do me a favor for once in your un-life!
Kill me!!
Ha. You're such a cliché.
So emo all the time about the tragedy of bloodlust like some bad Twilight fanfic.
But you're just a poseur.
You're not really a monster at all.
Let me show you how it's done.

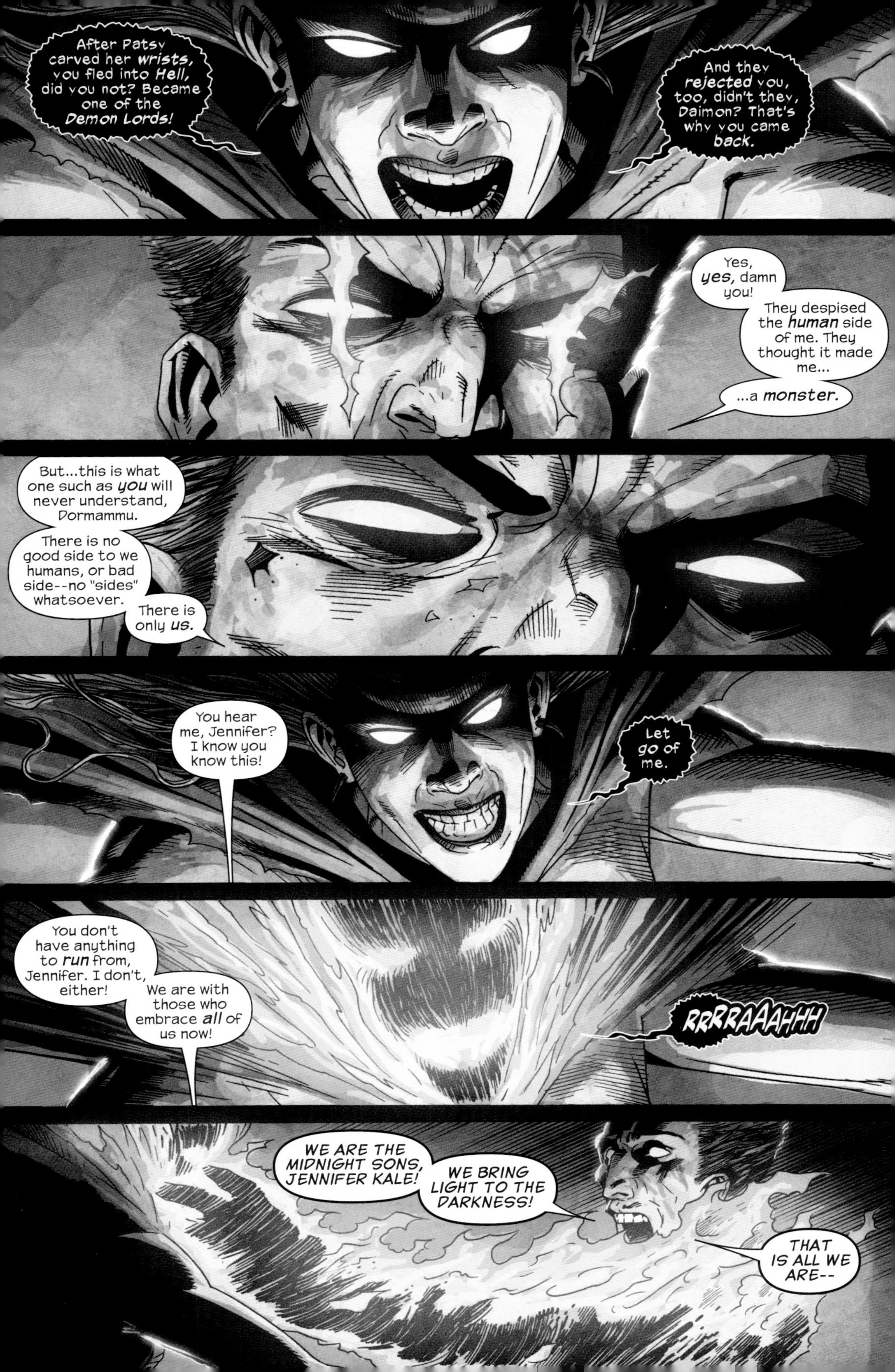
After Patsy carved her wrists, you fled into Hell, did you not? Became one of the Demon Lords!
And they rejected you, too, didn't they, Daimon? That's why you came back.
Yes, yes, damn you!
They despised the human side of me. They thought it made me...
...a monster.
But...this is what one such as you will never understand, Dormammu.
There is no good side to we humans, or bad side--no "sides" whatsoever.
There is only us.
You hear me, Jennifer? I know you know this!
Let go of me.
You don't have anything to run from, Jennifer. I don't, either!
We are with those who embrace all of us now!
RRRRAAAHHH
WE ARE THE MIDNIGHT SONS, JENNIFER KALE!
WE BRING LIGHT TO THE DARKNESS!
THAT IS ALL WE ARE--

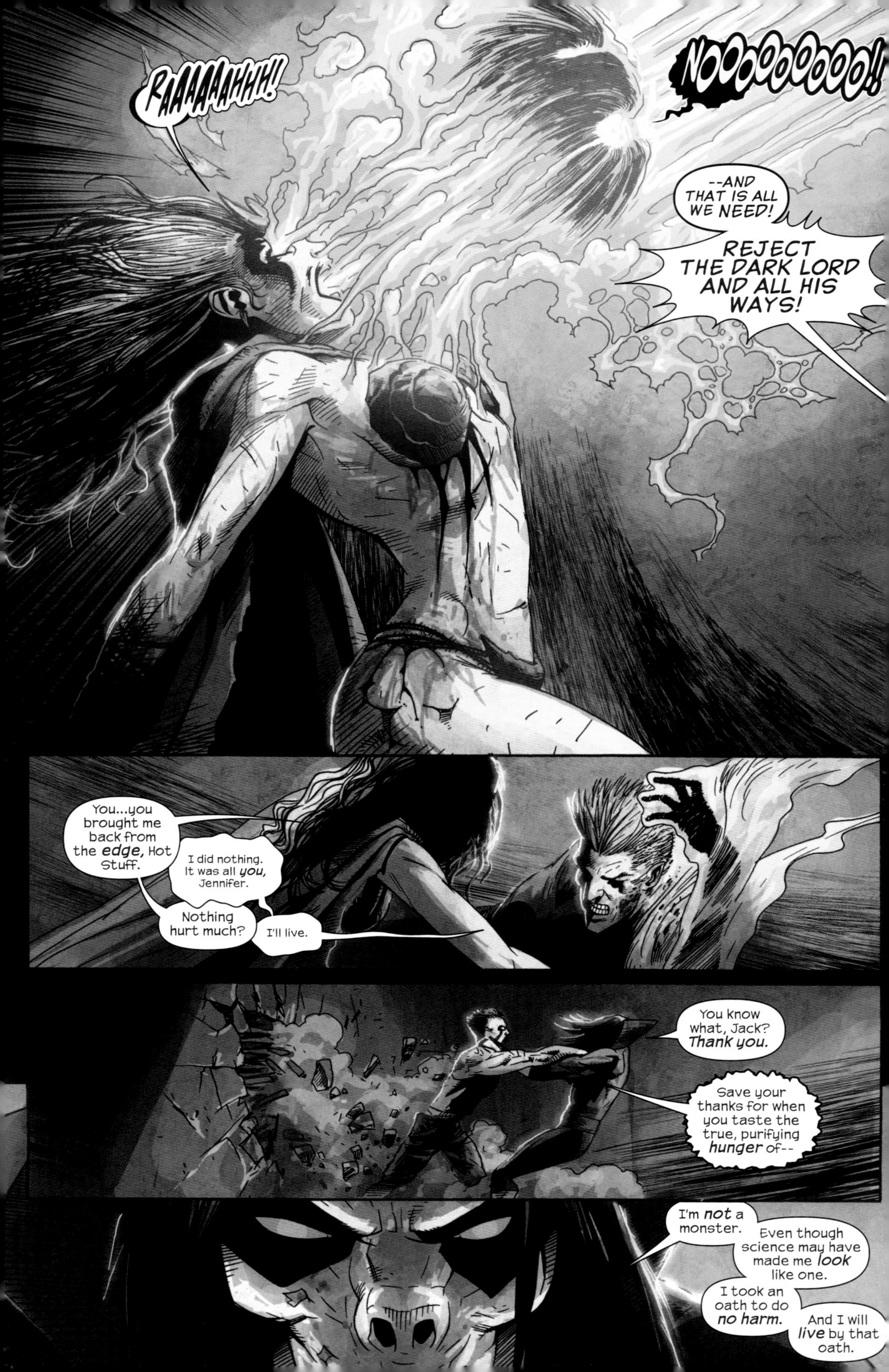
RAAAAAAHHH!!
NOOOOOOOOOO!!
--AND THAT IS ALL WE NEED!
REJECT THE DARK LORD AND ALL HIS WAYS!
You...you brought me back from the *edge,* Hot Stuff.
I did nothing. It was all *you,* Jennifer.
Nothing hurt much?
I'll live.
You know what, Jack? *Thank you.*
Save your thanks for when you taste the true, purifying *hunger* of--
I'm *not* a monster.
Even though science may have made me *look* like one.
I took an oath to do *no harm.*
And I will *live* by that oath.

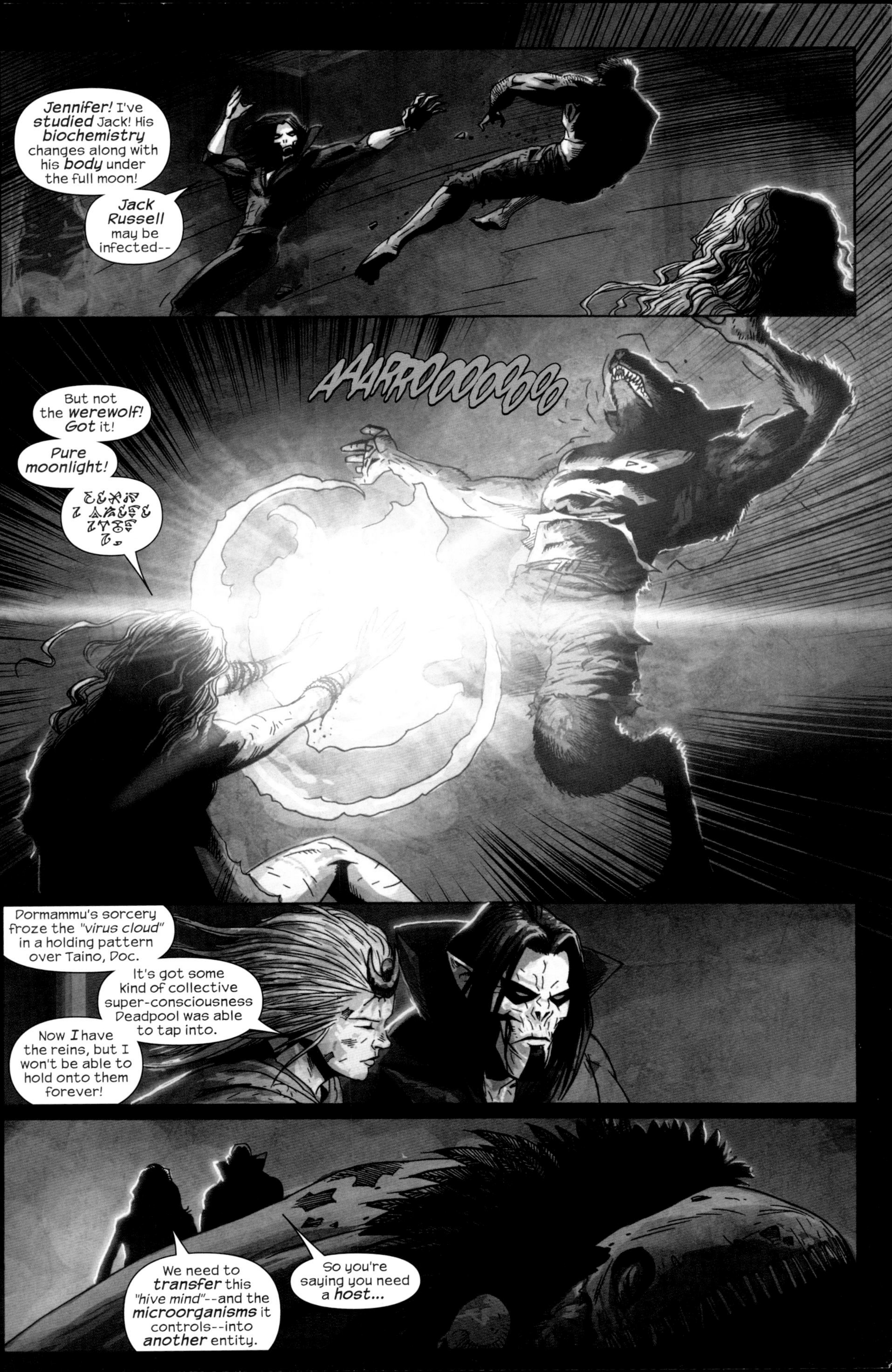
Jennifer! I've studied Jack! His biochemistry changes along with his body under the full moon!
Jack Russell may be infected--
AAARROOOOOOOOO
But not the werewolf! Got it!
Pure moonlight!
Dormammu's sorcery froze the "virus cloud" in a holding pattern over Taino, Doc.
It's got some kind of collective super-consciousness Deadpool was able to tap into.
Now I have the reins, but I won't be able to hold onto them forever!
We need to transfer this "hive mind"--and the microorganisms it controls--into another entity.
So you're saying you need a host...

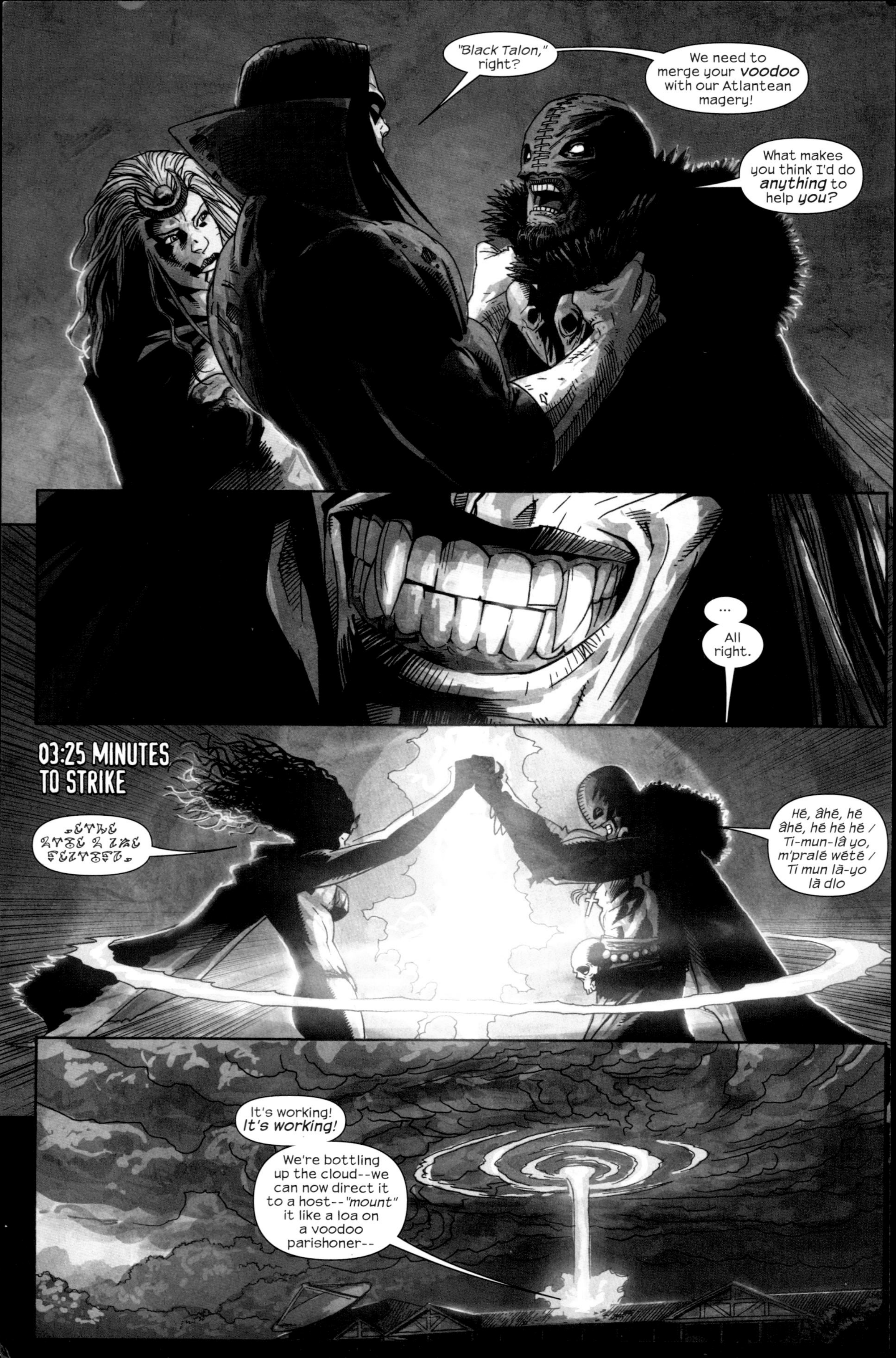
"Black Talon," right?
We need to merge your *voodoo* with our Atlantean magery!
What makes you think I'd do ***anything*** to help ***you?***
...
All right.
03:25 MINUTES TO STRIKE
Hē, âhē, hē âhē, hē hē hē / Ti-mun-lâ yo, m'pralē wētē / Ti mun là-yo là dlo
It's working! ***It's working!***
We're bottling up the cloud--we can now direct it to a host--*"mount"* it like a loa on a voodoo parishoner--

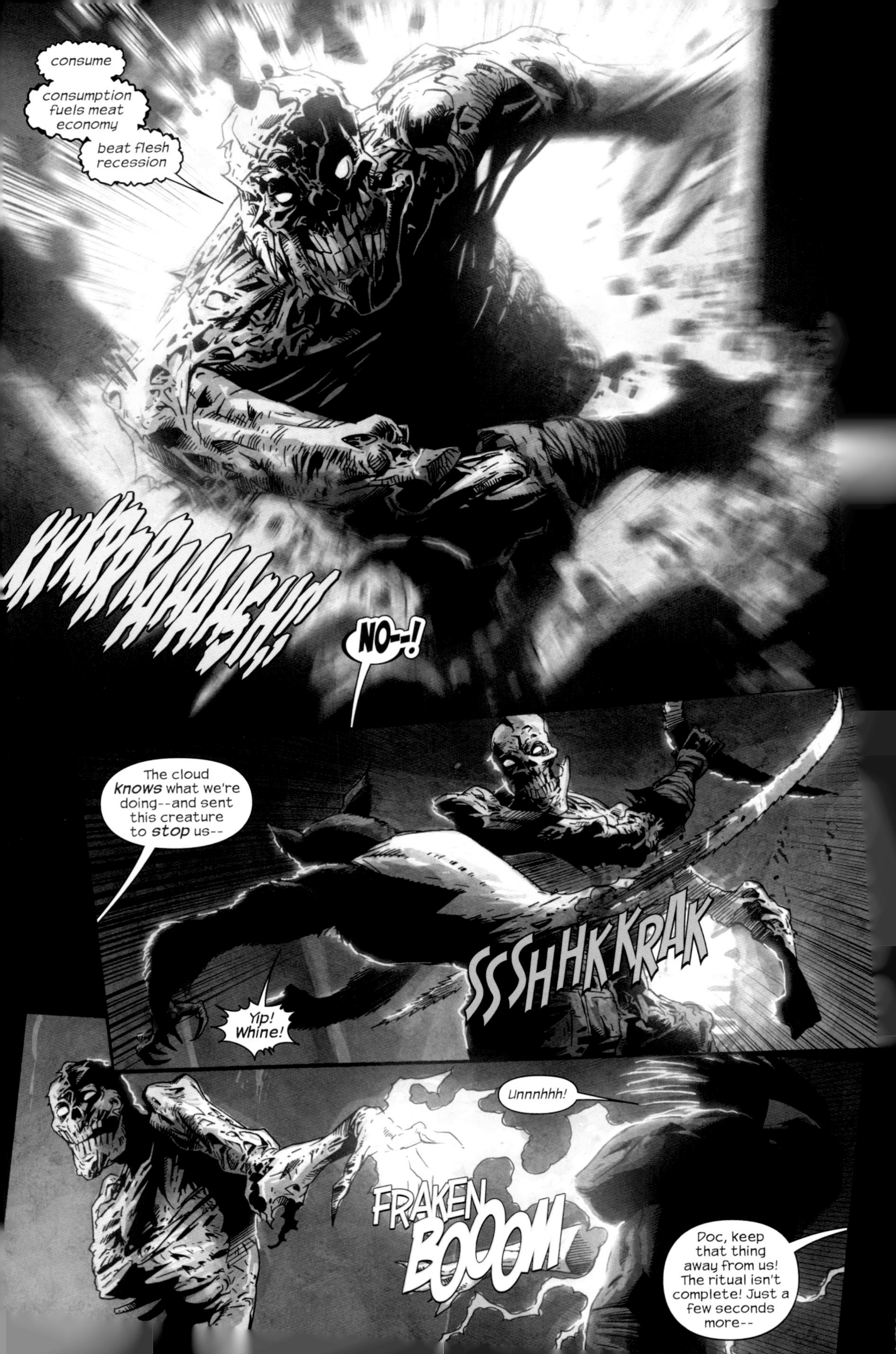
consume
consumption fuels meat economy
beat flesh recession
KKKKRAAAAASH!!
NO--!
The cloud knows what we're doing--and sent this creature to stop us--
SSHHKKRAK
Yip! Whine!
Unnnhhh!
FRAKEN BOOOM
Doc, keep that thing away from us! The ritual isn't complete! Just a few seconds more--

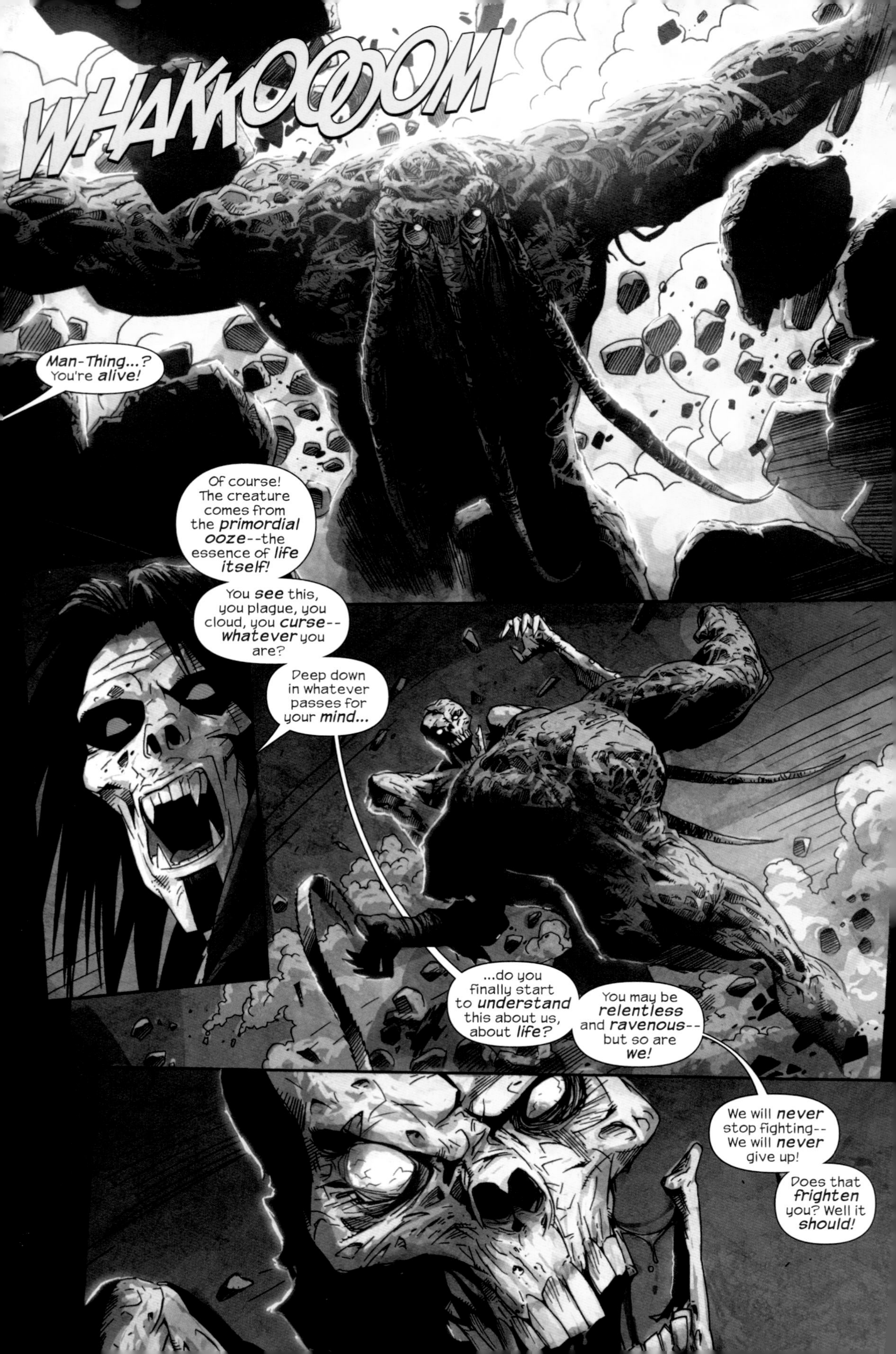
WHAKOOOOM
Man-Thing...? You're alive!
Of course! The creature comes from the primordial ooze--the essence of life itself!
You see this, you plague, you cloud, you curse--whatever you are?
Deep down in whatever passes for your mind...
...do you finally start to understand this about us, about life?
You may be relentless and ravenous--but so are we!
We will never stop fighting--We will never give up!
Does that frighten you? Well it should!

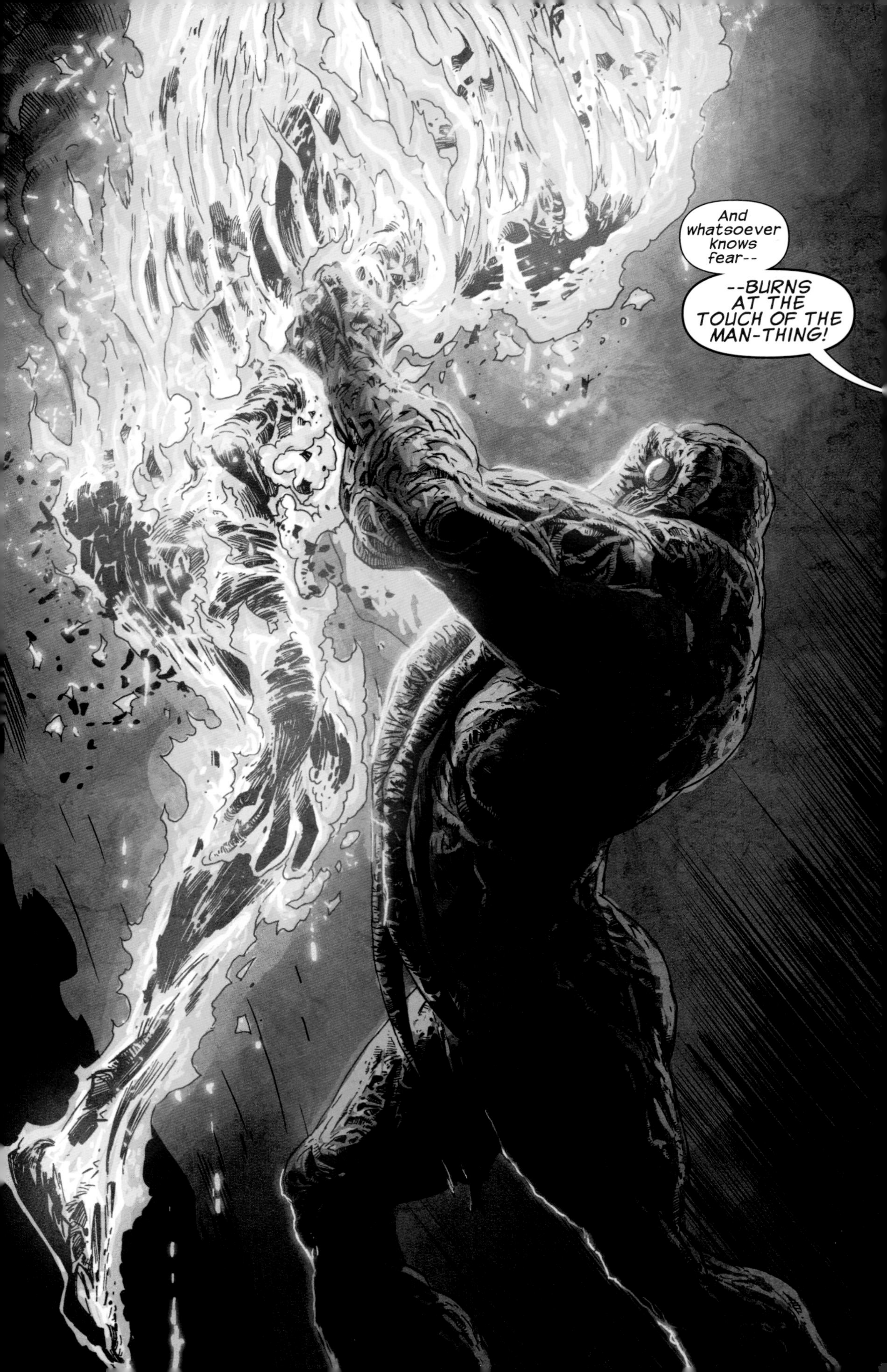
And whatsoever knows fear--
--BURNS AT THE TOUCH OF THE MAN-THING!

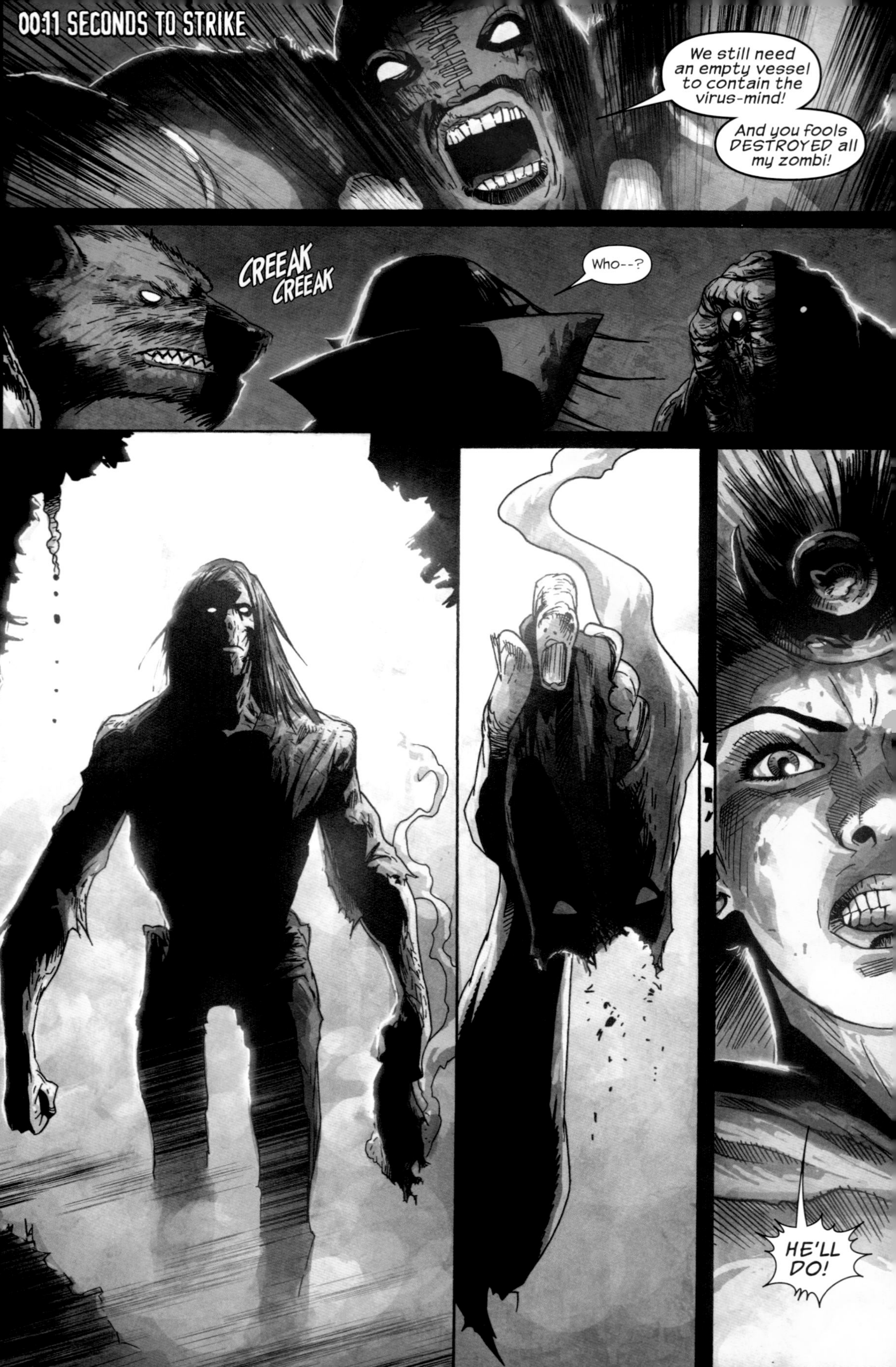
00:11 SECONDS TO STRIKE
We still need an empty vessel to contain the virus-mind!
And you fools DESTROYED all my zombi!
CREEAK CREEAK
Who--?
HE'LL DO!

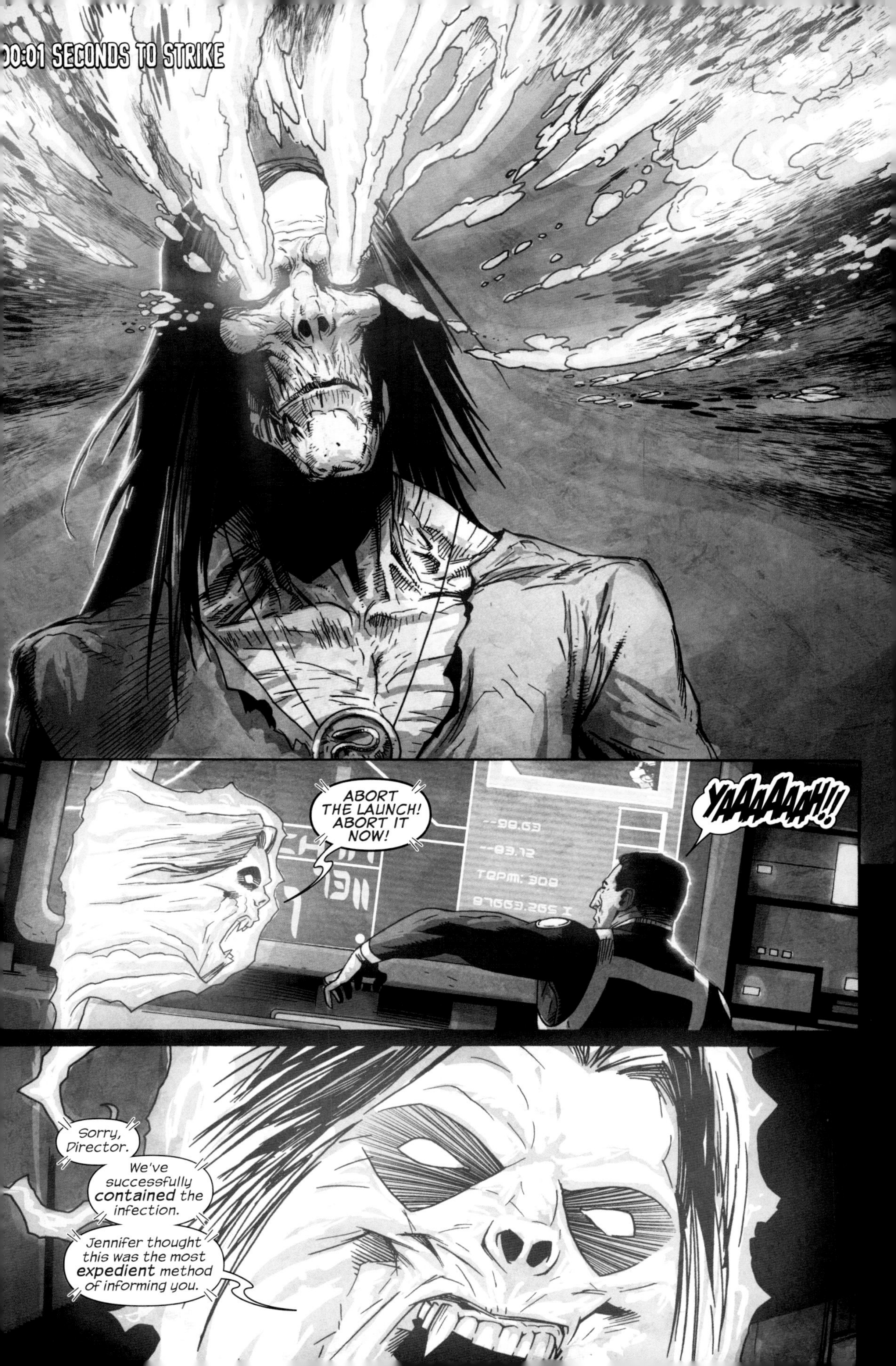
00:01 SECONDS TO STRIKE
ABORT THE LAUNCH! ABORT IT NOW!
YAAAAAAH!!
--98.63
--83.12
TQPM: 308
Sorry, Director.
We've successfully contained the infection.
Jennifer thought this was the most expedient method of informing you.

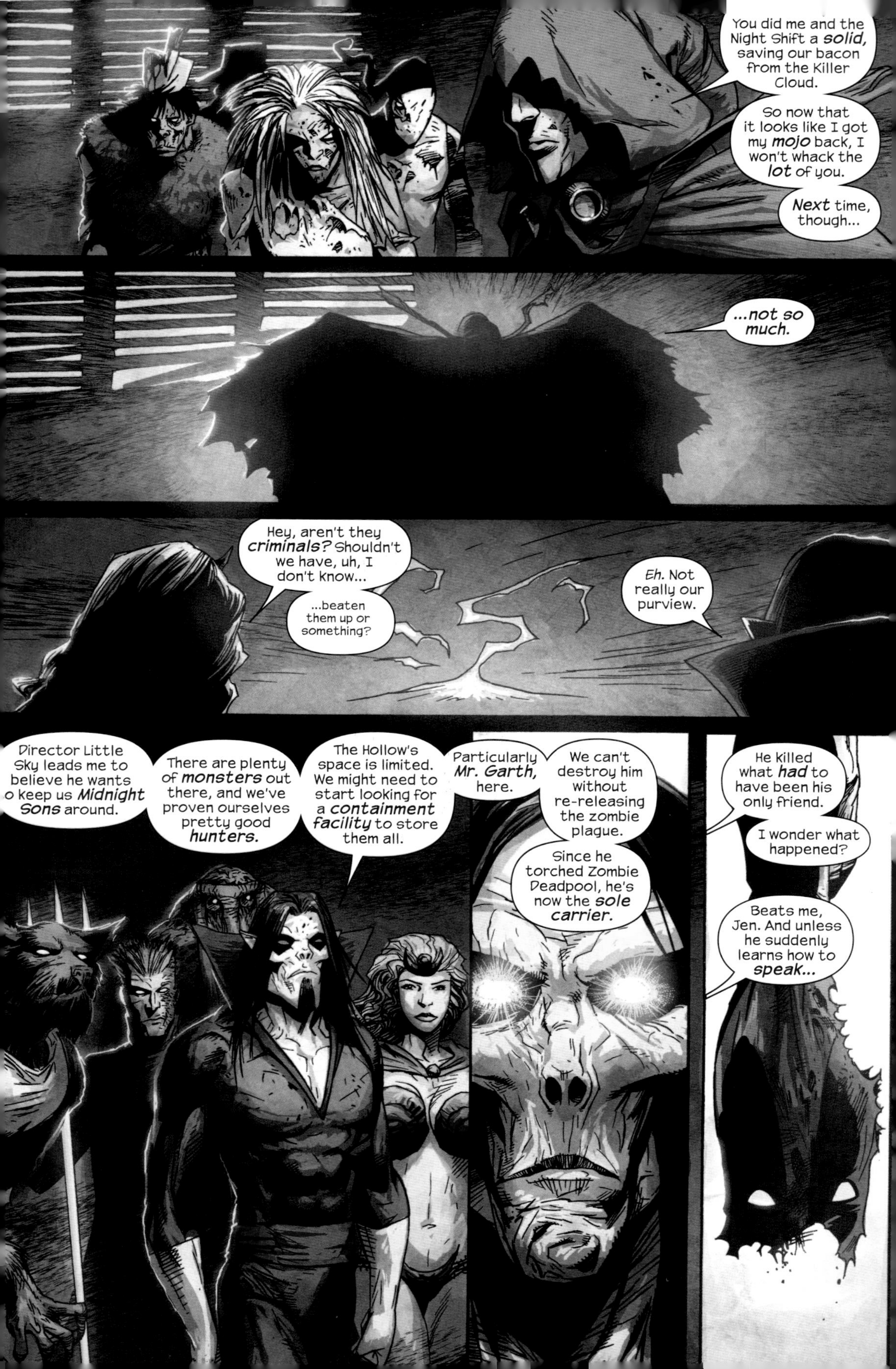
You did me and the Night Shift a solid, saving our bacon from the Killer Cloud.
So now that it looks like I got my mojo back, I won't whack the lot of you.
Next time, though...
...not so much.
Hey, aren't they criminals? Shouldn't we have, uh, I don't know...
...beaten them up or something?
Eh. Not really our purview.
Director Little Sky leads me to believe he wants o keep us Midnight Sons around.
There are plenty of monsters out there, and we've proven ourselves pretty good hunters.
The Hollow's space is limited. We might need to start looking for a containment facility to store them all.
Particularly Mr. Garth, here.
We can't destroy him without re-releasing the zombie plague.
Since he torched Zombie Deadpool, he's now the sole carrier.
He killed what had to have been his only friend.
I wonder what happened?
Beats me, Jen. And unless he suddenly learns how to speak...

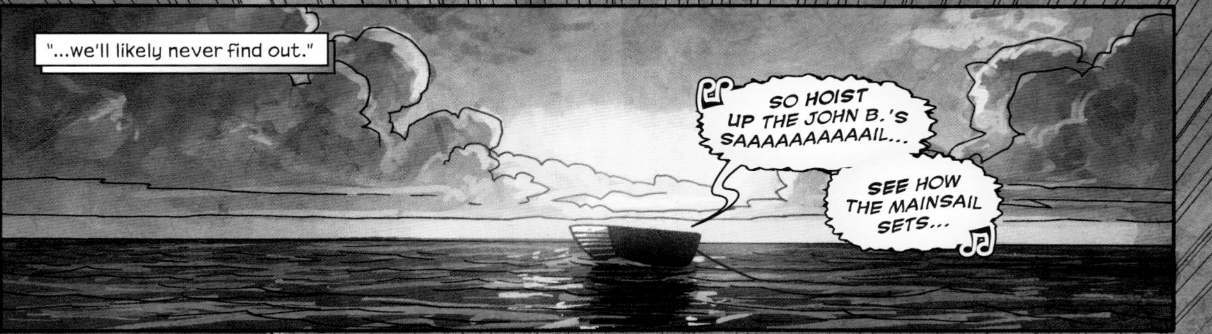
"...we'll likely never find out."
SO HOIST UP THE JOHN B.'S SAAAAAAAAAAIL...
SEE HOW THE MAINSAIL SETS...

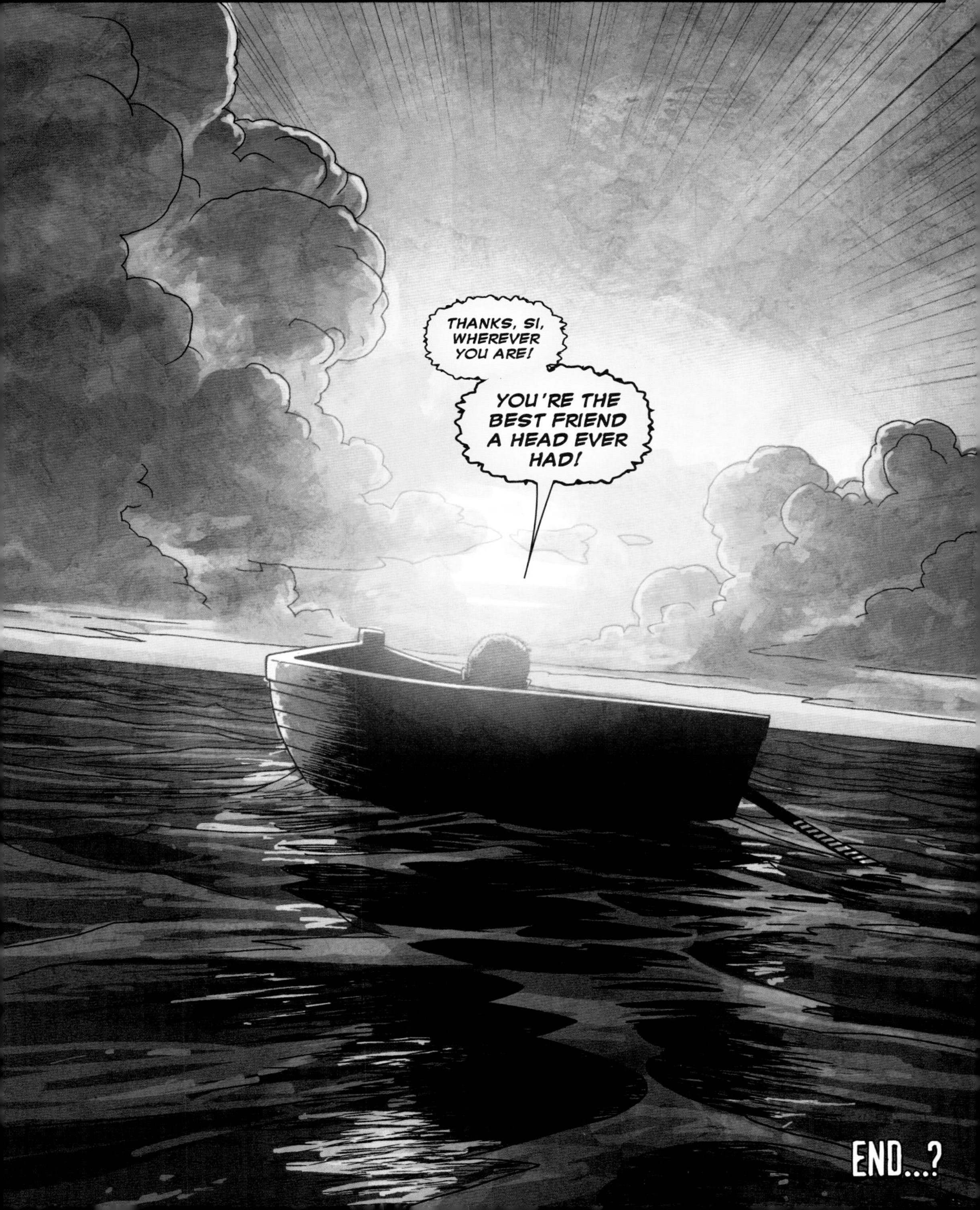
THANKS, SI, WHEREVER YOU ARE!
YOU'RE THE BEST FRIEND A HEAD EVER HAD!
END...?

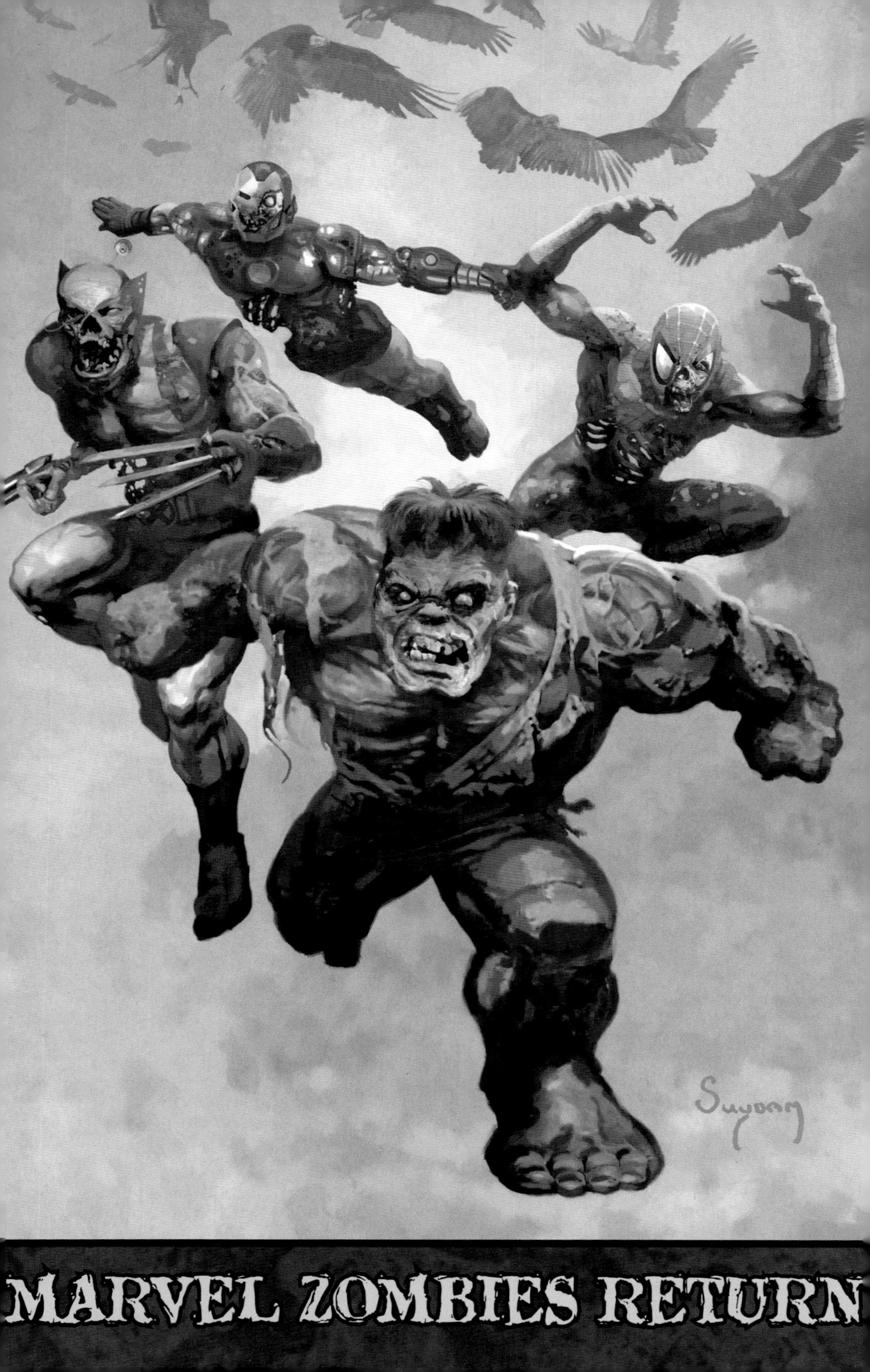
Suydam
MARVEL ZOMBIES RETURN

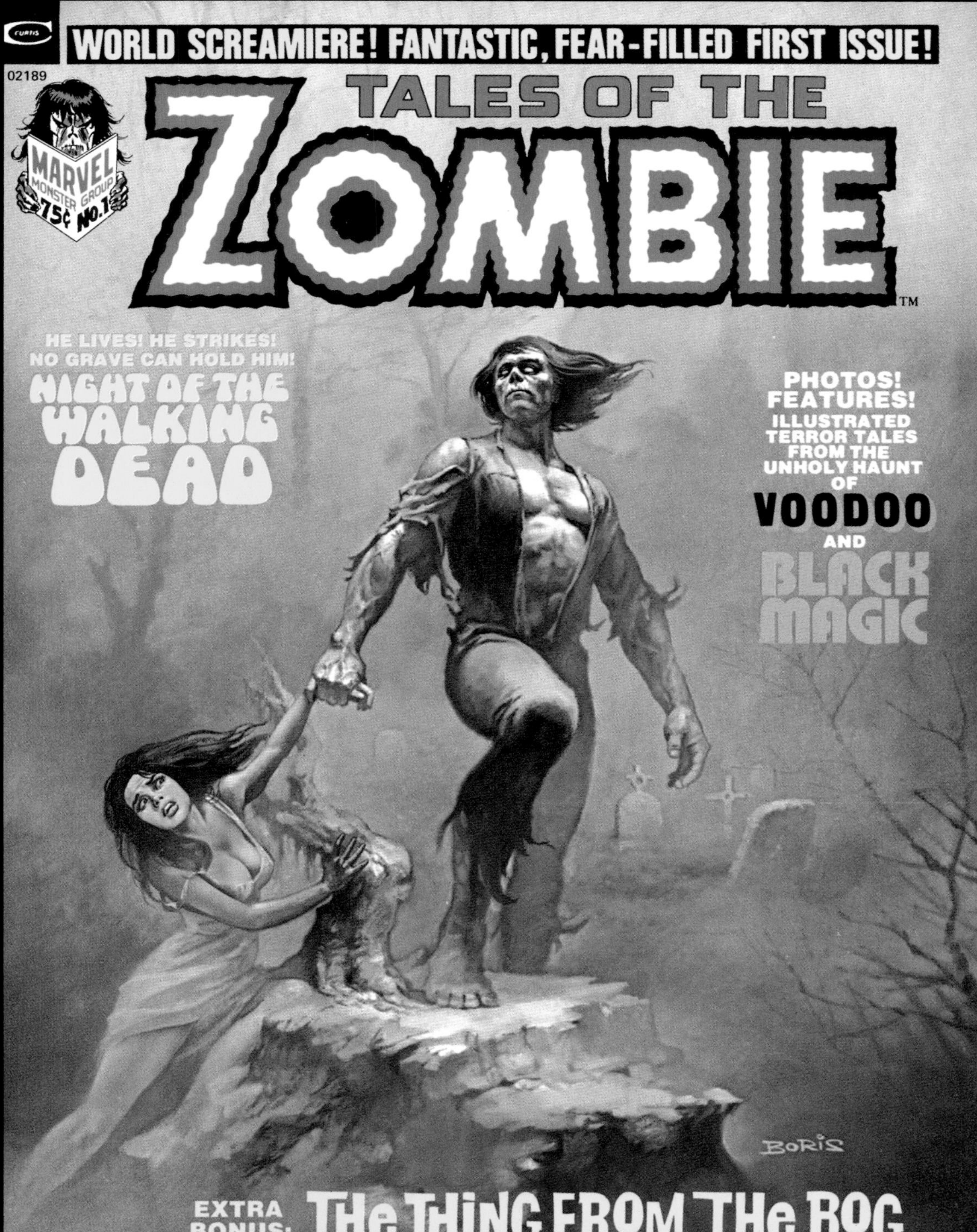
CURTIS
WORLD SCREAMIERE! FANTASTIC, FEAR-FILLED FIRST ISSUE!
02189
MARVEL MONSTER GROUP
75¢ NO.1
TALES OF THE
ZOMBIE™
HE LIVES! HE STRIKES! NO GRAVE CAN HOLD HIM!
NIGHT OF THE WALKING DEAD
PHOTOS! FEATURES! ILLUSTRATED TERROR TALES FROM THE UNHOLY HAUNT OF
VOODOO
AND
BLACK MAGIC
BORIS
EXTRA BONUS: THE THING FROM THE BOG

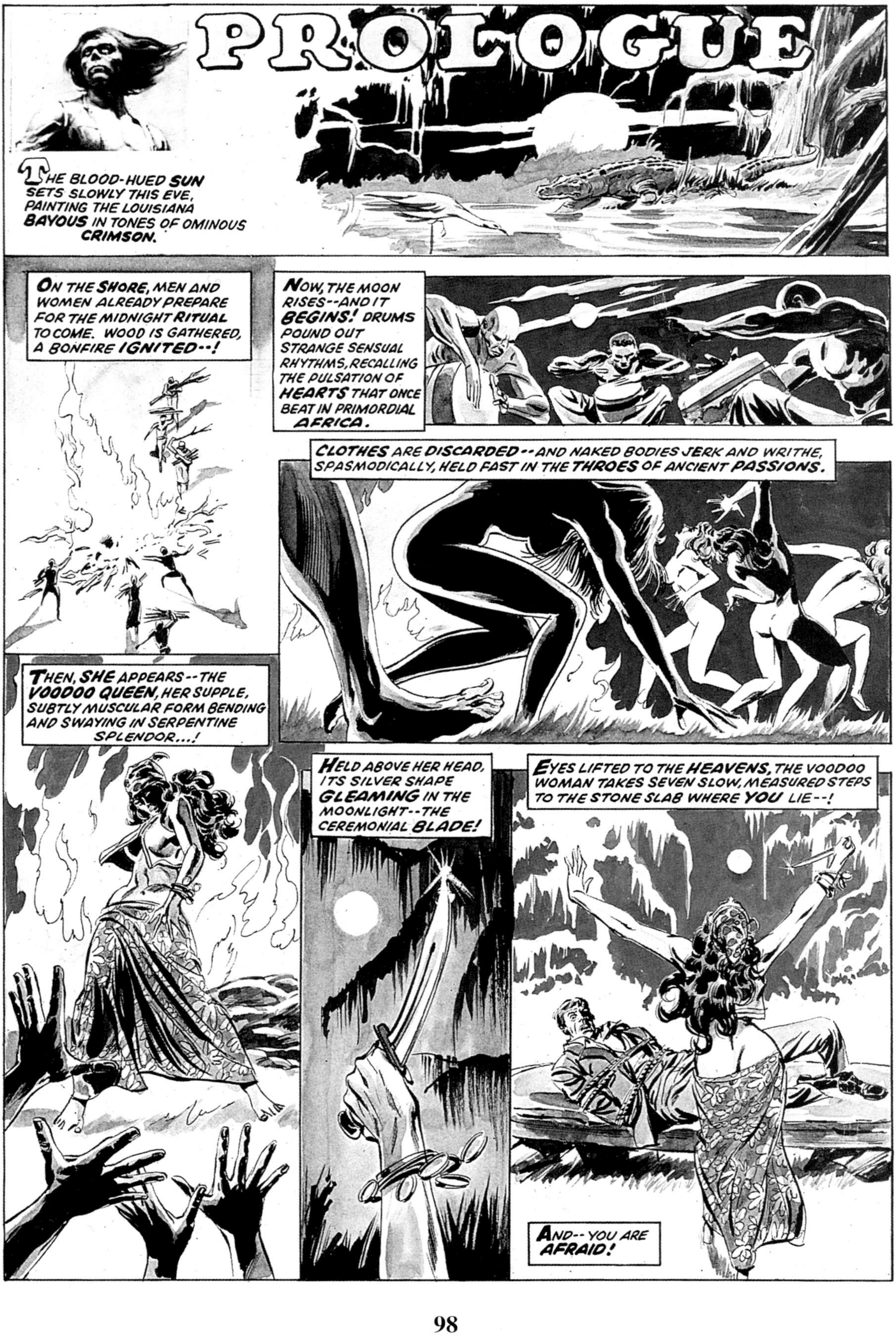
PROLOGUE
THE BLOOD-HUED SUN SETS SLOWLY THIS EVE, PAINTING THE LOUISIANA BAYOUS IN TONES OF OMINOUS CRIMSON.
ON THE SHORE, MEN AND WOMEN ALREADY PREPARE FOR THE MIDNIGHT RITUAL TO COME. WOOD IS GATHERED, A BONFIRE IGNITED--!
NOW, THE MOON RISES--AND IT BEGINS! DRUMS POUND OUT STRANGE SENSUAL RHYTHMS, RECALLING THE PULSATION OF HEARTS THAT ONCE BEAT IN PRIMORDIAL AFRICA.
CLOTHES ARE DISCARDED--AND NAKED BODIES JERK AND WRITHE, SPASMODICALLY, HELD FAST IN THE THROES OF ANCIENT PASSIONS.
THEN, SHE APPEARS--THE VOODOO QUEEN, HER SUPPLE, SUBTLY MUSCULAR FORM BENDING AND SWAYING IN SERPENTINE SPLENDOR...!
HELD ABOVE HER HEAD, ITS SILVER SHAPE GLEAMING IN THE MOONLIGHT--THE CEREMONIAL BLADE!
EYES LIFTED TO THE HEAVENS, THE VOODOO WOMAN TAKES SEVEN SLOW, MEASURED STEPS TO THE STONE SLAB WHERE YOU LIE--!
AND--YOU ARE AFRAID!

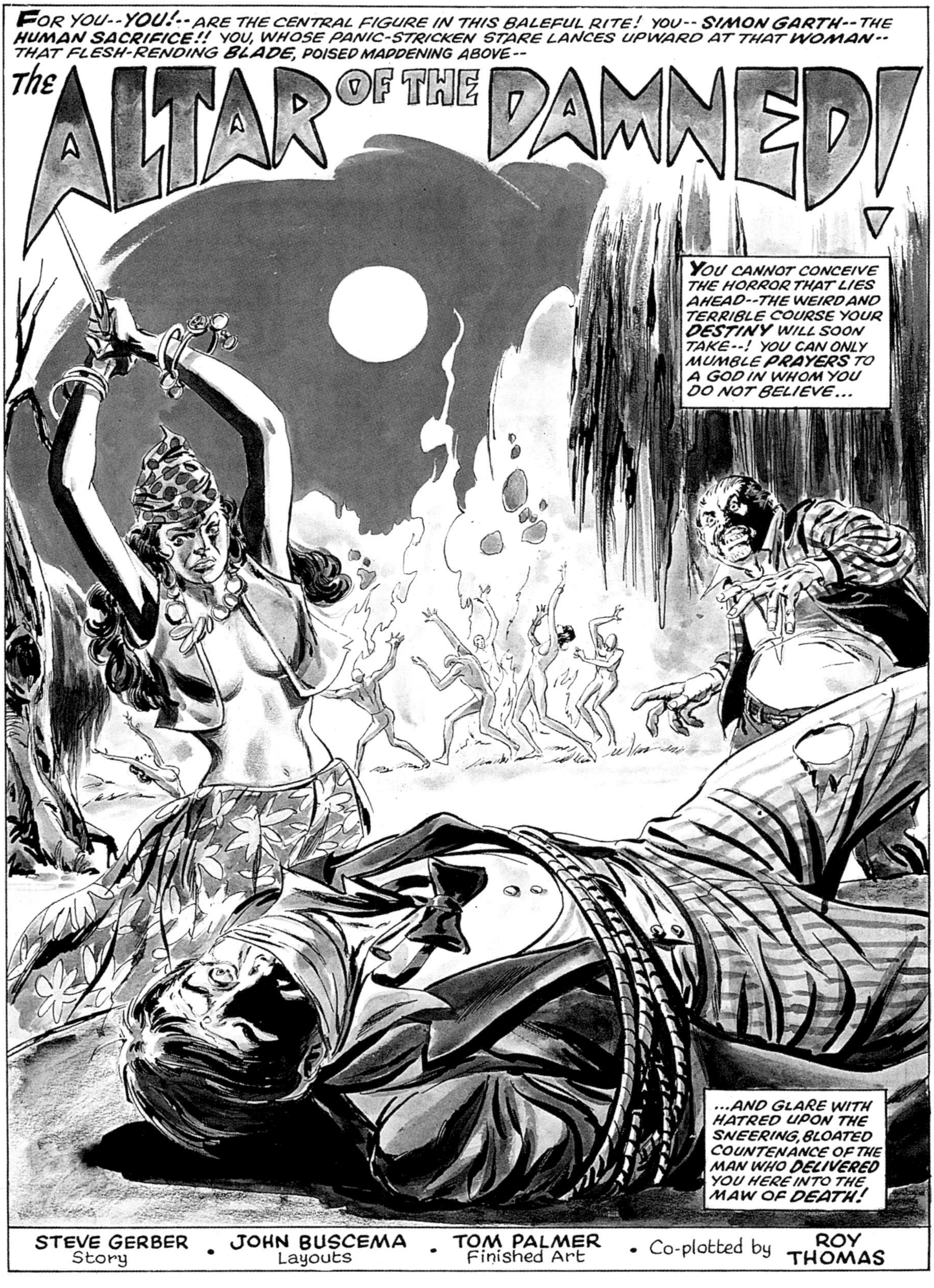
FOR YOU--YOU!--ARE THE CENTRAL FIGURE IN THIS BALEFUL RITE! YOU--SIMON GARTH--THE HUMAN SACRIFICE!! YOU, WHOSE PANIC-STRICKEN STARE LANCES UPWARD AT THAT WOMAN--THAT FLESH-RENDING BLADE, POISED MADDENING ABOVE--
THE ALTAR OF THE DAMNED!
YOU CANNOT CONCEIVE THE HORROR THAT LIES AHEAD--THE WEIRD AND TERRIBLE COURSE YOUR DESTINY WILL SOON TAKE--! YOU CAN ONLY MUMBLE PRAYERS TO A GOD IN WHOM YOU DO NOT BELIEVE...
...AND GLARE WITH HATRED UPON THE SNEERING, BLOATED COUNTENANCE OF THE MAN WHO DELIVERED YOU HERE INTO THE MAW OF DEATH!
STEVE GERBER Story • JOHN BUSCEMA Layouts • TOM PALMER Finished Art • Co-plotted by ROY THOMAS

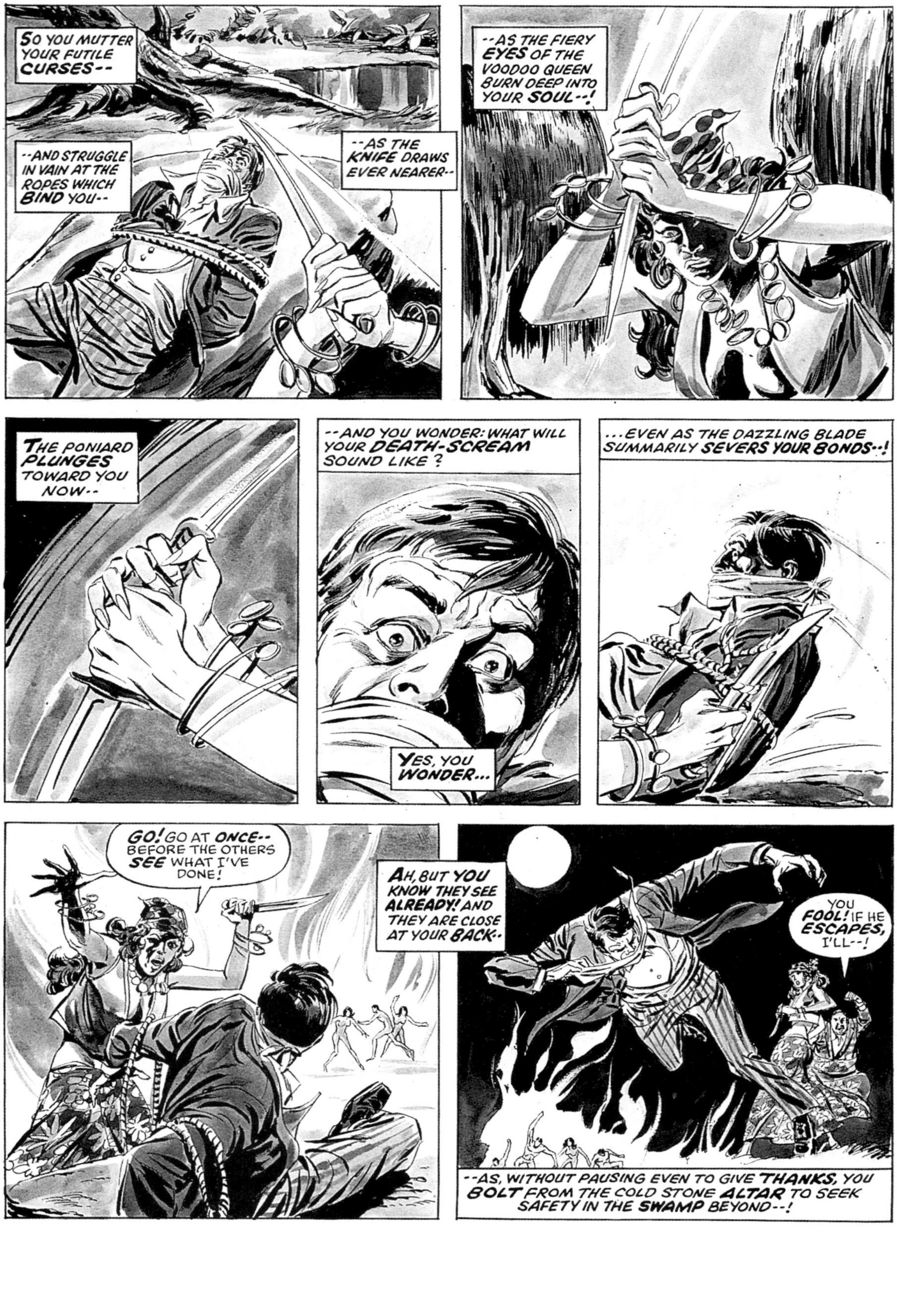
SO YOU MUTTER YOUR FUTILE CURSES--
--AND STRUGGLE IN VAIN AT THE ROPES WHICH BIND YOU--
--AS THE KNIFE DRAWS EVER NEARER--
--AS THE FIERY EYES OF THE VOODOO QUEEN BURN DEEP INTO YOUR SOUL--!
THE PONIARD PLUNGES TOWARD YOU NOW--
--AND YOU WONDER: WHAT WILL YOUR DEATH-SCREAM SOUND LIKE?
YES, YOU WONDER...
...EVEN AS THE DAZZLING BLADE SUMMARILY SEVERS YOUR BONDS--!
GO! GO AT ONCE-- BEFORE THE OTHERS SEE WHAT I'VE DONE!
AH, BUT YOU KNOW THEY SEE ALREADY! AND THEY ARE CLOSE AT YOUR BACK--
YOU FOOL! IF HE ESCAPES, I'LL--!
--AS, WITHOUT PAUSING EVEN TO GIVE THANKS, YOU BOLT FROM THE COLD STONE ALTAR TO SEEK SAFETY IN THE SWAMP BEYOND--!

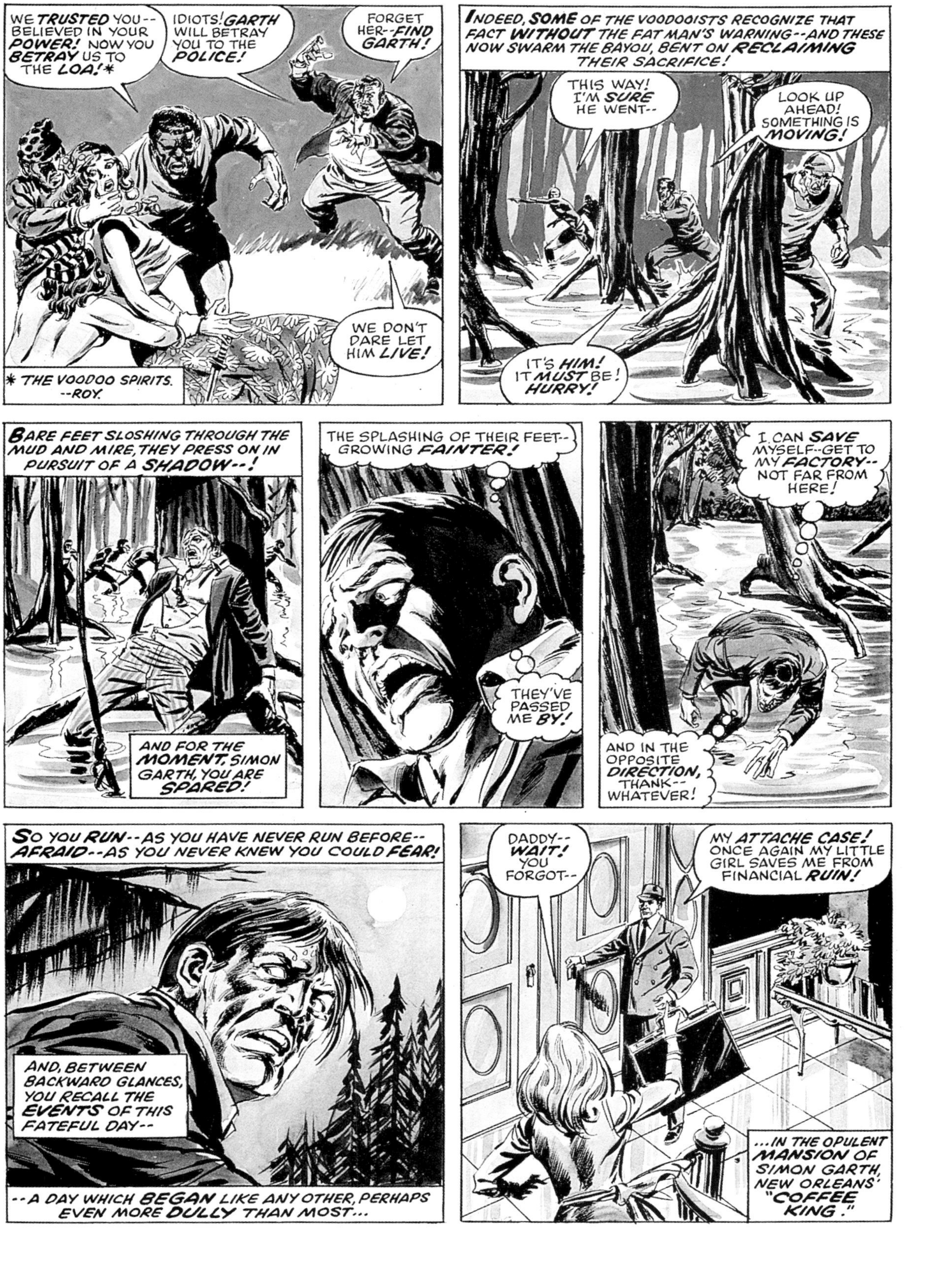

WE TRUSTED YOU--BELIEVED IN YOUR POWER! NOW YOU BETRAY US TO THE LOA!*
IDIOTS! GARTH WILL BETRAY YOU TO THE POLICE!
FORGET HER--FIND GARTH!
WE DON'T DARE LET HIM LIVE!
* THE VOODOO SPIRITS. --ROY.
INDEED, SOME OF THE VOODOOISTS RECOGNIZE THAT FACT WITHOUT THE FAT MAN'S WARNING--AND THESE NOW SWARM THE BAYOU, BENT ON RECLAIMING THEIR SACRIFICE!
THIS WAY! I'M SURE HE WENT--
LOOK UP AHEAD! SOMETHING IS MOVING!
IT'S HIM! IT MUST BE! HURRY!
BARE FEET SLOSHING THROUGH THE MUD AND MIRE, THEY PRESS ON IN PURSUIT OF A SHADOW--!
AND FOR THE MOMENT, SIMON GARTH, YOU ARE SPARED!
THE SPLASHING OF THEIR FEET--GROWING FAINTER!
THEY'VE PASSED ME BY!
I CAN SAVE MYSELF--GET TO MY FACTORY--NOT FAR FROM HERE!
AND IN THE OPPOSITE DIRECTION, THANK--WHATEVER!
SO YOU RUN--AS YOU HAVE NEVER RUN BEFORE--AFRAID--AS YOU NEVER KNEW YOU COULD FEAR!
AND, BETWEEN BACKWARD GLANCES, YOU RECALL THE EVENTS OF THIS FATEFUL DAY--
--A DAY WHICH BEGAN LIKE ANY OTHER, PERHAPS EVEN MORE DULLY THAN MOST...
DADDY--WAIT! YOU FORGOT--
MY ATTACHE CASE! ONCE AGAIN MY LITTLE GIRL SAVES ME FROM FINANCIAL RUIN!
...IN THE OPULENT MANSION OF SIMON GARTH, NEW ORLEANS' "COFFEE KING."

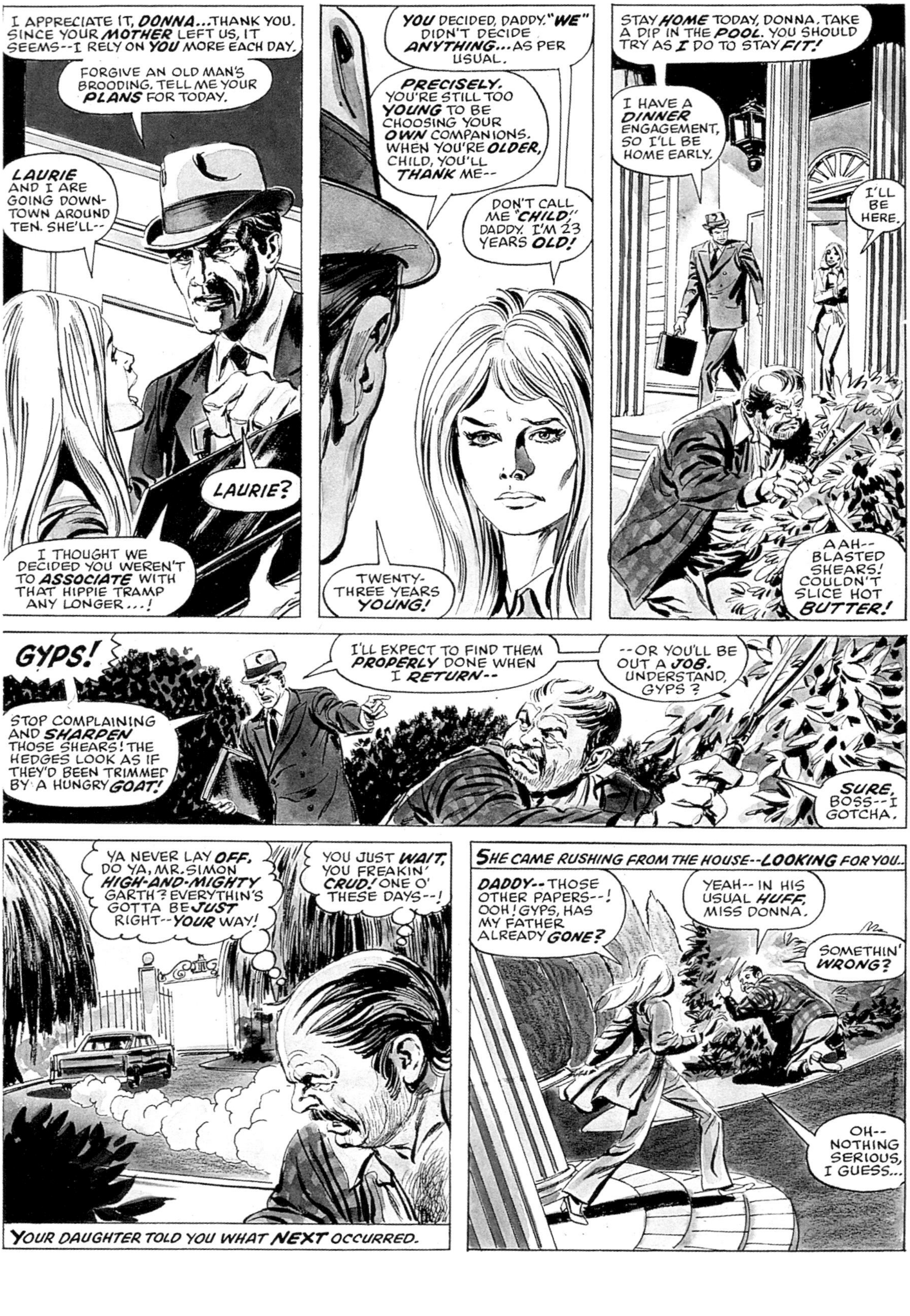

I APPRECIATE IT, DONNA... THANK YOU. SINCE YOUR MOTHER LEFT US, IT SEEMS--I RELY ON YOU MORE EACH DAY.
FORGIVE AN OLD MAN'S BROODING. TELL ME YOUR PLANS FOR TODAY.
LAURIE AND I ARE GOING DOWN-TOWN AROUND TEN. SHE'LL--
LAURIE?
I THOUGHT WE DECIDED YOU WEREN'T TO ASSOCIATE WITH THAT HIPPIE TRAMP ANY LONGER...!
YOU DECIDED, DADDY. "WE" DIDN'T DECIDE ANYTHING... AS PER USUAL.
PRECISELY. YOU'RE STILL TOO YOUNG TO BE CHOOSING YOUR OWN COMPANIONS. WHEN YOU'RE OLDER, CHILD, YOU'LL THANK ME--
DON'T CALL ME "CHILD," DADDY. I'M 23 YEARS OLD!
TWENTY-THREE YEARS YOUNG!
STAY HOME TODAY, DONNA. TAKE A DIP IN THE POOL. YOU SHOULD TRY AS I DO TO STAY FIT!
I HAVE A DINNER ENGAGEMENT, SO I'LL BE HOME EARLY.
I'LL BE HERE.
AAH-- BLASTED SHEARS! COULDN'T SLICE HOT BUTTER!
GYPS!
STOP COMPLAINING AND SHARPEN THOSE SHEARS! THE HEDGES LOOK AS IF THEY'D BEEN TRIMMED BY A HUNGRY GOAT!
I'LL EXPECT TO FIND THEM PROPERLY DONE WHEN I RETURN--
--OR YOU'LL BE OUT A JOB. UNDERSTAND, GYPS?
SURE, BOSS--I GOTCHA.
YA NEVER LAY OFF, DO YA, MR. SIMON HIGH-AND-MIGHTY GARTH? EVERYTHIN'S GOTTA BE JUST RIGHT--YOUR WAY!
YOU JUST WAIT, YOU FREAKIN' CRUD! ONE O' THESE DAYS--!
YOUR DAUGHTER TOLD YOU WHAT NEXT OCCURRED.
SHE CAME RUSHING FROM THE HOUSE--LOOKING FOR YOU...
DADDY--THOSE OTHER PAPERS--! OOH! GYPS, HAS MY FATHER ALREADY GONE?
YEAH--IN HIS USUAL HUFF, MISS DONNA.
SOMETHIN' WRONG?
OH-- NOTHING SERIOUS, I GUESS...

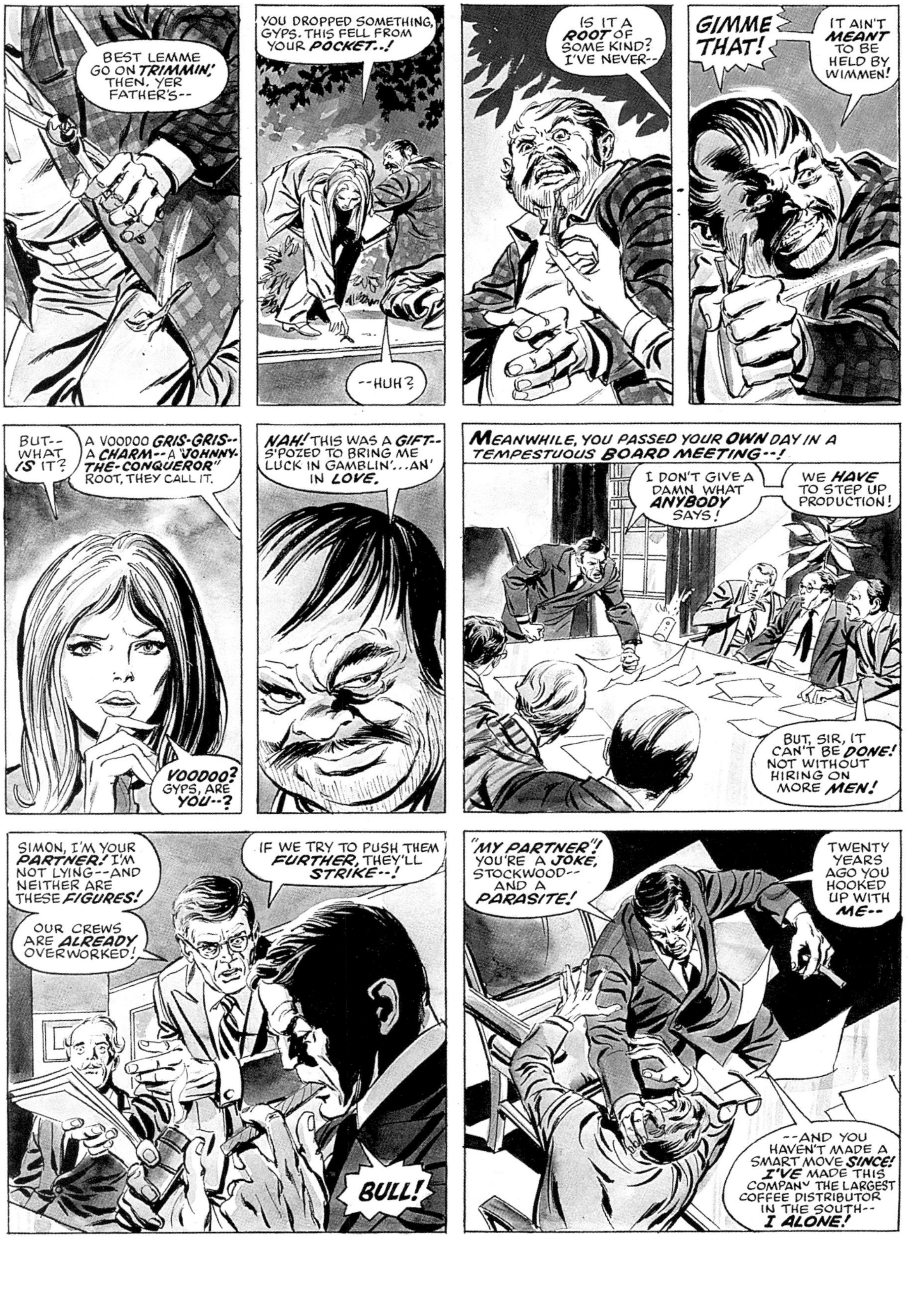
BEST LEMME GO ON TRIMMIN,' THEN. YER FATHER'S--
YOU DROPPED SOMETHING, GYPS. THIS FELL FROM YOUR POCKET..!
--HUH?
IS IT A ROOT OF SOME KIND? I'VE NEVER--
GIMME THAT!
IT AIN'T MEANT TO BE HELD BY WIMMEN!
BUT--WHAT IS IT?
A VOODOO GRIS-GRIS--A CHARM--A 'JOHNNY-THE-CONQUEROR" ROOT, THEY CALL IT.
VOODOO? GYPS, ARE YOU--?
NAH! THIS WAS A GIFT--S'POZED TO BRING ME LUCK IN GAMBLIN'...AN' IN LOVE.
MEANWHILE, YOU PASSED YOUR OWN DAY IN A TEMPESTUOUS BOARD MEETING--!
I DON'T GIVE A DAMN WHAT ANYBODY SAYS!
WE HAVE TO STEP UP PRODUCTION!
BUT, SIR, IT CAN'T BE DONE! NOT WITHOUT HIRING ON MORE MEN!
SIMON, I'M YOUR PARTNER! I'M NOT LYING--AND NEITHER ARE THESE FIGURES!
OUR CREWS ARE ALREADY OVERWORKED!
IF WE TRY TO PUSH THEM FURTHER, THEY'LL STRIKE--!
BULL!
"MY PARTNER"! YOU'RE A JOKE, STOCKWOOD--AND A PARASITE!
TWENTY YEARS AGO YOU HOOKED UP WITH ME--
--AND YOU HAVEN'T MADE A SMART MOVE SINCE! I'VE MADE THIS COMPANY THE LARGEST COFFEE DISTRIBUTOR IN THE SOUTH--I ALONE!

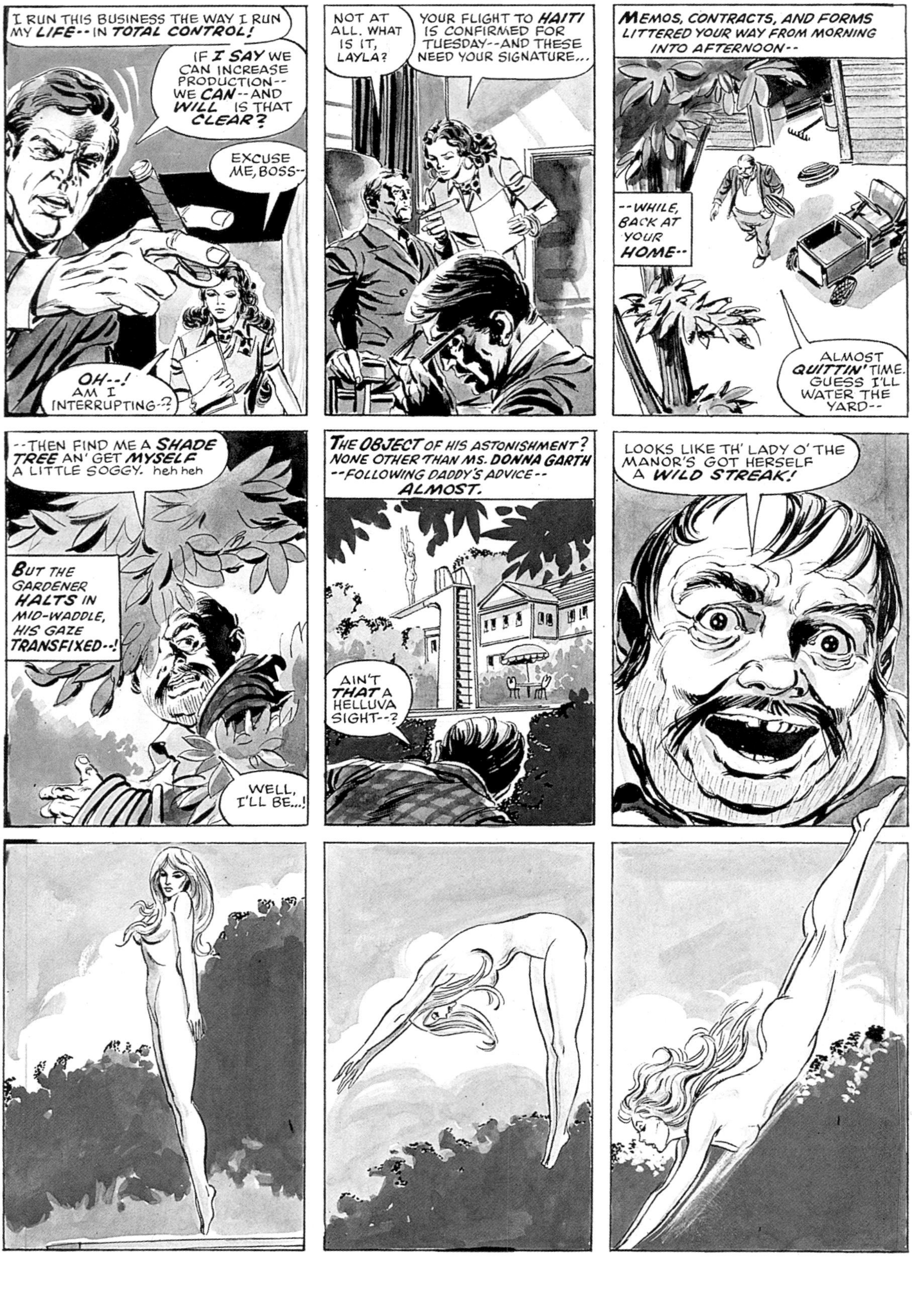
I RUN THIS BUSINESS THE WAY I RUN MY LIFE--IN TOTAL CONTROL!
IF I SAY WE CAN INCREASE PRODUCTION--WE CAN--AND WILL IS THAT CLEAR?
EXCUSE ME, BOSS--
OH--! AM I INTERRUPTING--?
NOT AT ALL. WHAT IS IT, LAYLA?
YOUR FLIGHT TO HAITI IS CONFIRMED FOR TUESDAY--AND THESE NEED YOUR SIGNATURE...
MEMOS, CONTRACTS, AND FORMS LITTERED YOUR WAY FROM MORNING INTO AFTERNOON--
--WHILE, BACK AT YOUR HOME--
ALMOST QUITTIN' TIME. GUESS I'LL WATER THE YARD--
--THEN FIND ME A SHADE TREE AN' GET MYSELF A LITTLE SOGGY. heh heh
BUT THE GARDENER HALTS IN MID-WADDLE, HIS GAZE TRANSFIXED--!
WELL, I'LL BE...!
THE OBJECT OF HIS ASTONISHMENT? NONE OTHER THAN MS. DONNA GARTH --FOLLOWING DADDY'S ADVICE-- ALMOST.
AIN'T THAT A HELLUVA SIGHT--?
LOOKS LIKE TH' LADY O' THE MANOR'S GOT HERSELF A WILD STREAK!

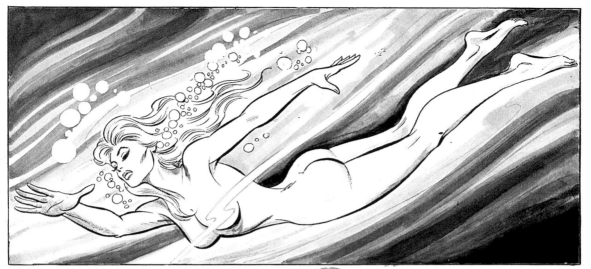

HI THERE, MISS DONNA--THAT'S SOME *STROKE* YOU GOT!

HOPE YA DIDN'T *MIND MY WATCHIN'!*

OOH--! GYPS-- YOU *SAW...?*

SURE...AN' DON'T TELL ME I WEREN'T *S'POZED* TO! OL' GYPS *KNOWS,* HONEY-- HE KNOWS *PLENTY!*

AN' HE'S JUST *ACHIN'* TA--

ACHING TO *WHAT,* GYPS? TELL *ME,* TOO!

HUH--?

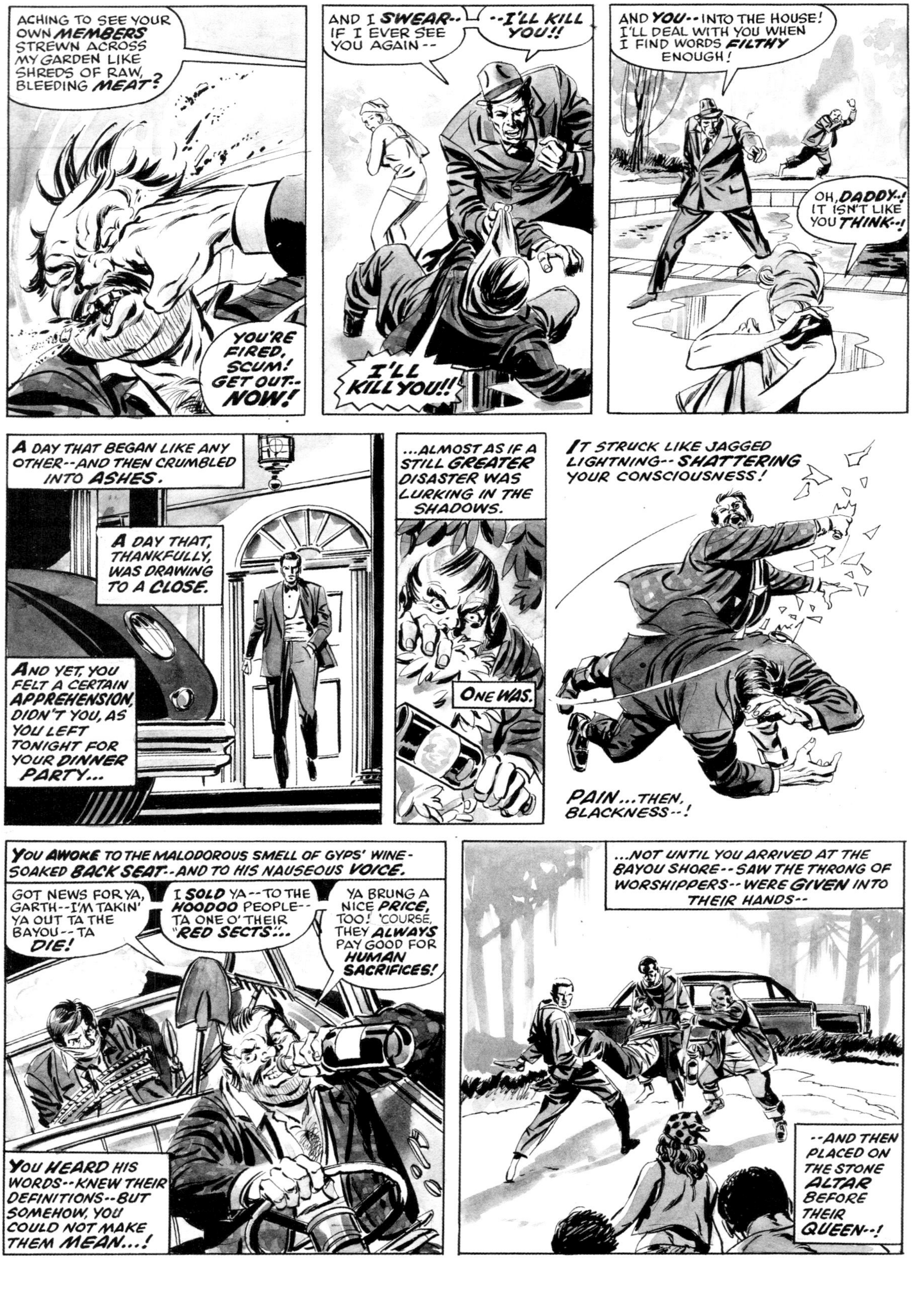

ACHING TO SEE YOUR OWN MEMBERS STREWN ACROSS MY GARDEN LIKE SHREDS OF RAW, BLEEDING MEAT?
YOU'RE FIRED, SCUM! GET OUT-- NOW!
AND I SWEAR-- IF I EVER SEE YOU AGAIN --
--I'LL KILL YOU!!
I'LL KILL YOU!!
AND YOU-- INTO THE HOUSE! I'LL DEAL WITH YOU WHEN I FIND WORDS FILTHY ENOUGH!
OH, DADDY--! IT ISN'T LIKE YOU THINK--!
A DAY THAT BEGAN LIKE ANY OTHER--AND THEN CRUMBLED INTO ASHES.
A DAY THAT, THANKFULLY, WAS DRAWING TO A CLOSE.
AND YET, YOU FELT A CERTAIN APPREHENSION, DIDN'T YOU, AS YOU LEFT TONIGHT FOR YOUR DINNER PARTY...
...ALMOST AS IF A STILL GREATER DISASTER WAS LURKING IN THE SHADOWS.
ONE WAS.
IT STRUCK LIKE JAGGED LIGHTNING-- SHATTERING YOUR CONSCIOUSNESS!
PAIN...THEN, BLACKNESS--!
YOU AWOKE TO THE MALODOROUS SMELL OF GYPS' WINE-SOAKED BACK SEAT--AND TO HIS NAUSEOUS VOICE.
GOT NEWS FOR YA, GARTH--I'M TAKIN' YA OUT TA THE BAYOU--TA DIE!
I SOLD YA--TO THE HOODOO PEOPLE--TA ONE O' THEIR "RED SECTS"...
YA BRUNG A NICE PRICE, TOO! 'COURSE, THEY ALWAYS PAY GOOD FOR HUMAN SACRIFICES!
YOU HEARD HIS WORDS--KNEW THEIR DEFINITIONS--BUT SOMEHOW, YOU COULD NOT MAKE THEM MEAN...!
...NOT UNTIL YOU ARRIVED AT THE BAYOU SHORE--SAW THE THRONG OF WORSHIPPERS--WERE GIVEN INTO THEIR HANDS--
--AND THEN PLACED ON THE STONE ALTAR BEFORE THEIR QUEEN--!

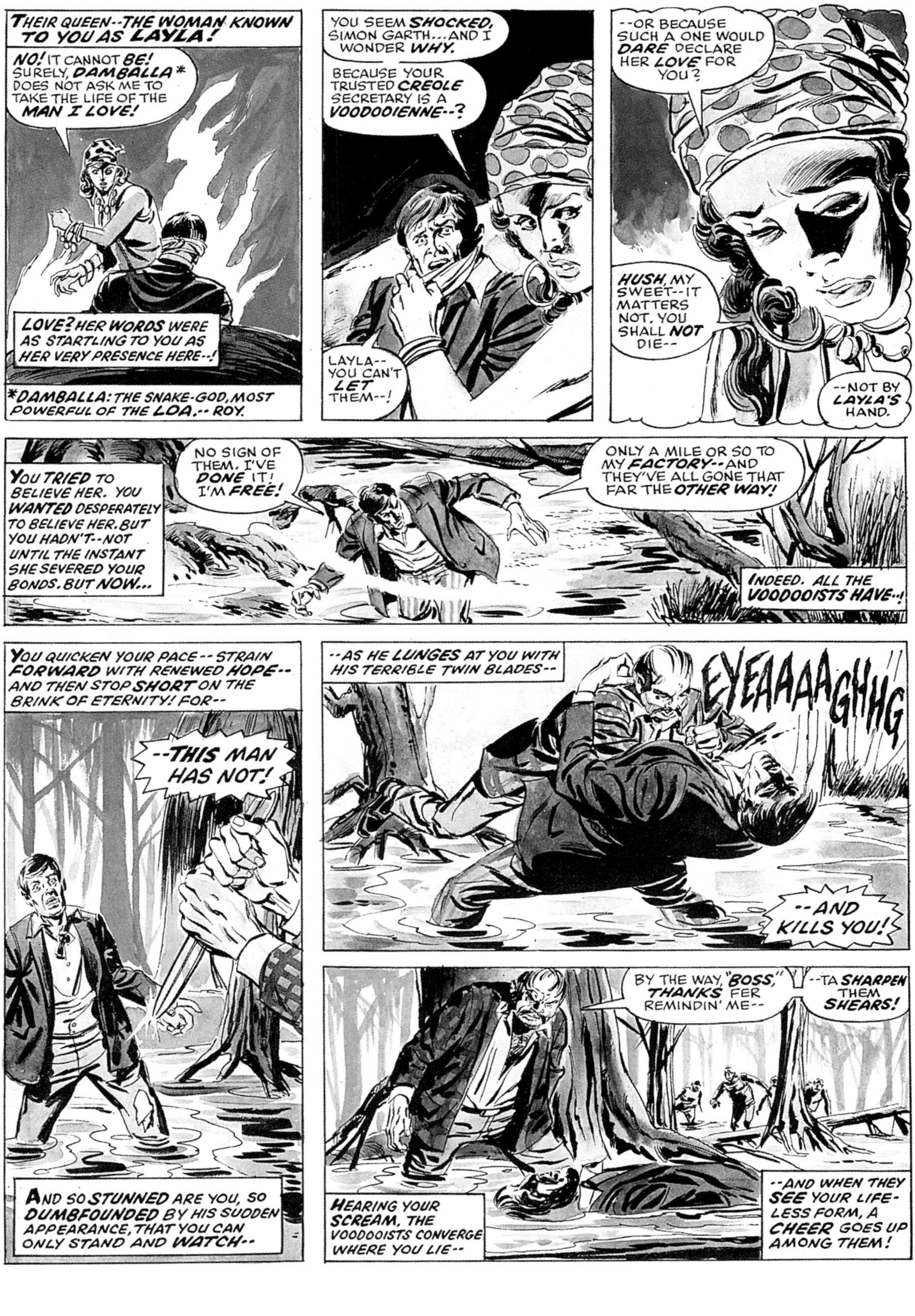

THEIR QUEEN--THE WOMAN KNOWN TO YOU AS LAYLA!
NO! IT CANNOT BE! SURELY, DAMBALLA* DOES NOT ASK ME TO TAKE THE LIFE OF THE MAN I LOVE!
LOVE? HER WORDS WERE AS STARTLING TO YOU AS HER VERY PRESENCE HERE--!
*DAMBALLA: THE SNAKE-GOD, MOST POWERFUL OF THE LOA.--ROY.
YOU SEEM SHOCKED, SIMON GARTH... AND I WONDER WHY.
BECAUSE YOUR TRUSTED CREOLE SECRETARY IS A VOODOOIENNE--?
LAYLA--YOU CAN'T LET THEM--!
--OR BECAUSE SUCH A ONE WOULD DARE DECLARE HER LOVE FOR YOU?
HUSH, MY SWEET--IT MATTERS NOT. YOU SHALL NOT DIE--
--NOT BY LAYLA'S HAND.
YOU TRIED TO BELIEVE HER. YOU WANTED DESPERATELY TO BELIEVE HER. BUT YOU HADN'T--NOT UNTIL THE INSTANT SHE SEVERED YOUR BONDS. BUT NOW...
NO SIGN OF THEM. I'VE DONE IT! I'M FREE!
ONLY A MILE OR SO TO MY FACTORY--AND THEY'VE ALL GONE THAT FAR THE OTHER WAY!
INDEED. ALL THE VOODOOISTS HAVE--!
YOU QUICKEN YOUR PACE--STRAIN FORWARD WITH RENEWED HOPE--AND THEN STOP SHORT ON THE BRINK OF ETERNITY! FOR--
--THIS MAN HAS NOT!
AND SO STUNNED ARE YOU, SO DUMBFOUNDED BY HIS SUDDEN APPEARANCE, THAT YOU CAN ONLY STAND AND WATCH--
--AS HE LUNGES AT YOU WITH HIS TERRIBLE TWIN BLADES--
EYEAAAAGHHG
--AND KILLS YOU!
BY THE WAY, "BOSS," THANKS FER REMINDIN' ME--
--TA SHARPEN THEM SHEARS!
HEARING YOUR SCREAM, THE VOODOOISTS CONVERGE WHERE YOU LIE--
--AND WHEN THEY SEE YOUR LIFELESS FORM, A CHEER GOES UP AMONG THEM!

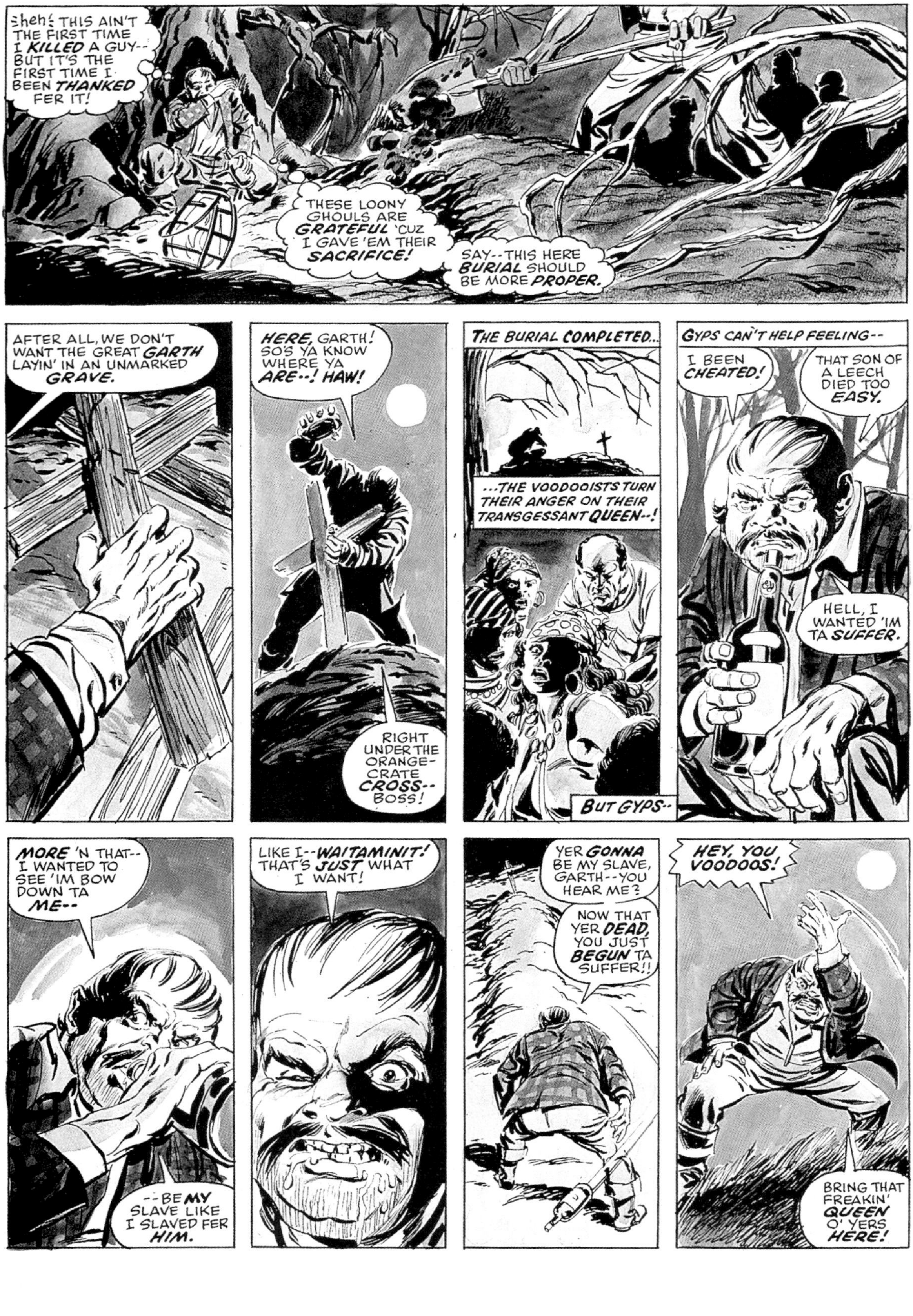

heh! THIS AIN'T THE FIRST TIME I KILLED A GUY-- BUT IT'S THE FIRST TIME I BEEN THANKED FER IT!
THESE LOONY GHOULS ARE GRATEFUL 'CUZ I GAVE 'EM THEIR SACRIFICE!
SAY--THIS HERE BURIAL SHOULD BE MORE PROPER.
AFTER ALL, WE DON'T WANT THE GREAT GARTH LAYIN' IN AN UNMARKED GRAVE.
HERE, GARTH! SO'S YA KNOW WHERE YA ARE--! HAW!
RIGHT UNDER THE ORANGE-CRATE CROSS-- BOSS!
THE BURIAL COMPLETED...
...THE VOODOOISTS TURN THEIR ANGER ON THEIR TRANSGESSANT QUEEN--!
BUT GYPS--
GYPS CAN'T HELP FEELING--
I BEEN CHEATED!
THAT SON OF A LEECH DIED TOO EASY.
HELL, I WANTED 'IM TA SUFFER.
MORE 'N THAT-- I WANTED TO SEE 'IM BOW DOWN TA ME--
--BE MY SLAVE LIKE I SLAVED FER HIM.
LIKE I--WAITAMINIT! THAT'S JUST WHAT I WANT!
YER GONNA BE MY SLAVE, GARTH--YOU HEAR ME?
NOW THAT YER DEAD, YOU JUST BEGUN TA SUFFER!!
HEY, YOU VOODOOS!
BRING THAT FREAKIN' QUEEN O' YERS HERE!

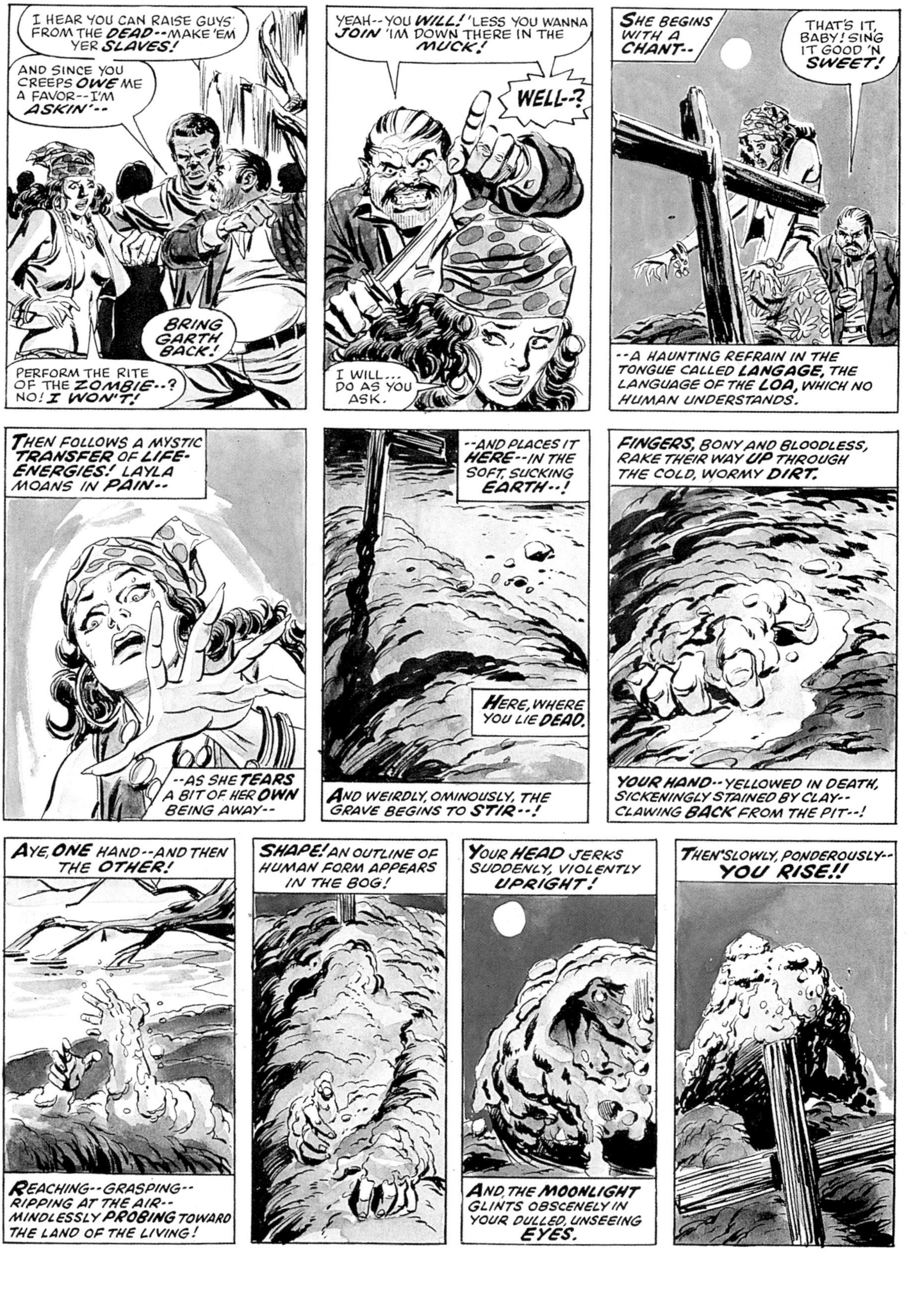

I HEAR YOU CAN RAISE GUYS FROM THE DEAD--MAKE 'EM YER SLAVES!
AND SINCE YOU CREEPS OWE ME A FAVOR--I'M ASKIN'--
BRING GARTH BACK!
PERFORM THE RITE OF THE ZOMBIE--? NO! I WON'T!
YEAH--YOU WILL! 'LESS YOU WANNA JOIN 'IM DOWN THERE IN THE MUCK!
WELL--?
I WILL... DO AS YOU ASK.
SHE BEGINS WITH A CHANT--
THAT'S IT, BABY! SING IT GOOD 'N SWEET!
--A HAUNTING REFRAIN IN THE TONGUE CALLED LANGAGE, THE LANGUAGE OF THE LOA, WHICH NO HUMAN UNDERSTANDS.
THEN FOLLOWS A MYSTIC TRANSFER OF LIFE-ENERGIES! LAYLA MOANS IN PAIN--
--AS SHE TEARS A BIT OF HER OWN BEING AWAY--
--AND PLACES IT HERE--IN THE SOFT, SUCKING EARTH--!
HERE, WHERE YOU LIE DEAD.
AND WEIRDLY, OMINOUSLY, THE GRAVE BEGINS TO STIR--!
FINGERS, BONY AND BLOODLESS, RAKE THEIR WAY UP THROUGH THE COLD, WORMY DIRT.
YOUR HAND--YELLOWED IN DEATH, SICKENINGLY STAINED BY CLAY--CLAWING BACK FROM THE PIT--!
AYE, ONE HAND--AND THEN THE OTHER!
REACHING--GRASPING--RIPPING AT THE AIR--MINDLESSLY PROBING TOWARD THE LAND OF THE LIVING!
SHAPE! AN OUTLINE OF HUMAN FORM APPEARS IN THE BOG!
YOUR HEAD JERKS SUDDENLY, VIOLENTLY UPRIGHT!
AND THE MOONLIGHT GLINTS OBSCENELY IN YOUR DULLED, UNSEEING EYES.
THEN SLOWLY, PONDEROUSLY--YOU RISE!!

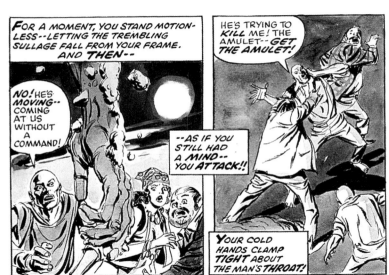

FOR A MOMENT, YOU STAND MOTIONLESS--LETTING THE TREMBLING SULLAGE FALL FROM YOUR FRAME. AND **THEN**--

NO! HE'S MOVING--COMING AT US WITHOUT A COMMAND!

HE'S TRYING TO **KILL** ME! THE AMULET--**GET THE AMULET!**

--AS IF YOU STILL HAD A **MIND**--YOU **ATTACK!!**

YOUR COLD HANDS CLAMP **TIGHT** ABOUT THE MAN'S **THROAT!**

YOU CANNOT **FEEL**--BUT YOU **KNOW** HE MUST DIE! AND SO YOU PRESS STILL **HARDER!**

THEN, ABRUPTLY--YOU **STOP**--AS A STRANGE **TALISMAN** IS TOSSED OVER YOUR HEAD, AROUND YOUR NECK.

THE AMULET--IT HAS **POWER** TO **CONTROL** HIM!

I DON'T **GET** IT--! WHAT MADE 'IM **QUIT?**

WHILE HE WEARS IT, HE IS YOURS TO **COMMAND.**

PROVIDING, OF COURSE, THAT **YOU** CARRY THIS **MATCHING** TALISMAN!

LEMME **HAVE** THAT!

INTA THE SWAMP, GARTH! NOW! AN' DON'T COME OUT TILL I CALL YA!

HEY! IT WORKS!!

I'VE DONE IT! SIMON GARTH IS MY **SLAVE!**

NO. NOT QUITE.

FOR YOU ARE NO **LONGER** SIMON GARTH--ONLY HIS SOULLESS **SHELL.**

HIS... REMAINS.

AND SO YOU WILL WAIT. AND WHEN CALLED, YOU WILL **ANSWER.** IN TRUTH, YOU HAVE NO **CHOICE.**

DEAD MEN... NEVER DO.

Finis...?

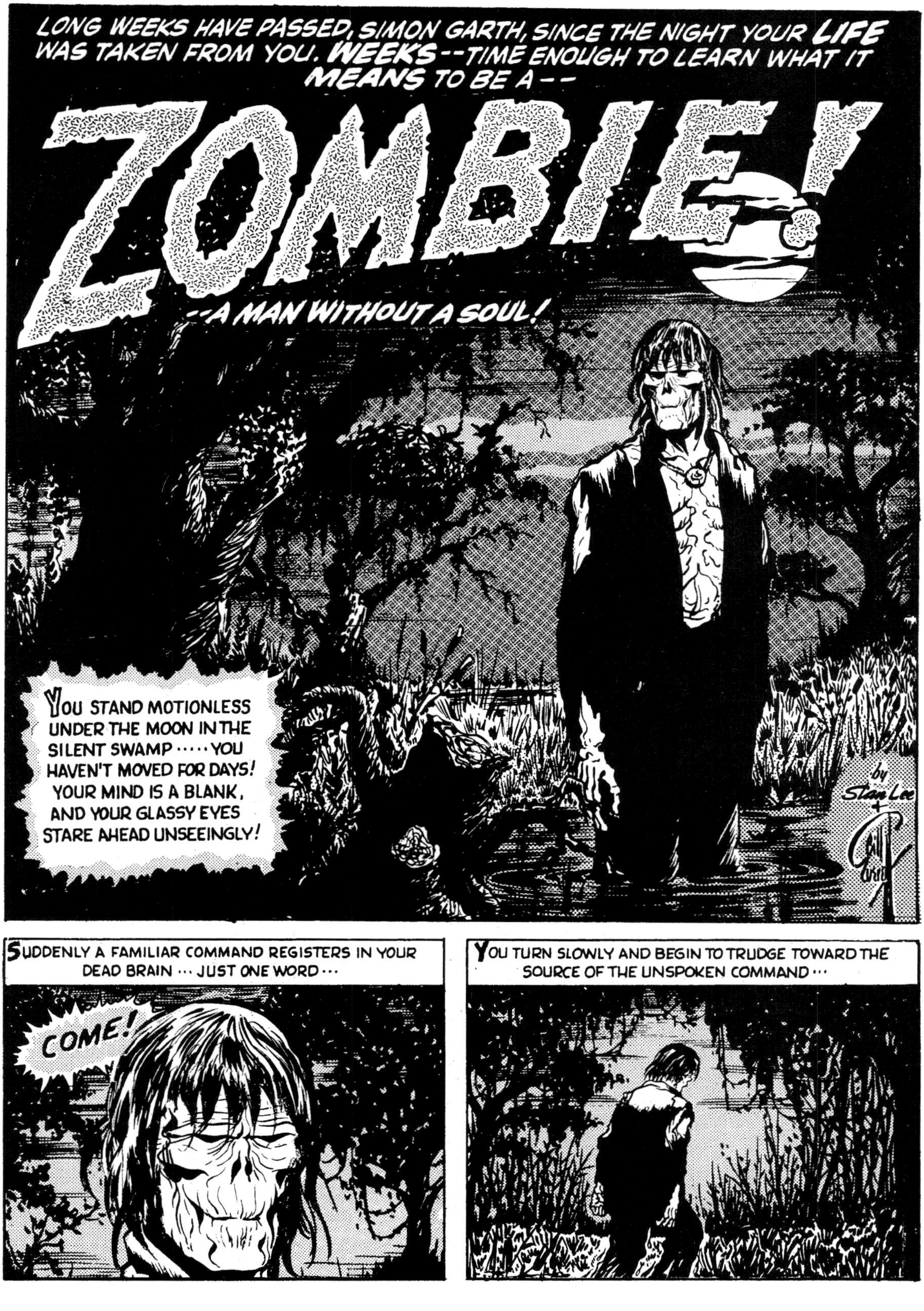
LONG WEEKS HAVE PASSED, SIMON GARTH, SINCE THE NIGHT YOUR LIFE WAS TAKEN FROM YOU. WEEKS--TIME ENOUGH TO LEARN WHAT IT MEANS TO BE A--
ZOMBIE!
--A MAN WITHOUT A SOUL!
YOU STAND MOTIONLESS UNDER THE MOON IN THE SILENT SWAMP.....YOU HAVEN'T MOVED FOR DAYS! YOUR MIND IS A BLANK, AND YOUR GLASSY EYES STARE AHEAD UNSEEINGLY!
by Stan Lee +
SUDDENLY A FAMILIAR COMMAND REGISTERS IN YOUR DEAD BRAIN... JUST ONE WORD...
COME!
YOU TURN SLOWLY AND BEGIN TO TRUDGE TOWARD THE SOURCE OF THE UNSPOKEN COMMAND...

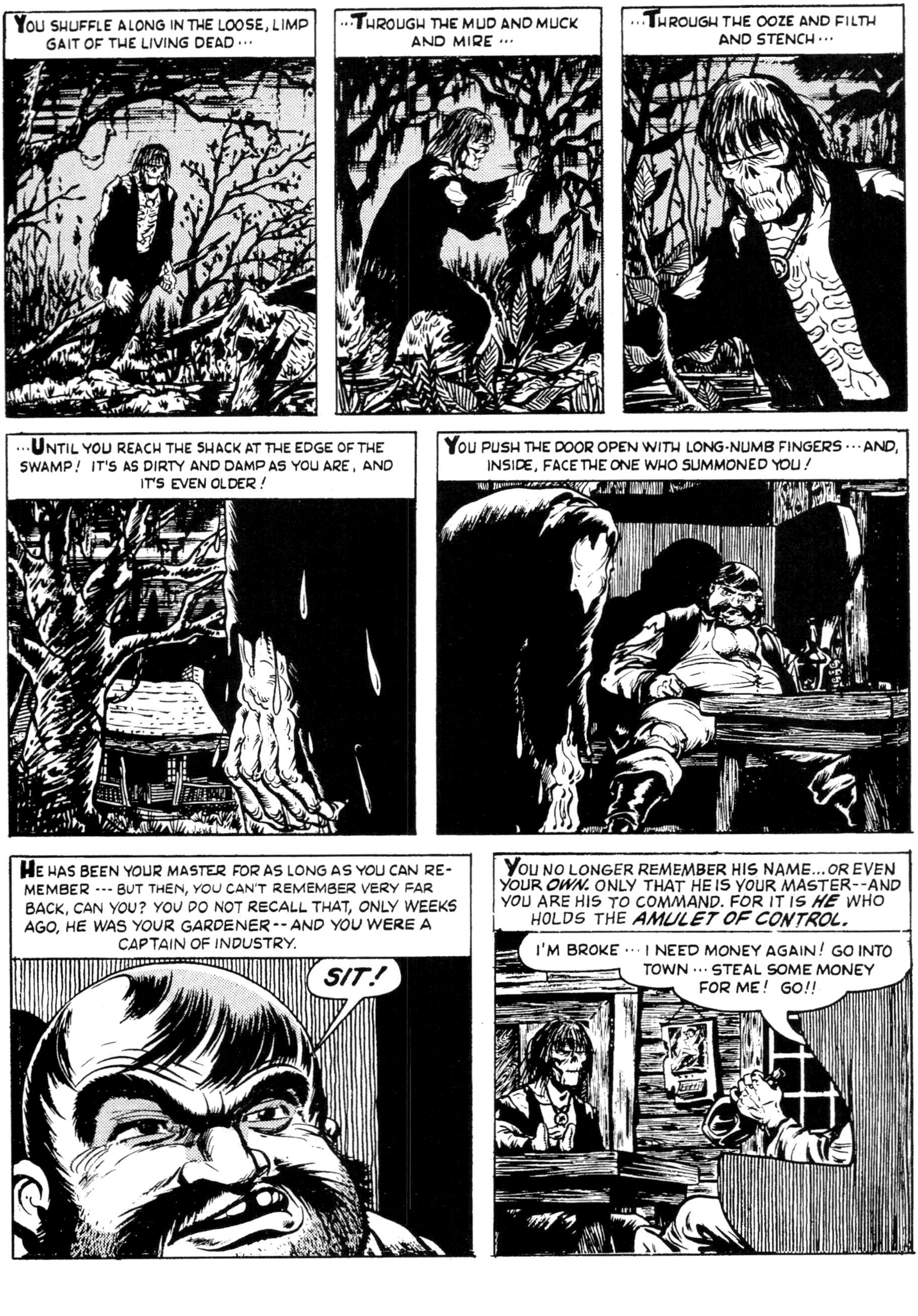
YOU SHUFFLE ALONG IN THE LOOSE, LIMP GAIT OF THE LIVING DEAD ···
···THROUGH THE MUD AND MUCK AND MIRE ···
···THROUGH THE OOZE AND FILTH AND STENCH ···
···UNTIL YOU REACH THE SHACK AT THE EDGE OF THE SWAMP! IT'S AS DIRTY AND DAMP AS YOU ARE, AND IT'S EVEN OLDER!
YOU PUSH THE DOOR OPEN WITH LONG-NUMB FINGERS ··· AND, INSIDE, FACE THE ONE WHO SUMMONED YOU!
HE HAS BEEN YOUR MASTER FOR AS LONG AS YOU CAN REMEMBER --- BUT THEN, YOU CAN'T REMEMBER VERY FAR BACK, CAN YOU? YOU DO NOT RECALL THAT, ONLY WEEKS AGO, HE WAS YOUR GARDENER -- AND YOU WERE A CAPTAIN OF INDUSTRY.
SIT!
YOU NO LONGER REMEMBER HIS NAME...OR EVEN YOUR OWN. ONLY THAT HE IS YOUR MASTER--AND YOU ARE HIS TO COMMAND. FOR IT IS HE WHO HOLDS THE AMULET OF CONTROL.
I'M BROKE ··· I NEED MONEY AGAIN! GO INTO TOWN ··· STEAL SOME MONEY FOR ME! GO!!

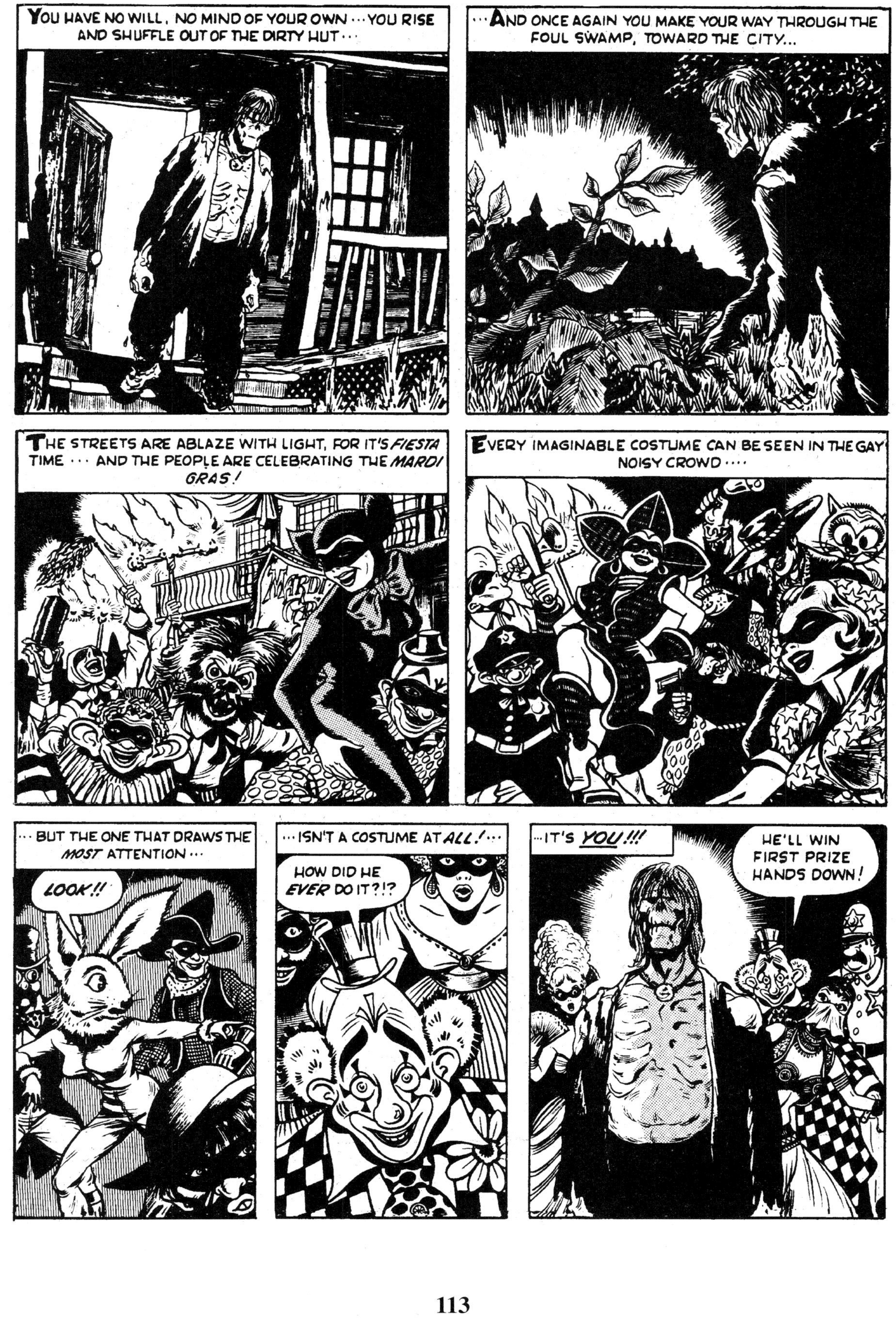
YOU HAVE NO WILL, NO MIND OF YOUR OWN ··· YOU RISE AND SHUFFLE OUT OF THE DIRTY HUT ···
··· AND ONCE AGAIN YOU MAKE YOUR WAY THROUGH THE FOUL SWAMP, TOWARD THE CITY...
THE STREETS ARE ABLAZE WITH LIGHT, FOR IT'S *FIESTA* TIME ··· AND THE PEOPLE ARE CELEBRATING THE *MARDI GRAS!*
EVERY IMAGINABLE COSTUME CAN BE SEEN IN THE GAY NOISY CROWD ····
··· BUT THE ONE THAT DRAWS THE *MOST* ATTENTION ···
LOOK!!
··· ISN'T A COSTUME AT *ALL!* ···
HOW DID HE *EVER* DO IT?!?
··· IT'S *YOU!!!*
HE'LL WIN FIRST PRIZE HANDS DOWN!

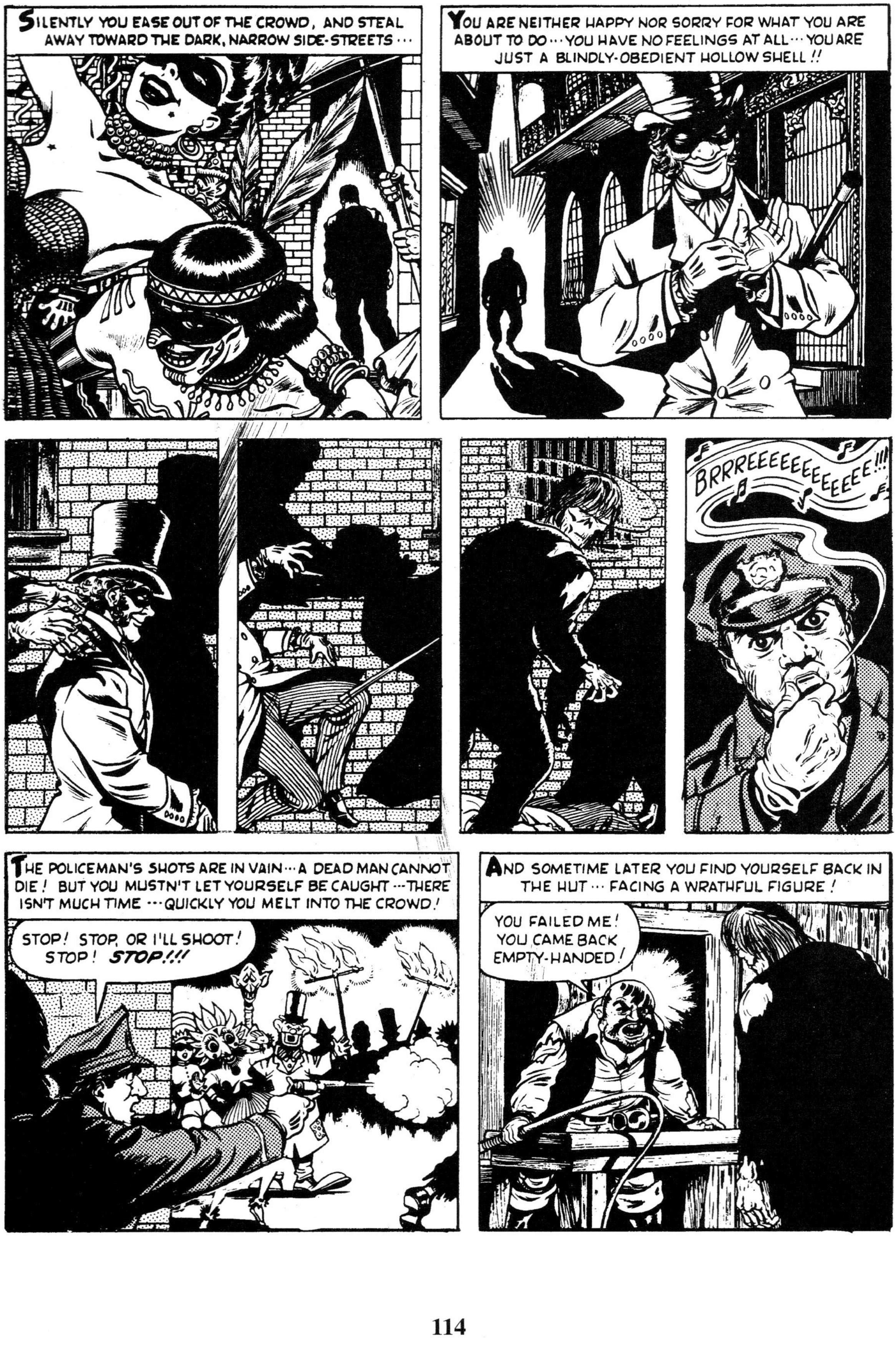
SILENTLY YOU EASE OUT OF THE CROWD, AND STEAL AWAY TOWARD THE DARK, NARROW SIDE-STREETS ···
YOU ARE NEITHER HAPPY NOR SORRY FOR WHAT YOU ARE ABOUT TO DO ··· YOU HAVE NO FEELINGS AT ALL ··· YOU ARE JUST A BLINDLY-OBEDIENT HOLLOW SHELL!!
BRRREEEEEEEEEEEEEE!!!
THE POLICEMAN'S SHOTS ARE IN VAIN ··· A DEAD MAN CANNOT DIE! BUT YOU MUSTN'T LET YOURSELF BE CAUGHT ··· THERE ISN'T MUCH TIME ··· QUICKLY YOU MELT INTO THE CROWD!
STOP! STOP, OR I'LL SHOOT! STOP! STOP!!!
AND SOMETIME LATER YOU FIND YOURSELF BACK IN THE HUT ··· FACING A WRATHFUL FIGURE!
YOU FAILED ME! YOU CAME BACK EMPTY-HANDED!

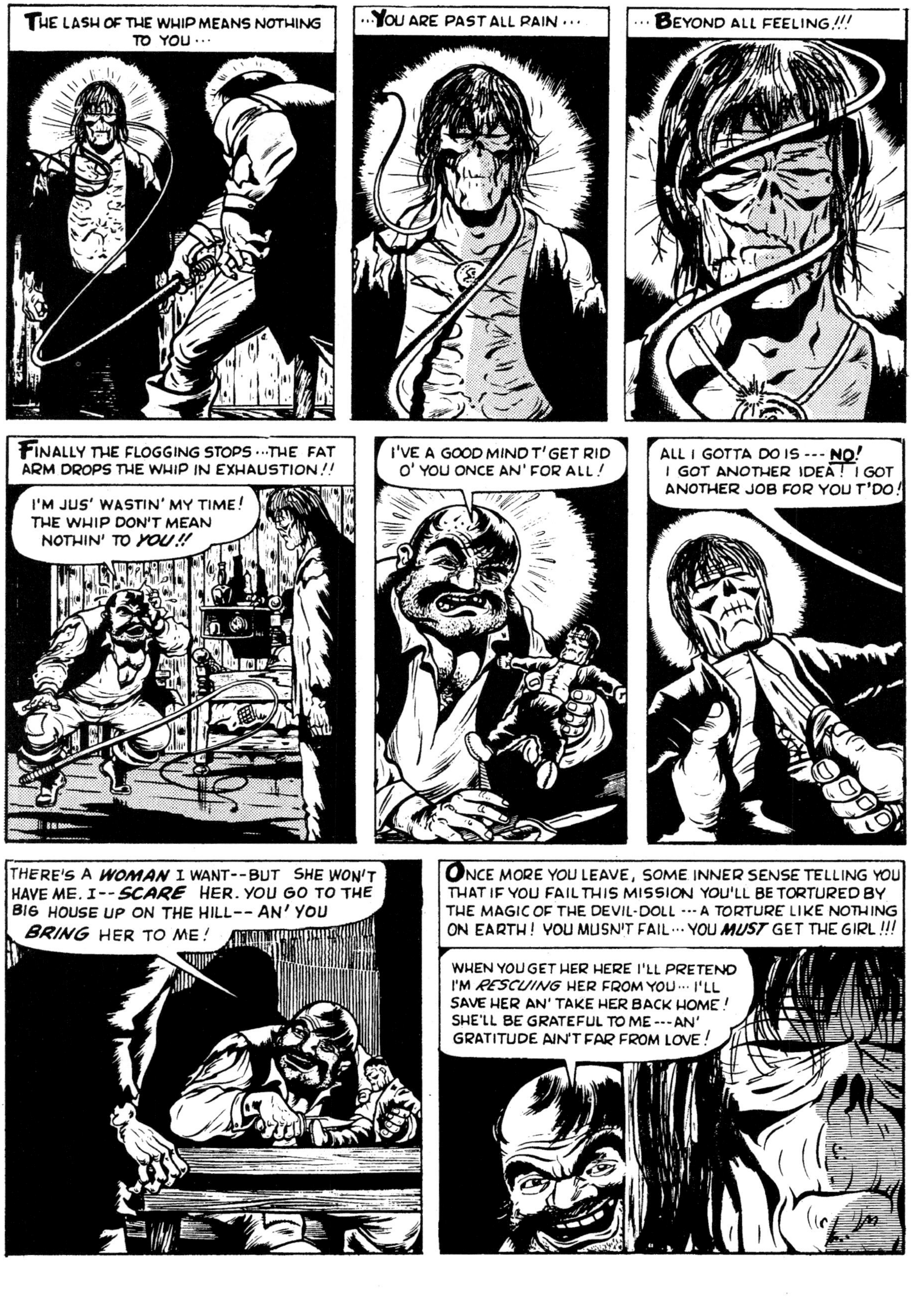
THE LASH OF THE WHIP MEANS NOTHING TO YOU...
...YOU ARE PAST ALL PAIN...
...BEYOND ALL FEELING!!!
FINALLY THE FLOGGING STOPS...THE FAT ARM DROPS THE WHIP IN EXHAUSTION!!
I'M JUS' WASTIN' MY TIME! THE WHIP DON'T MEAN NOTHIN' TO YOU!!
I'VE A GOOD MIND T' GET RID O' YOU ONCE AN' FOR ALL!
ALL I GOTTA DO IS --- NO! I GOT ANOTHER IDEA! I GOT ANOTHER JOB FOR YOU T'DO!
THERE'S A WOMAN I WANT--BUT SHE WON'T HAVE ME. I--SCARE HER. YOU GO TO THE BIG HOUSE UP ON THE HILL-- AN' YOU BRING HER TO ME!
ONCE MORE YOU LEAVE, SOME INNER SENSE TELLING YOU THAT IF YOU FAIL THIS MISSION YOU'LL BE TORTURED BY THE MAGIC OF THE DEVIL-DOLL --- A TORTURE LIKE NOTHING ON EARTH! YOU MUSN'T FAIL... YOU MUST GET THE GIRL!!!
WHEN YOU GET HER HERE I'LL PRETEND I'M RESCUING HER FROM YOU... I'LL SAVE HER AN' TAKE HER BACK HOME! SHE'LL BE GRATEFUL TO ME --- AN' GRATITUDE AIN'T FAR FROM LOVE!

THE NIGHT HAS GROWN EVEN DARKER AS YOU STALK TOWARD THE WHITE CABIN AT THE EDGE OF THE SWAMP...

SUDDENLY ITS SHAPE LOOMS UP AHEAD OF YOU --- YOU CREEP UP TO THE FRONT DOOR AND TRY THE KNOB --- IT'S LOCKED!

BUT LOCKED DOORS MEAN NOTHING TO YOU!

CRASH!

YOU'RE IN THE SHADOWS WHERE SHE CAN'T SEE YOU --- BUT *YOU* CAN SEE *HER!*

WHO --- WHO'S THERE???

AND SUDDENLY SOMETHING INSIDE OF YOU SNAPS! YOU CAN'T MOVE FORWARD! YOU CAN'T CARRY OUT YOUR ORDERS!! ALL YOU CAN DO IS FLEE BACK INTO THE MURKY, EVIL NIGHT!!!

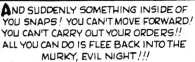

THE *FIRST* TIME YOU FAILED, YOU COULDN'T HELP YOURSELF...

BUT *THIS* TIME THERE'S NO EXCUSE! THIS TIME YOU'LL BE TORTURED FOR YOUR FAILURE!!

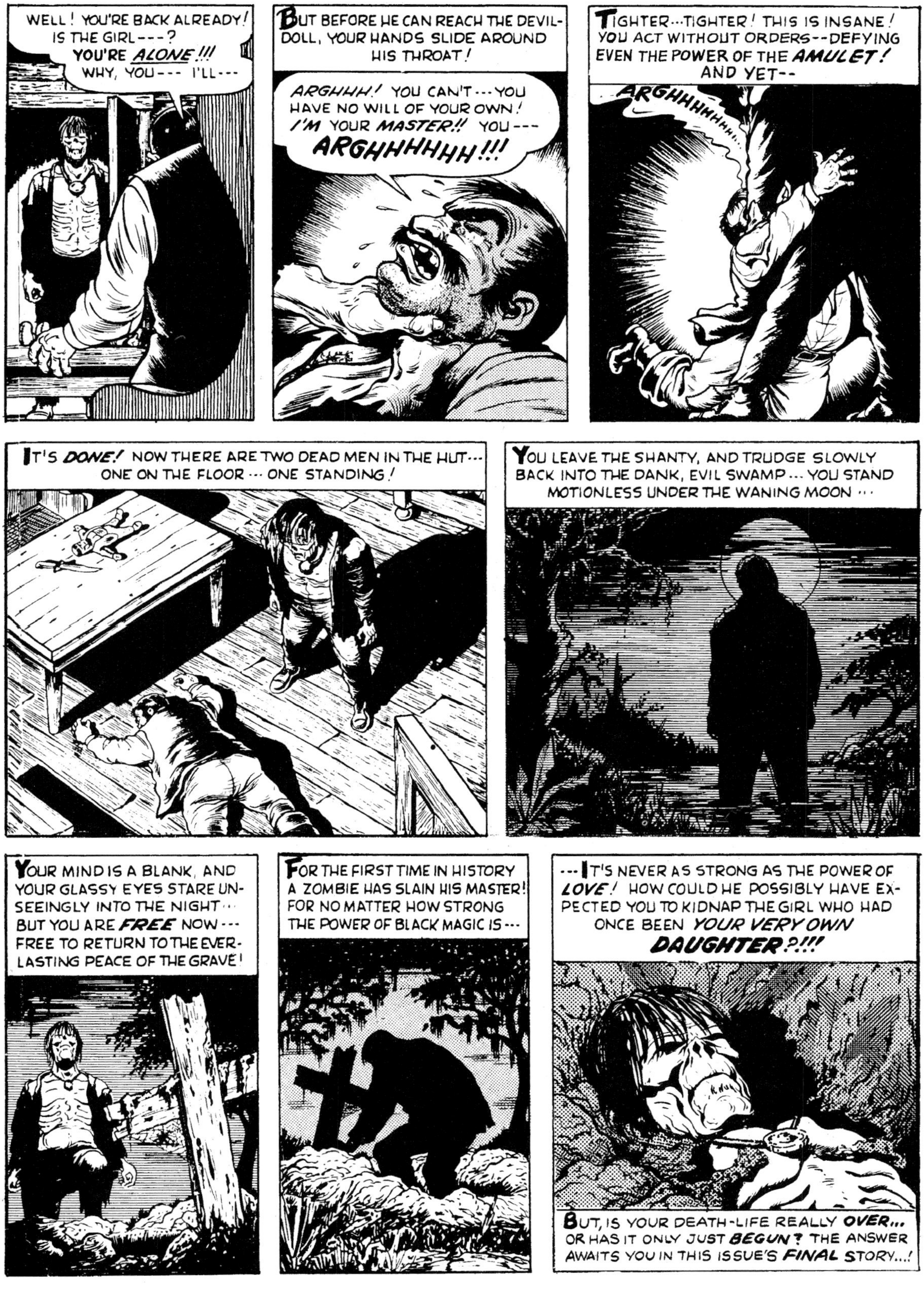
WELL! YOU'RE BACK ALREADY! IS THE GIRL---? YOU'RE ALONE!!! WHY, YOU--- I'LL---
BUT BEFORE HE CAN REACH THE DEVIL-DOLL, YOUR HANDS SLIDE AROUND HIS THROAT!
ARGHHH! YOU CAN'T---YOU HAVE NO WILL OF YOUR OWN! I'M YOUR MASTER!! YOU--- ARGHHHHHH!!!
TIGHTER---TIGHTER! THIS IS INSANE! YOU ACT WITHOUT ORDERS--DEFYING EVEN THE POWER OF THE AMULET! AND YET--
ARGHHHHHH
IT'S DONE! NOW THERE ARE TWO DEAD MEN IN THE HUT--- ONE ON THE FLOOR --- ONE STANDING!
YOU LEAVE THE SHANTY, AND TRUDGE SLOWLY BACK INTO THE DANK, EVIL SWAMP --- YOU STAND MOTIONLESS UNDER THE WANING MOON ---
YOUR MIND IS A BLANK, AND YOUR GLASSY EYES STARE UNSEEINGLY INTO THE NIGHT --- BUT YOU ARE FREE NOW --- FREE TO RETURN TO THE EVERLASTING PEACE OF THE GRAVE!
FOR THE FIRST TIME IN HISTORY A ZOMBIE HAS SLAIN HIS MASTER! FOR NO MATTER HOW STRONG THE POWER OF BLACK MAGIC IS ---
--- IT'S NEVER AS STRONG AS THE POWER OF LOVE! HOW COULD HE POSSIBLY HAVE EXPECTED YOU TO KIDNAP THE GIRL WHO HAD ONCE BEEN YOUR VERY OWN DAUGHTER?!!!
BUT, IS YOUR DEATH-LIFE REALLY OVER... OR HAS IT ONLY JUST BEGUN? THE ANSWER AWAITS YOU IN THIS ISSUE'S FINAL STORY...!

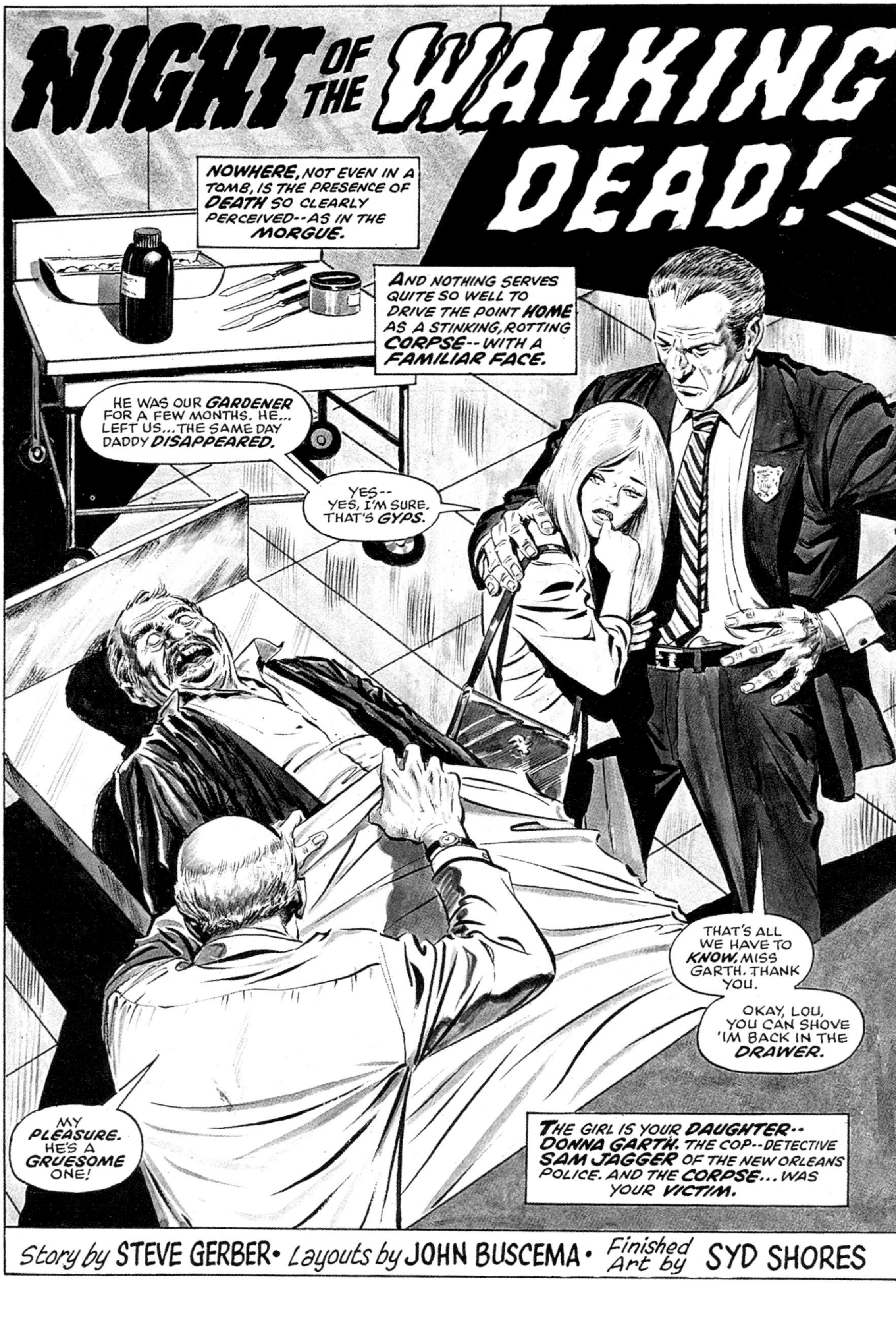
NIGHT OF THE WALKING DEAD!
NOWHERE, NOT EVEN IN A TOMB, IS THE PRESENCE OF DEATH SO CLEARLY PERCEIVED--AS IN THE MORGUE.
AND NOTHING SERVES QUITE SO WELL TO DRIVE THE POINT HOME AS A STINKING, ROTTING CORPSE-- WITH A FAMILIAR FACE.
HE WAS OUR GARDENER FOR A FEW MONTHS. HE... LEFT US... THE SAME DAY DADDY DISAPPEARED.
YES-- YES, I'M SURE. THAT'S GYPS.
THAT'S ALL WE HAVE TO KNOW, MISS GARTH. THANK YOU.
OKAY, LOU, YOU CAN SHOVE 'IM BACK IN THE DRAWER.
MY PLEASURE. HE'S A GRUESOME ONE!
THE GIRL IS YOUR DAUGHTER-- DONNA GARTH. THE COP--DETECTIVE SAM JAGGER OF THE NEW ORLEANS POLICE. AND THE CORPSE... WAS YOUR VICTIM.
Story by STEVE GERBER • Layouts by JOHN BUSCEMA • Finished Art by SYD SHORES

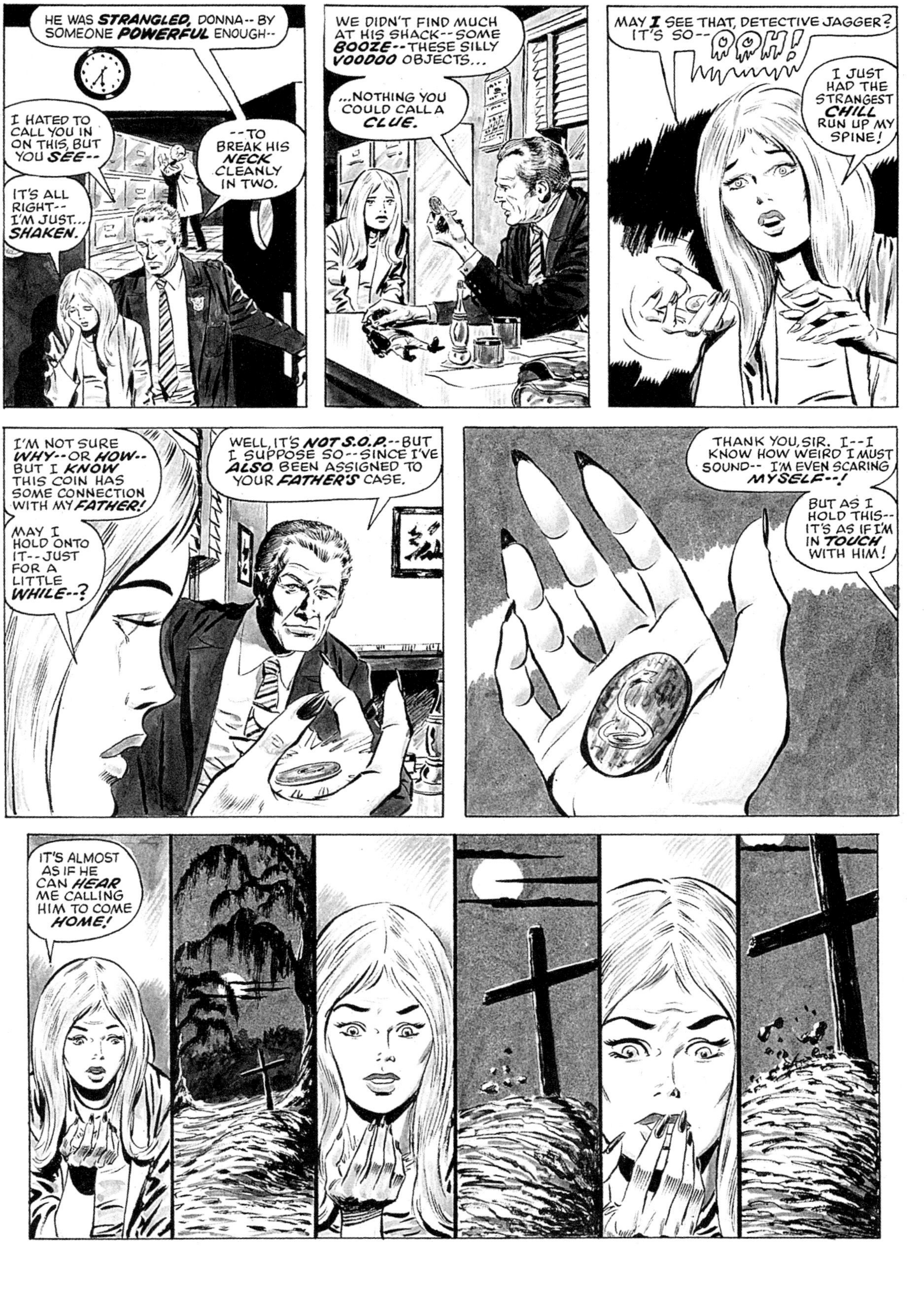

HE WAS STRANGLED, DONNA-- BY SOMEONE POWERFUL ENOUGH--
I HATED TO CALL YOU IN ON THIS, BUT YOU SEE--
--TO BREAK HIS NECK CLEANLY IN TWO.
IT'S ALL RIGHT-- I'M JUST... SHAKEN.
WE DIDN'T FIND MUCH AT HIS SHACK--SOME BOOZE--THESE SILLY VOODOO OBJECTS...
...NOTHING YOU COULD CALL A CLUE.
MAY I SEE THAT, DETECTIVE JAGGER? IT'S SO--
OOH!
I JUST HAD THE STRANGEST CHILL RUN UP MY SPINE!
I'M NOT SURE WHY--OR HOW--BUT I KNOW THIS COIN HAS SOME CONNECTION WITH MY FATHER!
MAY I HOLD ONTO IT--JUST FOR A LITTLE WHILE--?
WELL, IT'S NOT S.O.P.--BUT I SUPPOSE SO--SINCE I'VE ALSO BEEN ASSIGNED TO YOUR FATHER'S CASE.
THANK YOU, SIR. I--I KNOW HOW WEIRD I MUST SOUND-- I'M EVEN SCARING MYSELF--!
BUT AS I HOLD THIS-- IT'S AS IF I'M IN TOUCH WITH HIM!
IT'S ALMOST AS IF HE CAN HEAR ME CALLING HIM TO COME HOME!

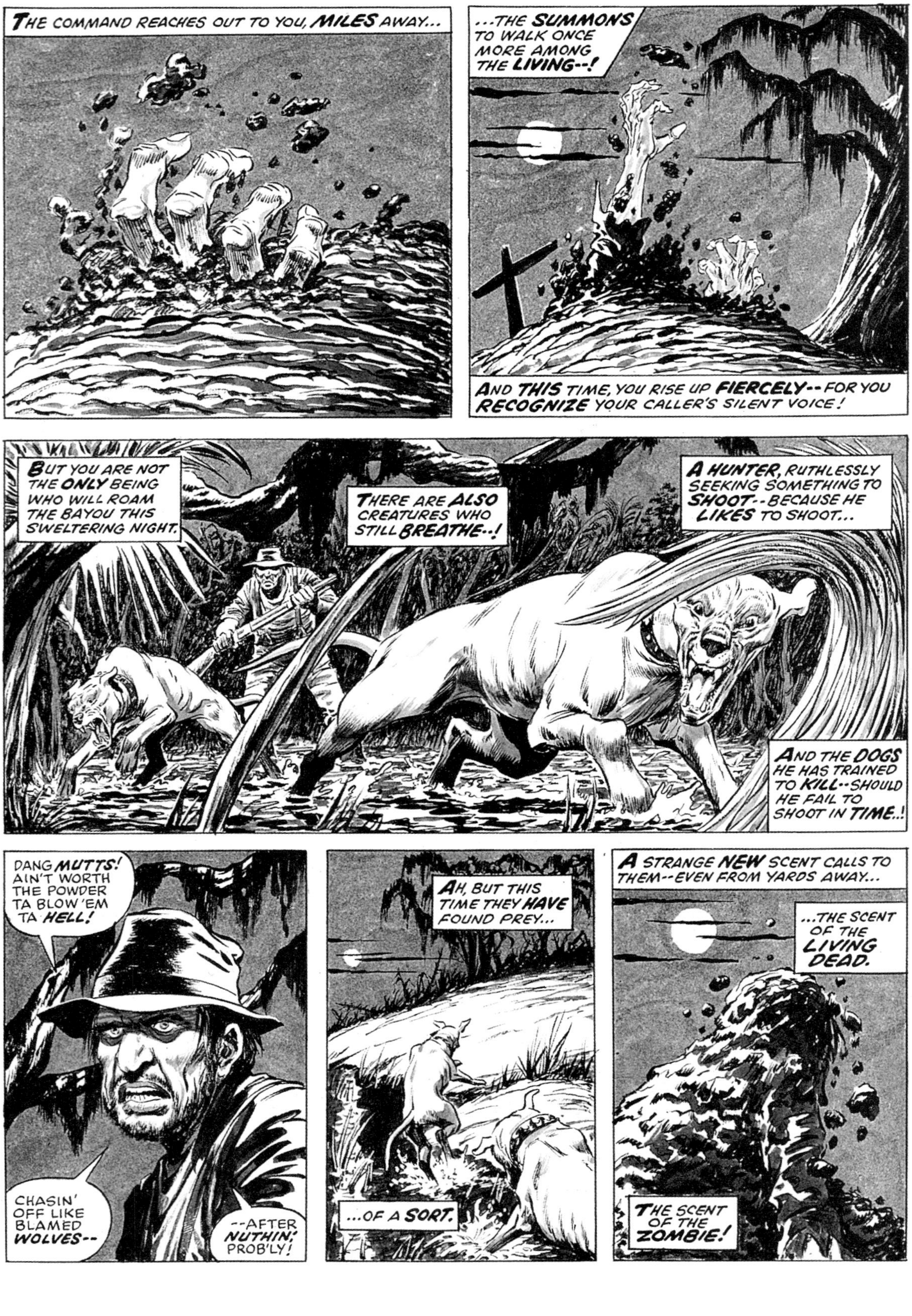
THE COMMAND REACHES OUT TO YOU, MILES AWAY...
...THE SUMMONS TO WALK ONCE MORE AMONG THE LIVING--!
AND THIS TIME, YOU RISE UP FIERCELY-- FOR YOU RECOGNIZE YOUR CALLER'S SILENT VOICE!
BUT YOU ARE NOT THE ONLY BEING WHO WILL ROAM THE BAYOU THIS SWELTERING NIGHT.
THERE ARE ALSO CREATURES WHO STILL BREATHE--!
A HUNTER, RUTHLESSLY SEEKING SOMETHING TO SHOOT--BECAUSE HE LIKES TO SHOOT...
AND THE DOGS HE HAS TRAINED TO KILL--SHOULD HE FAIL TO SHOOT IN TIME..!
DANG MUTTS! AIN'T WORTH THE POWDER TA BLOW 'EM TA HELL!
CHASIN' OFF LIKE BLAMED WOLVES--
--AFTER NUTHIN', PROB'LY!
AH, BUT THIS TIME THEY HAVE FOUND PREY...
...OF A SORT.
A STRANGE NEW SCENT CALLS TO THEM--EVEN FROM YARDS AWAY...
...THE SCENT OF THE LIVING DEAD.
THE SCENT OF THE ZOMBIE!

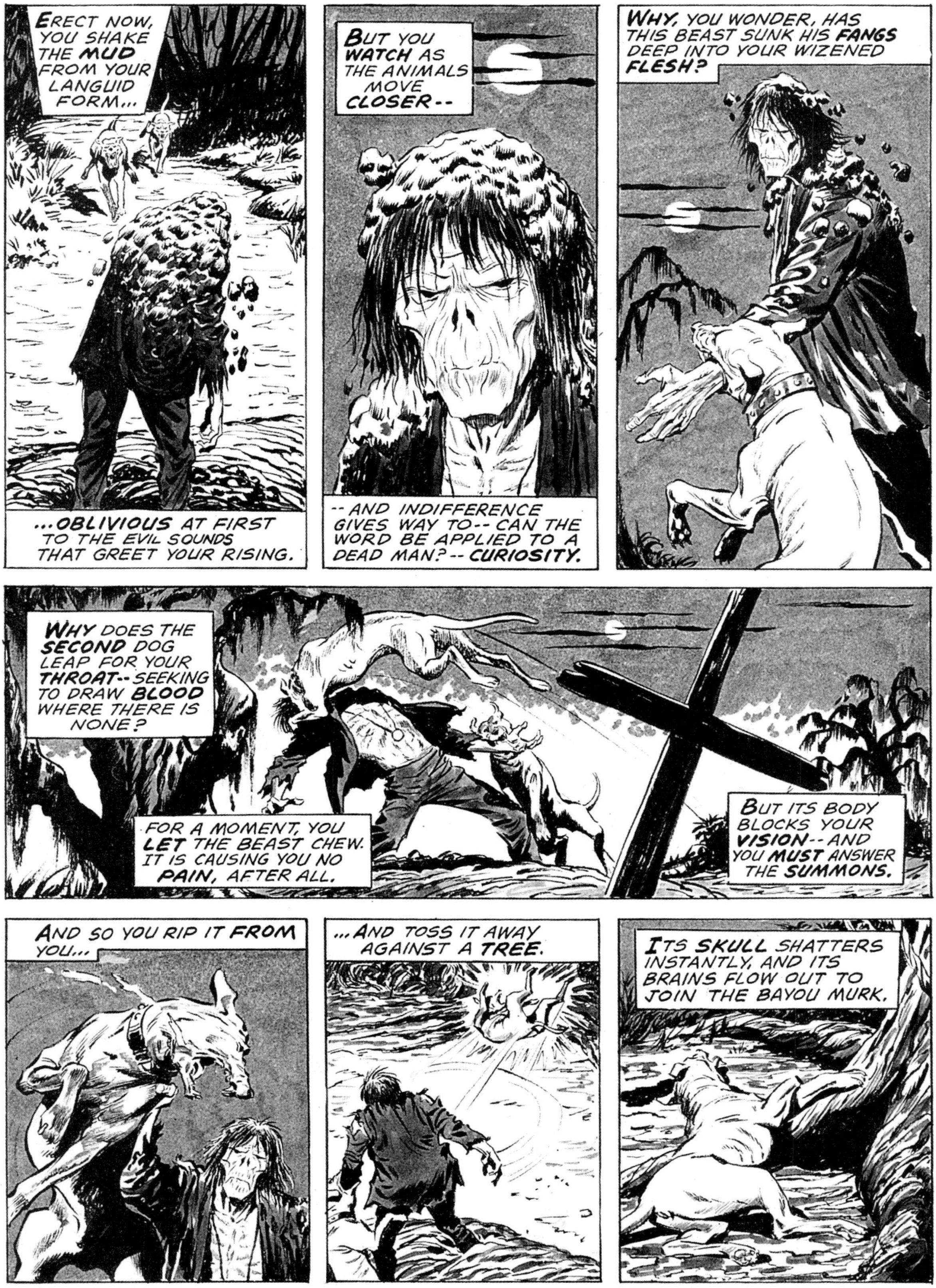

ERECT NOW, YOU SHAKE THE MUD FROM YOUR LANGUID FORM...
...OBLIVIOUS AT FIRST TO THE EVIL SOUNDS THAT GREET YOUR RISING.
BUT YOU WATCH AS THE ANIMALS MOVE CLOSER--
--AND INDIFFERENCE GIVES WAY TO-- CAN THE WORD BE APPLIED TO A DEAD MAN?-- CURIOSITY.
WHY, YOU WONDER, HAS THIS BEAST SUNK HIS FANGS DEEP INTO YOUR WIZENED FLESH?
WHY DOES THE SECOND DOG LEAP FOR YOUR THROAT-- SEEKING TO DRAW BLOOD WHERE THERE IS NONE?
FOR A MOMENT, YOU LET THE BEAST CHEW. IT IS CAUSING YOU NO PAIN, AFTER ALL.
BUT ITS BODY BLOCKS YOUR VISION-- AND YOU MUST ANSWER THE SUMMONS.
AND SO YOU RIP IT FROM YOU...
...AND TOSS IT AWAY AGAINST A TREE.
ITS SKULL SHATTERS INSTANTLY, AND ITS BRAINS FLOW OUT TO JOIN THE BAYOU MURK.

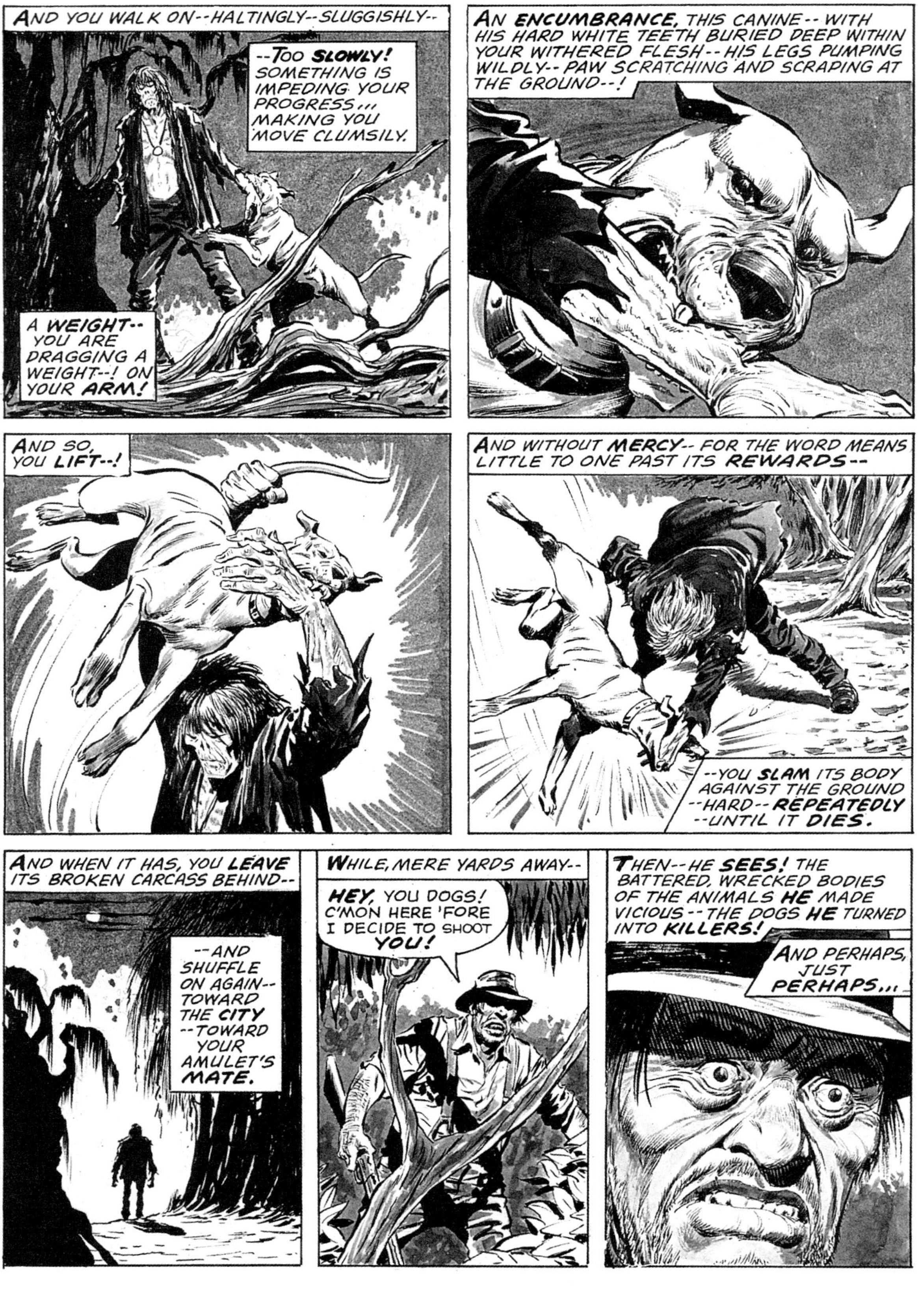

AND YOU WALK ON--HALTINGLY--SLUGGISHLY--
--TOO SLOWLY! SOMETHING IS IMPEDING YOUR PROGRESS... MAKING YOU MOVE CLUMSILY.
A WEIGHT-- YOU ARE DRAGGING A WEIGHT--! ON YOUR ARM!
AN ENCUMBRANCE, THIS CANINE-- WITH HIS HARD WHITE TEETH BURIED DEEP WITHIN YOUR WITHERED FLESH--HIS LEGS PUMPING WILDLY--PAW SCRATCHING AND SCRAPING AT THE GROUND--!
AND SO, YOU LIFT--!
AND WITHOUT MERCY-- FOR THE WORD MEANS LITTLE TO ONE PAST ITS REWARDS--
--YOU SLAM ITS BODY AGAINST THE GROUND --HARD--REPEATEDLY --UNTIL IT DIES.
AND WHEN IT HAS, YOU LEAVE ITS BROKEN CARCASS BEHIND--
--AND SHUFFLE ON AGAIN-- TOWARD THE CITY --TOWARD YOUR AMULET'S MATE.
WHILE, MERE YARDS AWAY--
HEY, YOU DOGS! C'MON HERE 'FORE I DECIDE TO SHOOT YOU!
THEN--HE SEES! THE BATTERED, WRECKED BODIES OF THE ANIMALS HE MADE VICIOUS--THE DOGS HE TURNED INTO KILLERS!
AND PERHAPS, JUST PERHAPS...

...HE CATCHES A GLIMPSE OF THE SICKNESS IN HIS **OWN** SOUL -- OF THE **PRICE** OF KILLING FOR **PLEASURE** --

--AND HE **RUNS.** AND HE DOESN'T LOOK **BACK.**

MILES DISTANT, A **DIFFERENT** SORT OF **DRAMA** BEGINS TO TAKE SHAPE.

SO **MUCH** HAS HAPPENED THESE PAST FEW WEEKS. MY **FATHER,** MISSING...

...NOW **GYPS** DEAD -- AND EVERYWHERE, THE SPECTRE OF **VOODOO!**

WHAT CAN IT ALL **MEAN?**

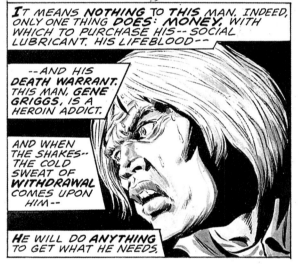

IT MEANS **NOTHING** TO **THIS** MAN. INDEED, ONLY ONE THING **DOES:** MONEY. WITH WHICH TO PURCHASE HIS -- SOCIAL LUBRICANT. HIS LIFEBLOOD --

--AND HIS **DEATH WARRANT.** THIS MAN, **GENE GRIGGS,** IS A HEROIN ADDICT.

AND WHEN THE SHAKES-- THE COLD SWEAT OF **WITHDRAWAL** COMES UPON HIM --

HE WILL DO **ANYTHING** TO GET WHAT HE NEEDS.

THINK I GOT ME A **HOT** ONE THIS TIME--!

HEY! STOP! WHAT ARE YOU--?

HE WIELDS HIS KNIFE LIKE A **SURGEON** --

--SLASHING DONNA GARTH'S PURSE-STRAP THEN **FLEEING** INTO THE SHADOWLAND OF THE ALLEYWAYS OF NEW ORLEANS --!

STOP! THIEF! HELP-- POLICE!

HE WILL BE **GONE** LONG BEFORE THE POLICE ARRIVE.

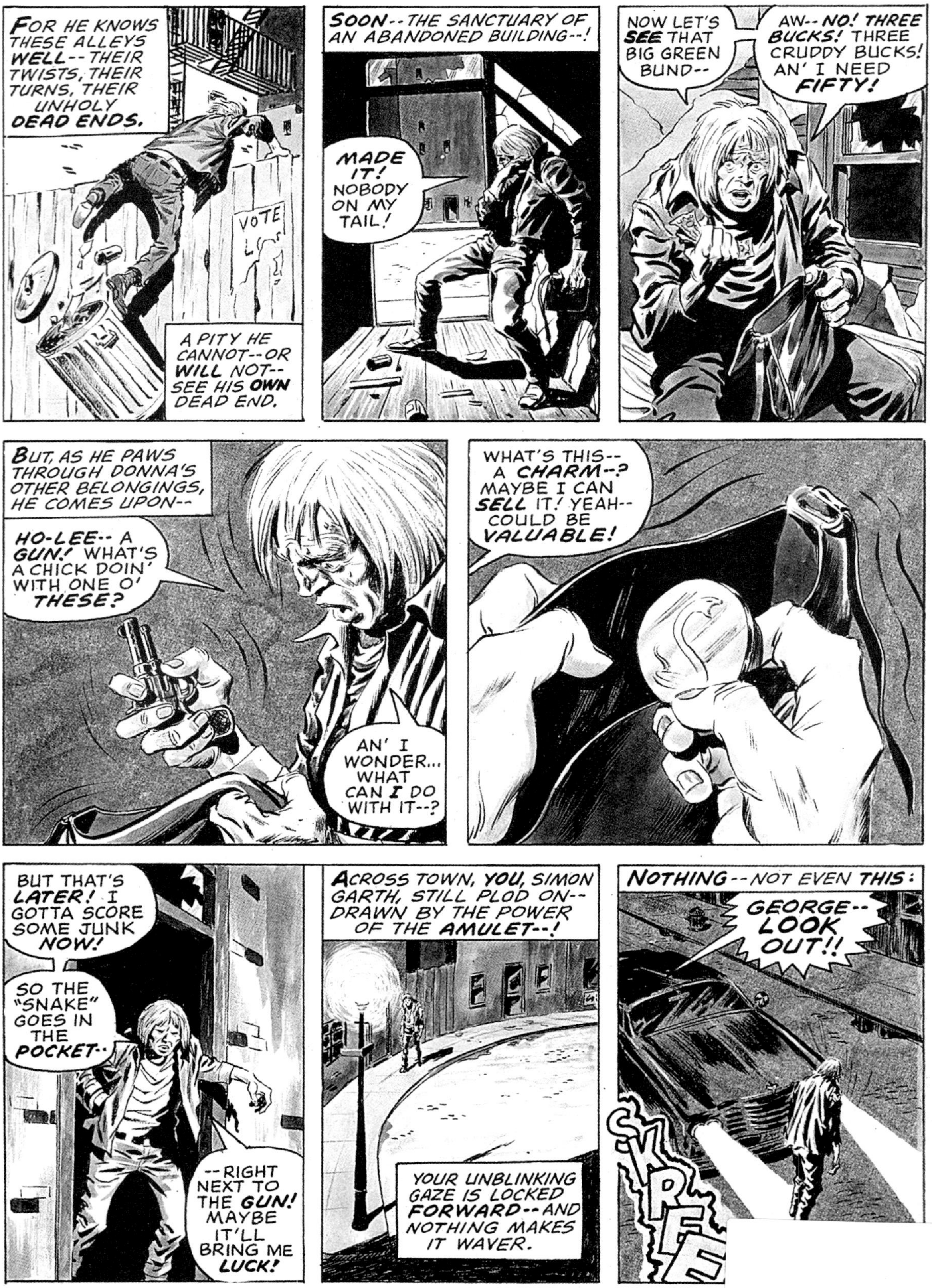
FOR HE KNOWS THESE ALLEYS WELL--THEIR TWISTS, THEIR TURNS, THEIR UNHOLY DEAD ENDS.
VOTE
A PITY HE CANNOT--OR WILL NOT--SEE HIS OWN DEAD END.
SOON--THE SANCTUARY OF AN ABANDONED BUILDING--!
MADE IT! NOBODY ON MY TAIL!
NOW LET'S SEE THAT BIG GREEN BUND--
AW--NO! THREE BUCKS! THREE CRUDDY BUCKS! AN' I NEED FIFTY!
BUT, AS HE PAWS THROUGH DONNA'S OTHER BELONGINGS, HE COMES UPON--
HO-LEE--A GUN! WHAT'S A CHICK DOIN' WITH ONE O' THESE?
AN' I WONDER... WHAT CAN I DO WITH IT--?
WHAT'S THIS--A CHARM--? MAYBE I CAN SELL IT! YEAH--COULD BE VALUABLE!
BUT THAT'S LATER! I GOTTA SCORE SOME JUNK NOW!
SO THE "SNAKE" GOES IN THE POCKET--
--RIGHT NEXT TO THE GUN! MAYBE IT'LL BRING ME LUCK!
ACROSS TOWN, YOU, SIMON GARTH, STILL PLOD ON--DRAWN BY THE POWER OF THE AMULET--!
YOUR UNBLINKING GAZE IS LOCKED FORWARD--AND NOTHING MAKES IT WAVER.
NOTHING--NOT EVEN THIS:
GEORGE--LOOK OUT!!

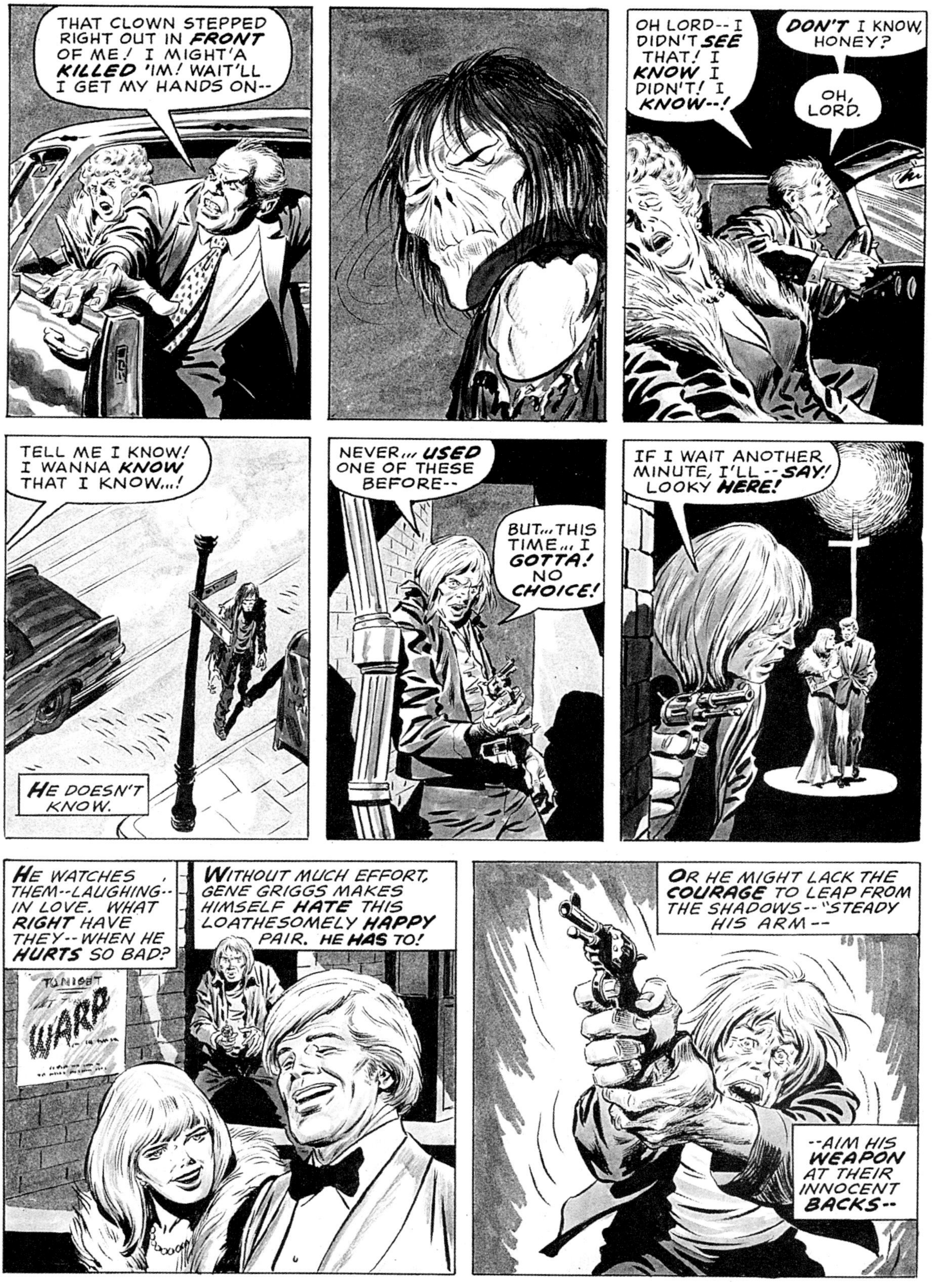
THAT CLOWN STEPPED RIGHT OUT IN FRONT OF ME! I MIGHT'A KILLED 'IM! WAIT'LL I GET MY HANDS ON--
OH LORD-- I DIDN'T SEE THAT! I KNOW I DIDN'T! I KNOW--!
DON'T I KNOW, HONEY?
OH, LORD.
TELL ME I KNOW! I WANNA KNOW THAT I KNOW...!
HE DOESN'T KNOW.
NEVER... USED ONE OF THESE BEFORE--
BUT... THIS TIME... I GOTTA! NO CHOICE!
IF I WAIT ANOTHER MINUTE, I'LL --SAY! LOOKY HERE!
HE WATCHES THEM--LAUGHING--IN LOVE. WHAT RIGHT HAVE THEY--WHEN HE HURTS SO BAD?
WITHOUT MUCH EFFORT, GENE GRIGGS MAKES HIMSELF HATE THIS LOATHESOMELY HAPPY PAIR. HE HAS TO!
TONIGHT
WARP
OR HE MIGHT LACK THE COURAGE TO LEAP FROM THE SHADOWS--"STEADY HIS ARM--
--AIM HIS WEAPON AT THEIR INNOCENT BACKS--

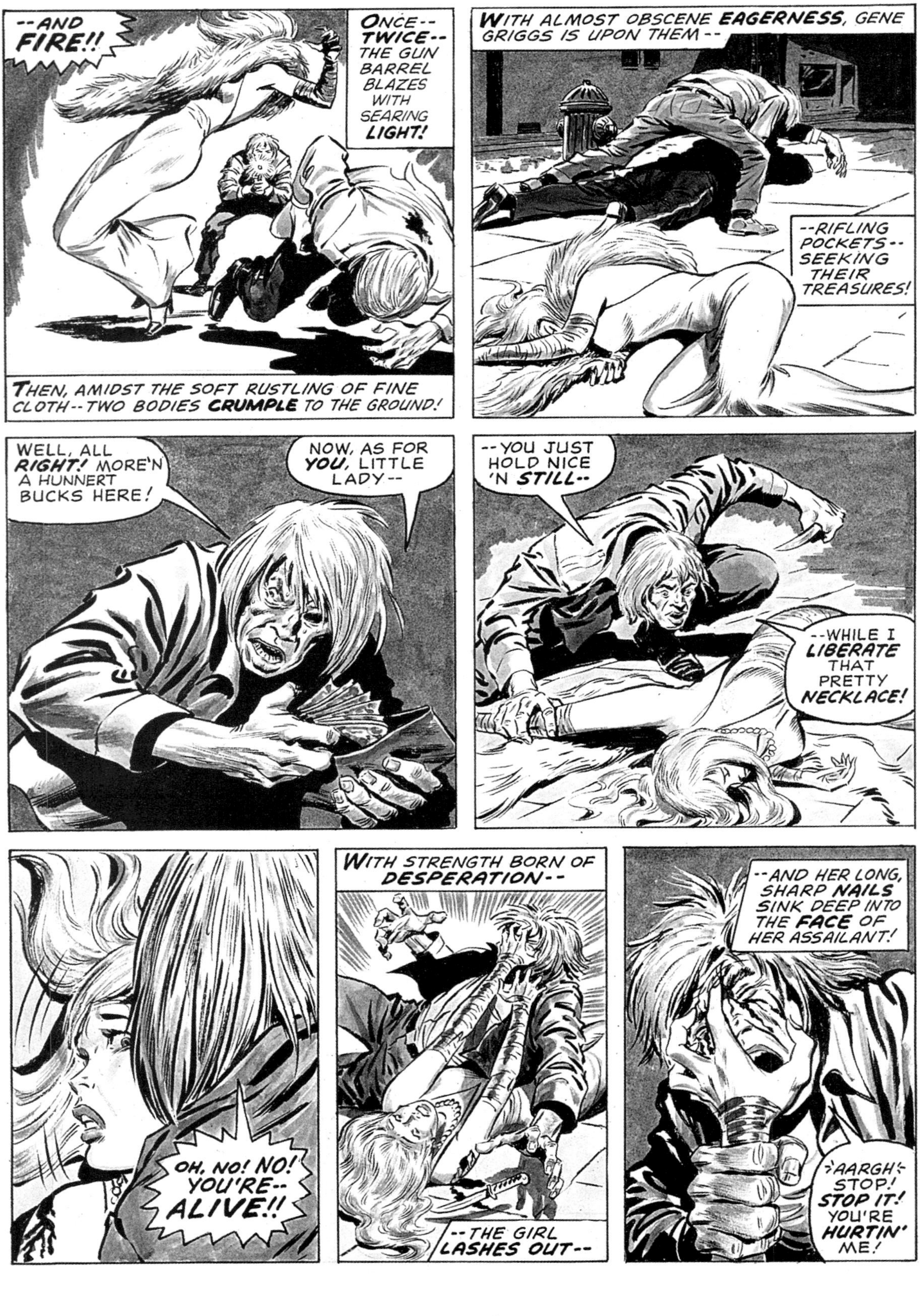
--AND FIRE!!
ONCE-- TWICE-- THE GUN BARREL BLAZES WITH SEARING LIGHT!
THEN, AMIDST THE SOFT RUSTLING OF FINE CLOTH--TWO BODIES CRUMPLE TO THE GROUND!
WITH ALMOST OBSCENE EAGERNESS, GENE GRIGGS IS UPON THEM--
--RIFLING POCKETS--SEEKING THEIR TREASURES!
WELL, ALL RIGHT! MORE'N A HUNNERT BUCKS HERE!
NOW, AS FOR YOU, LITTLE LADY--
--YOU JUST HOLD NICE 'N STILL--
--WHILE I LIBERATE THAT PRETTY NECKLACE!
OH, NO! NO! YOU'RE--ALIVE!!
WITH STRENGTH BORN OF DESPERATION--
--THE GIRL LASHES OUT--
--AND HER LONG, SHARP NAILS SINK DEEP INTO THE FACE OF HER ASSAILANT!
AARGH! STOP! STOP IT! YOU'RE HURTIN' ME!

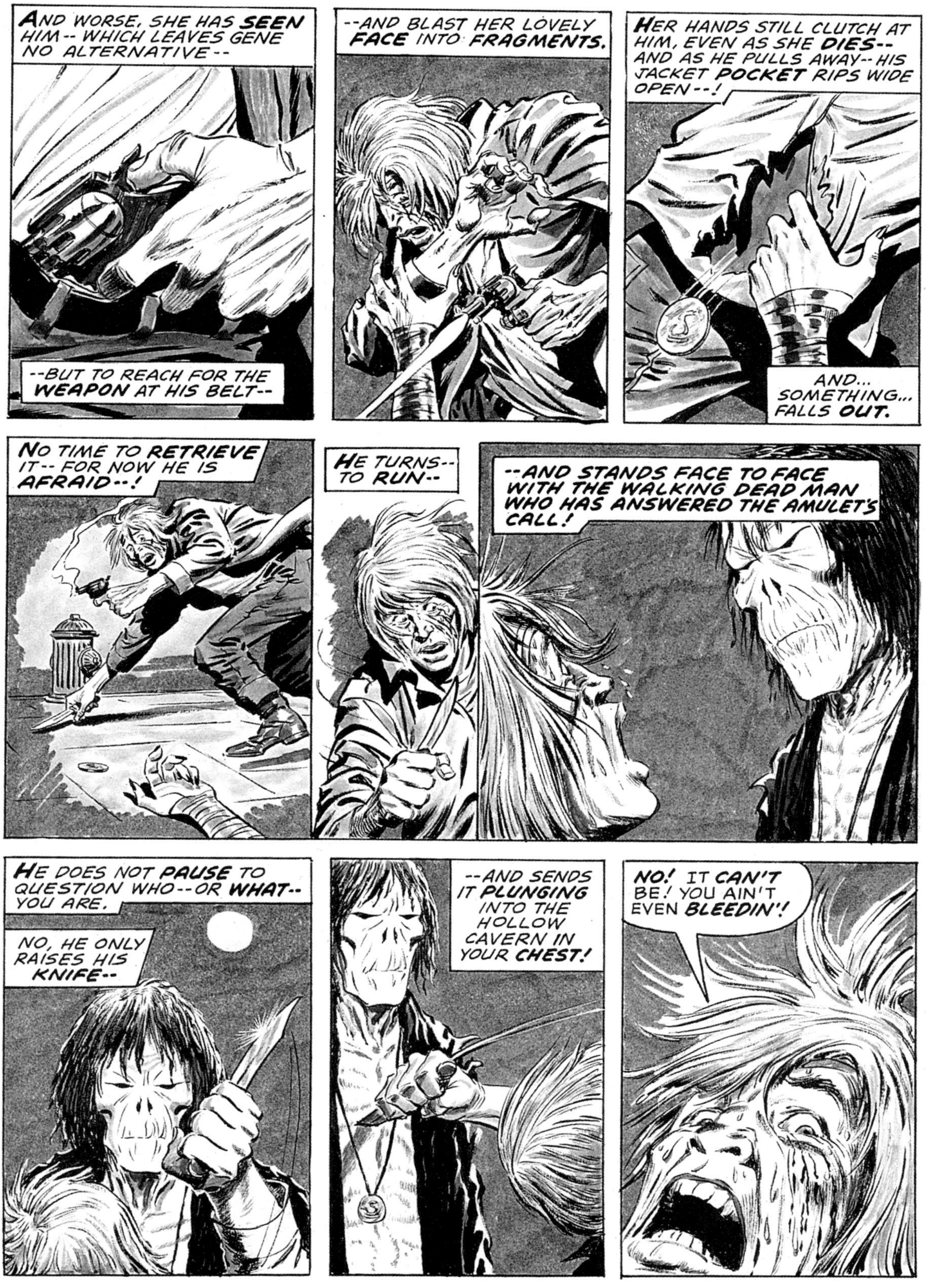
AND WORSE, SHE HAS SEEN HIM -- WHICH LEAVES GENE NO ALTERNATIVE --
--BUT TO REACH FOR THE WEAPON AT HIS BELT--
--AND BLAST HER LOVELY FACE INTO FRAGMENTS.
HER HANDS STILL CLUTCH AT HIM, EVEN AS SHE DIES-- AND AS HE PULLS AWAY-- HIS JACKET POCKET RIPS WIDE OPEN--!
AND... SOMETHING... FALLS OUT.
NO TIME TO RETRIEVE IT-- FOR NOW HE IS AFRAID--!
HE TURNS-- TO RUN--
--AND STANDS FACE TO FACE WITH THE WALKING DEAD MAN WHO HAS ANSWERED THE AMULET'S CALL!
HE DOES NOT PAUSE TO QUESTION WHO--OR WHAT-- YOU ARE.
NO, HE ONLY RAISES HIS KNIFE--
--AND SENDS IT PLUNGING INTO THE HOLLOW CAVERN IN YOUR CHEST!
NO! IT CAN'T BE! YOU AIN'T EVEN BLEEDIN'!

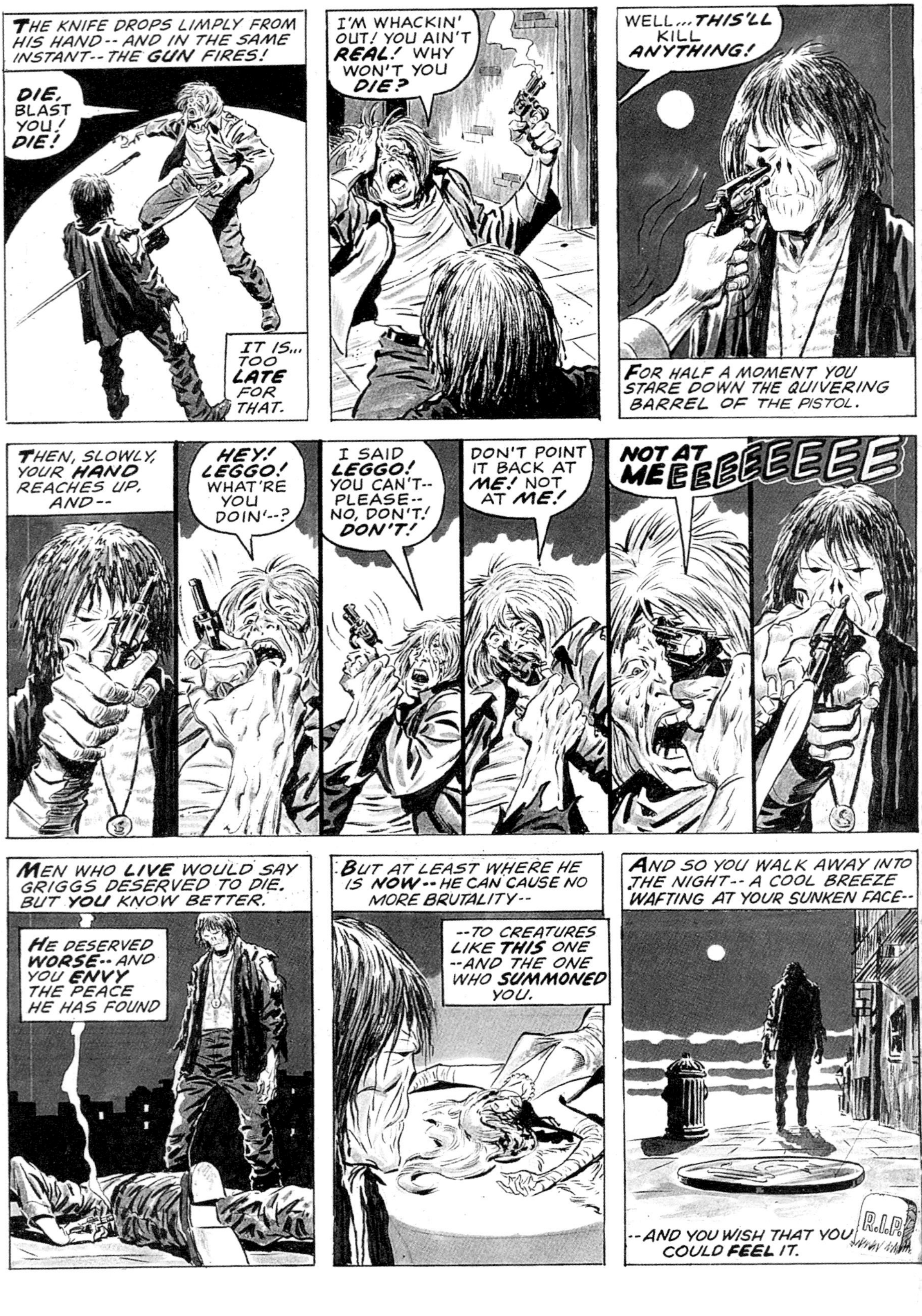
THE KNIFE DROPS LIMPLY FROM HIS HAND-- AND IN THE SAME INSTANT--THE GUN FIRES!
DIE, BLAST YOU! DIE!
IT IS... TOO LATE FOR THAT.
I'M WHACKIN' OUT! YOU AIN'T REAL! WHY WON'T YOU DIE?
WELL... THIS'LL KILL ANYTHING!
FOR HALF A MOMENT YOU STARE DOWN THE QUIVERING BARREL OF THE PISTOL.
THEN, SLOWLY, YOUR HAND REACHES UP, AND--
HEY! LEGGO! WHAT'RE YOU DOIN'--?
I SAID LEGGO! YOU CAN'T-- PLEASE-- NO, DON'T! DON'T!
DON'T POINT IT BACK AT ME! NOT AT ME!
NOT AT MEEEEEEEEE
MEN WHO LIVE WOULD SAY GRIGGS DESERVED TO DIE. BUT YOU KNOW BETTER.
HE DESERVED WORSE-- AND YOU ENVY THE PEACE HE HAS FOUND
BUT AT LEAST WHERE HE IS NOW-- HE CAN CAUSE NO MORE BRUTALITY--
--TO CREATURES LIKE THIS ONE --AND THE ONE WHO SUMMONED YOU.
AND SO YOU WALK AWAY INTO THE NIGHT-- A COOL BREEZE WAFTING AT YOUR SUNKEN FACE--
R.I.P.
--AND YOU WISH THAT YOU COULD FEEL IT.